PCs made easy

easy

STAGE

8

A PRACTICAL COURSE

PCs made easy

STAGE 8

A PRACTICAL COURSE

PUBLISHED BY THE READER'S DIGEST ASSOCIATION LIMITED
LONDON NEW YORK SYDNEY MONTREAL

PCS MADE EASY
A PRACTICAL COURSE – STAGE 8

Published by the Reader's Digest Association Limited, 2002

The Reader's Digest Association Limited
11 Westferry Circus, Canary Wharf, London E14 4HE
www.readersdigest.co.uk

We are committed to both the quality of our products and the service we
provide to our customers, so please feel free to contact us on 08705 113366,
or via our Web site at www.readersdigest.co.uk
If you have any comments or suggestions about the content
of this book, e-mail us at:
gbeditorial@readersdigest.co.uk

®Reader's Digest, The Reader's Digest and the Pegasus
logo are registered trademarks of The Reader's Digest
Association Inc, of Pleasantville, New York, USA

For Reader's Digest
Series Editor: Christine Noble
Assistant Editor: Caroline Boucher
Art Editor: Julie Bennett

Reader's Digest General Books
Editorial Director: Cortina Butler
Art Director: Nick Clark

PCs made easy was created and produced for
The Reader's Digest Association Limited by De Agostini UK Ltd,
from material originally published as the Partwork
Computer Success Plus.

Printing and binding: Printer Industria Gráfica S.A., Barcelona

ISBN 0 276 42640 1

CONTENTS

Windows

The Resource Meter

Monitoring how well your computer performs at different times will help you to work within its limits.

Using a number of programs at once can be a difficult business, particularly on a computer which has limited memory or a slow processor. You run the risk of your computer grinding to a halt or even crashing.

It's not easy to predict when this will happen. Sometimes the computer seems able to work quite happily with lots of programs and folders open, while at other times it can slow to a crawl with only a few programs running. However, Windows has a useful system tool, called Resource Meter, which indicates how much effort your computer is expending at any given time and so helps you to predict when things are likely to go wrong.

● Monitoring resources
The resources monitored by the Resource Meter are System, User and GDI, each of which is associated with a slightly different aspect of your computer's operations. The System resource indicates how much basic capacity your computer has for running programs; in a sense, it's a measure of its overall capacity. User resources relate to the actual programs you run and give an idea of how much of your computer's capacity the current programs are using. The GDI resource monitors the operations carried out by Windows to display itself on screen or on other output devices, such as printers.

● Running reports
The initial level of all the resources is set at 100 per cent; each resource level diminishes at

Like a set of performance gauges, the Resource Meter gives a constant running report on how much of your PC's capacity is free.

varying rates, depending on how much memory is being used. If you keep the Resource Meter visible all the time, you can see how your computer's resources are being used, anticipate a problem and take steps to prevent it. The exercise on the next page demonstrates two options available to keep the Resource Meter visible.

However, first make sure that the Resource Meter is installed on your PC, as it isn't always included as part of the original Windows installation. The procedure used to select and then install it from the Windows CD-ROM (using the Add/Remove Programs icon in the Control Panel) is covered in detail in Stage 3, on pages 18-21. The Resource Meter is listed under the Accessories options; go to System Tools, then tick the System Resource Meter entry to be able to access it from your Desktop.

WINDOWS ME

Windows Me closely follows the format of Windows 98, at least for the purposes of the average user. Therefore, unless indicated otherwise, all the exercises in *PCs made easy* work on both operating systems, with only minor differences in screen layout.

WHAT IT MEANS

GDI

The GDI (Graphics Device Interface) is the part of Windows that is concerned with displaying graphics and moving them around. Windows needs to keep track of the hundreds of items that must be drawn on the screen: icons, buttons, windows, menus and so on. Each one consumes a varying amount of GDI resources.

Checking resources with the Resource Meter

Here's how to run the Resource Meter and display it in two different ways. Both will help you to monitor your computer's performance and adjust the way you work to suit its capabilities.

1 To start up the Resource Meter, go to the Programs folder on the Start menu, click on the Accessories folder and select the Resource Meter option from the System Tools sub-folder.

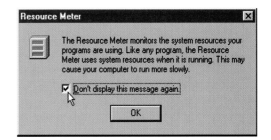

2 You'll see a reminder that the Resource Meter itself consumes some resources. Tick the Don't display this message again option and then click on the OK button.

3 This will load an additional icon into the Taskbar, located at the bottom right of your screen and next to the clock. The icon looks like a beaker with three horizontal lines across it. The more green on the icon, the more overall system resources you have. Anything up to the second horizontal line is fine, but below that you will probably find your computer starts slowing down and causing problems.

4 To test what effect the way you use your computer has on its resource levels, try opening as many programs as you can and then look at the Resource Meter. You'll see that as you open more programs, your computer begins to slow down a little. The Resource Meter level dips and changes to yellow (inset) to show that there are fewer resources available.

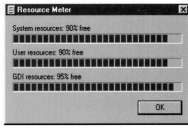

5 To expand the Resource Meter into a full-blown window, double-click on the Taskbar icon. A window will then appear showing three bar charts, which give a constantly updated, detailed picture of the system resources available to your computer.

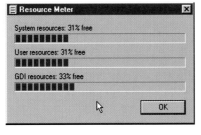

6 Close down all the programs you started up in Step 4. As you do, you'll notice the resource boxes gradually increasing to indicate resources being released for re-use.

7 Now try opening lots of different folders. Open as many as you can – we've opened rather more folders than we had programs open in Step 4.

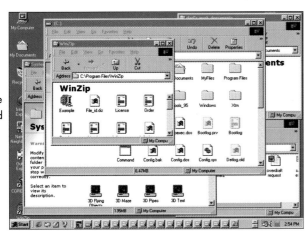

8 Bring up the Resource Meter window. As you can see, even though we have more folders open, there are more resources left than in Step 5. This shows that folders consume considerably fewer system resources than programs do. So if you find your system resources running low, it's more effective to find programs that you can close, rather than closing down folders.

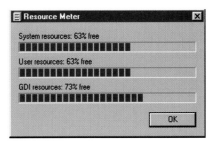

System Monitor

This useful tool allows you to check the resources and speed of your computer. Like Resource Meter, it will help you to see what tasks your computer is performing behind the scenes.

On pages 12-13, we looked at the Resource Meter system tool. Although useful for reviewing the overall system resources of your computer, it is not capable of measuring more specific resources, such as the amount of your computer's memory in use by Windows and the programs you are running.

If you want to go into more detail when measuring the performance of your computer's component parts, use System Monitor. This measures a variety of different resources: it can be used to predict when the computer is becoming over-worked and to log the performance of various devices. So, if your hard-disk drive is working slowly, measure its performance with System Monitor.

● Processor usage

When you first run System Monitor, it starts by measuring the amount of processor time that is spent idle – specifically, the amount that is not in use by the kernel. This information is displayed as a line graph, which is constantly updated (by default, every five seconds), thereby allowing you to measure exactly how much effort it takes for the computer to carry out certain functions. A number of different resources can be monitored at the same time, so you can check the effect on several resources when you perform one particular action.

System Monitor has a range of customizable options. These include various graph display options. The Bar chart and Numeric options display the monitoring information graphically, and they take up less space on screen as they make it easier to watch a large number of actions simultaneously. You can

also edit the axis of any graph, as well as its colour, to make System Monitor as user-friendly as possible.

The only problem with System Monitor is that, physically, it takes up a lot of space on screen and cannot be minimized to a Taskbar icon. For this reason it is best used to monitor a particular resource if a problem is thought to exist, rather than being permanently displayed as an early-warning system.

If System Monitor is not already installed on your computer, you will need to use the Add/Remove Programs dialog box to copy it from the Windows CD-ROM (see Stage 3, pages 18-21).

WHAT IT MEANS

KERNEL

The kernel is the central core of Windows. Once loaded, it remains in your computer's memory for as long as the computer is switched on. The kernel is responsible for vital basic tasks, such as memory, process, task and disk management. It is a very small and tightly programmed piece of code and so doesn't take up too much valuable memory.

System Monitor's kernel gives you a clear idea of how much time Windows is spending on certain tasks.

Using System Monitor

The System Monitor gives a detailed view of what's going on inside your PC while you work. Here's how to explore the inner workings of Windows.

1 The System Monitor program icon appears inside the System Tools folder, which is inside the Start menu's Accessories folder.

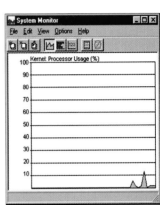

2 When you start it up, you'll initially see a large window with an almost blank graph. Leave the mouse idle for a few seconds and you'll see a light-blue coloured graph appear at the bottom right of the window. At the moment, there's not much activity, so the blue area is quite small.

3 Now start up some big programs – Word or Excel, for example. You'll soon see that the blue area of the graph increases to show the amount of processor capacity being used.

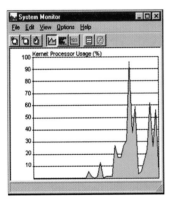

4 Click the fourth button from the right on the toolbar (inset). You'll see the graph change into a bar chart (below).

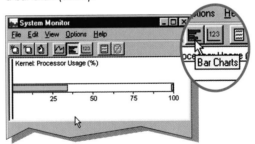

5 Now let's monitor some other aspects of the computer. Click on the Edit menu and then select the Add Item command.

6 When the dialog box pops up, select File System from the Category list and then Bytes read/second from the Item list. Click OK.

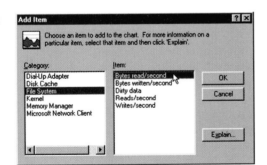

7 We've switched back to graph view (using the fifth button from the right on the toolbar). Continue to open and close programs and you'll see two graphs plotting processor and hard-disk activity in parallel.

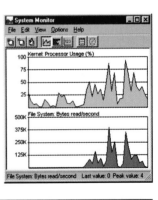

8 If you maximize the System Monitor window, you'll see that there's plenty of room to add several more graphs. Experiment by opening and closing programs and windows. You'll soon see that your computer is working very hard beneath its grey exterior.

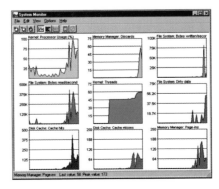

PC TIPS

Altering update speed

You can alter the speed at which the graphs update. Go to the Options menu and select Chart, then move the slider bar to make the update interval faster or slower. By default, it is set to five seconds so that the PC doesn't spend too long updating the charts, rather than dealing with more important programs.

Tweak your Windows settings

Some Windows 98 PCs have a useful – but hard to find – utility that can help you control many aspects of Windows. Here's how to install and use TweakUI.

In Stage 5, pages 8-9, we looked at a number of utilities that can be added to Windows. Microsoft itself also produces some useful small programs. These applets (small applications), known as PowerToys, were made by the programmers who created Windows 95.

The PowerToys were so useful that Microsoft made them 'semi-official' – free to download from the Microsoft Web site but not officially supported. That meant that if something went wrong with your computer while you were using them, Microsoft wouldn't help you to fix it. Despite this caveat, they were very popular.

TweakUI is a powerful piece of software, giving you lots more control over the Desktop and the way windows open and close on it.

● Tweaking Windows 98

When Windows 98 was launched, Microsoft cut out the PowerToys but included the best of the lot – TweakUI – on the CD-ROM. However, this useful utility is easily overlooked as it is not installed on your PC but hidden in an obscure folder on the CD-ROM. Once installed, TweakUI appears as a new icon in the Control Panel.

UI stands for user interface and you can use TweakUI to make many subtle changes to the way that Windows and the Desktop work. For example, you can change the speed at which program menus drop down when you click on them and fine-tune the way the mouse works. You can also remove some of the Desktop icons that are normally impossible to get rid of. For instance, if you try to drag the Network Neighborhood icon into the Recycle Bin, Windows won't let you. But, with TweakUI, you can just remove the icon with a few simple clicks.

● Safety first

TweakUI is very powerful and so should be used with care. It is possible to accidentally damage your Windows installation when using it. As a safety precaution, Microsoft recommends using a special backup program that can make a copy of the Windows Registry. Do this (see Registry safety box, opposite) before making changes, and it will be easier to recover from a mishap.

MISSING TWEAKUI?

Despite TweakUI's popularity, Microsoft decided not to release TweakUI with the Millennium Edition of Windows and it was also omitted from some later pressings of the Windows 98 CD-ROM. Although it's possible that your friends have it on their Windows 98 CD-ROM or that old versions are downloadable from unscrupulous Internet sites, it's best to steer clear of these unofficial versions which may harm your system.

Installing and using TweakUI

The TweakUI window lets you check and change many obscure but useful Windows and Desktop settings, making it a great tool.

1 TweakUI is powerful, so you should take precautions before using it (see PC Tips box, right). To install TweakUI, insert the Windows 98 CD-ROM and click the Browse This CD option.

2 Look in the CD-ROM's tools folder, then in the reskit folder and then in the powertoy folder. Right-click on the tweakui.inf file. Select Install from the pop-up menu.

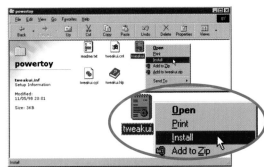

PC TIPS

Registry safety

Before using TweakUI, you should get Windows to make a backup copy of the system Registry – a vital system file that stores masses of data about your computer's settings. To do this, select Run from the Start menu and type SCANREGW into the Open box in the Run dialog box.

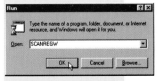

Click OK and Windows checks the Registry before asking you if you want to back it up.

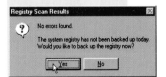

Click the Yes button. If you damage the Registry with TweakUI, Windows will restart using this backup Registry.

3 Once TweakUI has been installed, you can launch it through the Windows Control Panel by double-clicking on its icon.

4 The masses of TweakUI settings are held on 13 tabs. You can use the left and right arrow buttons (inset) to scroll through the tabs.

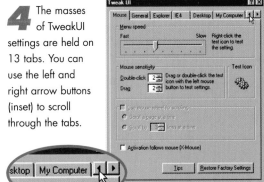

5 On the Mouse tab, drag the Menu speed slider to the left and click the Apply button. You can see the difference if you use the menus that appear when you right-click on the Test Icon. This setting affects the speed at which all program menus appear: experiment until you get the speed you like.

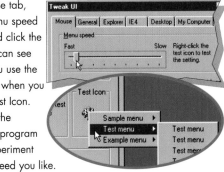

6 Similarly, if you don't like the delay that occurs between you clicking on a program menu and its list of commands sliding down, you can turn off this animation so the list pops up instantly. On the General tab, untick the Menu animation option and click Apply.

7 Scroll right to find the Paranoia tab which allows you to hide the Web pages and documents you most recently used.

8 There is no built-in help available in the TweakUI window, but you can use the Help file that's on the Windows 98 CD-ROM. Open the powertoy folder (see Step 2) and double-click on tweakui.hlp. The information supplied is brief, but it should get you started.

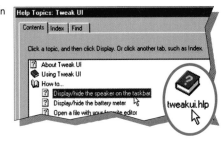

Customizing the Windows Taskbar

The Windows Taskbar is almost infinitely customizable. You can, for instance, add shortcut buttons for your favourite programs and documents, and even set up quick access links to Web sites.

If you haven't yet experimented with the extra features of the Windows Taskbar, you might have missed some very useful options. With a few adjustments you can add extra toolbars for faster access to programs, documents and even Web sites.

● Extra toolbars

There are four ready-made toolbars which you can add to the Taskbar. The first is the Address toolbar, which shows how Windows is integrated with the Internet. The Address toolbar allows you to type an Internet address into a text box on the Taskbar; Windows then starts your browser, dials up your Internet service provider and takes you to the Web site. You can also access an AutoSearch feature by typing Go, followed by a word or phrase to start an Internet search using a search engine (see Stage 2, pages 136-137).

The Links toolbar gives you easy access to your choice of Internet links from the Taskbar. Instead of a text box for the Internet address, you simply add buttons for each link, which you can click on to access the site.

The Desktop toolbar offers quick access to everything stored on your Desktop. With a single click, you can open any icon, document or folder stored on the Desktop itself.

By adding your own shortcut buttons to the Taskbar the system becomes a personal computing taskforce.

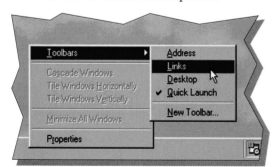

Right-click on the Windows Taskbar, select Toolbars, and you'll see the four standard options for Taskbar toolbars. Tick the ones you want to use and they will be added to the Taskbar.

The fourth ready-made toolbar is Quick Launch. This is probably the most useful of all, and by default is switched on when Windows is first installed (it's the set of four to six icons at the bottom of the screen, to the right of the Start button). The default icons are set up by Microsoft to launch particular programs, but you can change these. Some programs may also add an icon here, too.

Depending on how you use your computer, you can add some, none or all of the toolbars. You can also make your own toolbar using whichever shortcuts you want, such as documents, programs or links to Web sites. With some thought, you can create a single toolbar that will incorporate all of your favourite aspects of your computer without any unnecessary clutter.

Adding a custom toolbar to the Taskbar

Here we show you how to get more out of the Windows Taskbar by creating your own toolbar containing some shortcuts to documents and programs.

1 Start by creating a folder and adding shortcuts to your favourite programs and documents. You can use any name for the folder, but make it obvious. We have called it My toolbar.

2 Using the right-hand mouse button, click on a clear space on the Taskbar, select Toolbars from the menu and then New Toolbar from the sub-menu.

3 A New Toolbar window enables you to locate the folder that you created in Step 1. Select this folder and click OK.

4 You can now see a toolbar containing your own shortcuts on the Taskbar. Click on a button when you want to open an item.

5 Right-click on the Taskbar and untick the Show Text option (right) and then the Show Title option. The text on your toolbar disappears to conserve space. By pausing the mouse pointer over an icon you can still see the full title of the shortcut.

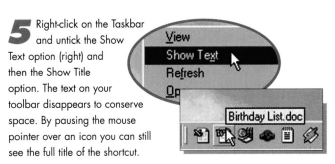

6 Drag your toolbar into the centre of the screen. It now appears in its own floating window instead of in the Taskbar.

7 Press the X button at the top right of the floating toolbar to close it. Windows then reminds you that you can reinstall it on the Taskbar whenever you like (below).

Housekeeping utilities

Just as your home needs a regular 'spring clean' to remove dirt and junk, so too does your computer. With housekeeping utilities, you can keep your PC neat and tidy so that it runs quickly and smoothly.

The world of Windows utilities has much to offer. In Stage 5, pages 8-9 we covered the extensive range of low-cost, or even free, high-quality software that is available. Some of these utilities add extra functionality to Windows itself whilst others let you customize Windows to make it work better for you.

The usefulness of utilities varies greatly from program to program, but there's one group of software that is consistently the most popular and successful: housekeeping programs. These can be simple one-function programs or complete suites of programs, each of which handles a specific task. The common factor is that they are dedicated to keeping your computer well organized. Your computer needs a regular clean-up to keep it running smoothly and the housekeeping utilities do just that. The more you use your computer – especially the more programs you install – the more important a housekeeping utility becomes.

● Removing drudgery

Housekeeping utilities are popular because they remove the drudgery of tidying up, leaving you free to use your computer for the activities it's designed to tackle, such as creating documents, using the Internet, playing games and so on.

Windows already includes a handful of basic housekeeping programs. For example, the Disk Defragmenter (see Stage 3, page 10) helps to ensure that your hard disk doesn't slow down by searching for data and parts of programs that are scattered all over the disk's magnetic surface. And ScanDisk (see Stage 3, page 9) checks your hard disk for errors, particularly chunks of data or programs that have become detached and whose origins can no longer be traced.

These built-in Windows housekeeping utilities are fine as such, but for many people, they don't go far enough. The most popular housekeeping suites include more advanced versions of these Windows utilities, and cover other functions not featured on them. Norton Utilities is by far the most successful and popular suite (see Stage 5, pages 10-13). It lets you recover a file even if it's been overwritten, or if something you have been working on decides it won't open any more. By running the Norton Utilities Disk Doctor you should be able to fix the problem quickly. System Doctor, another program in the suite, checks through the Windows system files for missing files, viruses and programs that have been wrongly set up.

Maintaining Windows can be a time-consuming job, but there is software available to help you.

SHAREWARE

Many housekeeping utilities are available as shareware. If you have an Internet account, you'll find that many are available for download from the software developer's Web site. Complete suites can be large (up to 45MB), whereas the simple one-function programs are small, typically less than 2MB and thus quick to download.

Which utility?

There's a wide choice of utilities, whether you want a whole suite of programs for every need or just one.

CleanSweep
Symantec Corp

This program focuses on the single most tricky area of housekeeping: installing and uninstalling programs. As we've seen, this is an area that Windows usually manages for itself (see Stage 3, pages 12-15).

However, when it does go wrong, Windows can easily lose track of the files that were copied and changed when a program was installed. CleanSweep performs the same service as the Windows uninstaller, but it has a greater success rate and many more options to offer. For example, it can search your hard drive for unwanted or unused files and then delete unnecessary copies, including old Web pages.

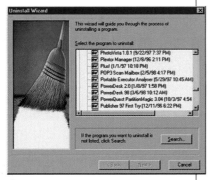

DirSize
Crystal Software

Monitoring the usage and contents of your hard drive is another useful function that many people wish Windows did itself. It can be very difficult to keep track of what is using the most space on your hard drive, without having to check individual files and folders using Windows Explorer.

DirSize, like many programs of its type, shows a graphical diagram of your computer's hard drive and all its contents. It gives the size of folders, as well as the percentage of hard disk space they take up. The same details are supplied for files, together with information about how much space is being used and how much is wasted. This program is perfect for working out just which programs or files to remove to free up more space on your hard drive.

EzDesk
Melissa Nguyen

EzDesk is typical of a small but useful housekeeping utility. It manages the layout of your Desktop icons so that they don't obscure each other, which can often happen when, for example, you need to switch between resolutions to use different programs to their full potential (see Stage 2, pages 12-13). EzDesk organizes the Desktop according to your specification and can save an arrangement so that it can be restored later. You can also configure EzDesk so that it automatically reorganizes your Desktop layout if you switch to a higher or lower resolution.

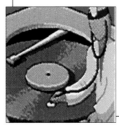

You can also choose a keyboard shortcut so that you can make changes with just the press of a button.

Norton Utilities
Symantec Corp

The concept behind Norton Utilities is that problems should be detected before they become serious. The

System Doctor can run in the background, monitoring your computer's system resources (see pages 12-13) and alerting you if a problem is spotted. You can use the Rescue Recovery Wizard to restore your system after a serious crash.

SITES TO @ VISIT

You can download many utilities, either as shareware or for a trial period:

Cleansweep
www.symantec.com/
DirSize
www.crystalsoftware.com.au
EzDesk
http://members.aol.com/EzDesk95
Norton Utilities
www.norton.com/

Don't forget to search shareware sites, such as:
Tucows
www.tucows.com/
C:NET
www.download.com/

Windows' printing options

Using Windows' centralized printer settings means that you can control the way your printer works, both for all the programs you use and for all the documents you want to print out.

Most computer users think about printing only just before they print out a document. Not surprisingly, therefore, the most common approach to adjusting printer settings is through the Print dialog box of the program used to prepare the document.

While there's nothing wrong with this, it can be wasteful of both time and paper because it changes the settings for each individual document only. If you need to change these settings often, you might find that a document doesn't print correctly if you forget to check. Sometimes the paper will be the wrong size, or perhaps the page might not appear in your preferred print quality.

● Paper problems
Some printers are initially set up to print on a popular American size of paper – US Letter. This measures 11x8.5 inches (279x216mm) as compared with A4 (297x210mm), which is the Europe-wide standard. The difference seems small, but a mismatch here can cause several types of problem, depending on the printer. For example, on many laser printers the page might not print at first. Instead, an error message appears on the display asking for US Letter size paper to be inserted. On other printers, the page might print but with different margins from the ones you specified in your document. Depending on the way the document was set up and the mismatch in page size, you might find that the type at the bottom of the page is truncated, ruining the whole print job.

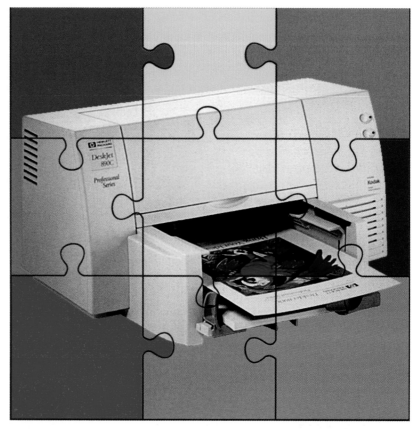

Save time, trouble and expense by setting printer options centrally in Windows. Default settings will then apply across your programs.

By using Windows' own centralized method of setting the printer options, you can avoid these and similar printer problems, thus saving time and money.

● A question of quality
For example, if you use a 'best' or 'top' print quality for most documents, it's tedious to have to change the setting from normal to best every time you print. By changing the default to best through Windows' centralized Printers folder, every document will print to the same high quality, without the need to alter the settings of each and every one.

You can use this technique to save money, too. If you use a colour printer, changing the default quality setting to draft will mean that you never accidentally waste ink printing a rough copy of a document at too high a quality. Once you've finalized the document, you can then print it at the highest quality setting (see Print properties box, right).

PC TIPS

Print properties
No matter how you set up your printer through Windows' centralized settings, you can always tweak print settings for individual documents from any Windows program. First, bring up the program's Print dialog box, but don't press the Print button. Instead, press the Properties button to see the full range of printer settings.

Using the Windows Printer folder

Windows offers a simple way to adjust print settings consistently for all your programs and documents.

1 Double-click on the Desktop's My Computer icon, then double-click on the Printers folder.

2 The window that appears has an icon for each printer (see Phantom printers box, below, if your PC has more than one printer). The printer with a tick next to it is the default printer – the one that Windows uses unless you specifically choose another. Right-click on this printer and select Properties from the pop-up menu.

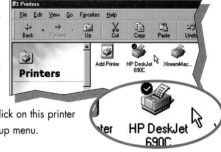

3 A dialog box pops up. The settings and options that appear depend on the printer you have attached to your computer. Most printers use several tabs to organize the many options available. Most will also have a Paper tab: click on it and you can see the range of paper sizes that your printer can use.

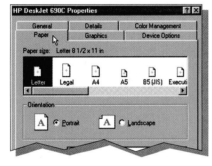

4 In this case, the default paper size for this printer is currently US Letter – inappropriate for Europe, where the predominant size is A4. Click on the A4 page icon and click the Apply button.

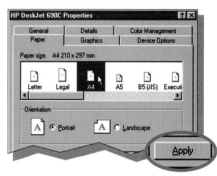

5 Most people print documents with portrait orientation, but you can change this if most of your documents are landscape. Just select the Landscape option and click the Apply button.

6 If you have a colour printer, find the tab that has the settings for colour print quality (here it's the Graphics tab) and change the Resolution and any other quality settings to suit the majority of the documents you create. Opting for a lower resolution can save ink and time if you print lots of drafts, for example.

PHANTOM PRINTERS

Don't worry if your computer's Printers folder shows that you have an extra printer. It's not unusual for 'phantom' printers to appear. The most common explanation is that your fax software has installed an extra printer driver for its use.

If this is the case, you can send a fax from any program that has a Print command – you select the phantom printer in the Print dialog box and the software sends it using your modem (see Stage 5, pages 26-27).

7 Check the settings on the other tabs and then press OK when you're finished. (Note: you should leave the settings on the Details tab as they are, as errors here can lead to pages not printing out at all.)

8 Now, whenever you print a document from a program, it will use your new settings. You can check this by bringing up the Print dialog box for another document and clicking the Properties button to see its settings.

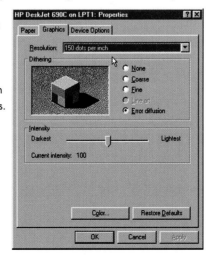

More troubleshooting wizards

Here we take another look at Windows' Help system, with more details on how it can assist you to solve problems with your computer and its software.

The complex nature of modern PCs means that when they malfunction it can be difficult to work out exactly what has gone wrong, let alone what the solution might be. Fortunately, the Windows troubleshooting wizards give you a hand with the kind of complex hardware and software problems that were once the preserve of the specialist.

In Stage 7, pages 24-27, we looked at how complex computer problems can be solved by using Windows troubleshooting wizards. These are interactive help files designed to present you with a series of different suggestions and tips, depending on the symptoms you describe – rather like getting advice on an ailment from a doctor over the phone. They are easy to use and, although they cover some quite complex ground, all the actions you have to perform are explained simply.

● Solving complex problems

We've already looked at the basics of how the troubleshooting wizards work. For example, in Stage 7, on pages 26-27, we

Explore the power of the Windows troubleshooting wizards and soon you'll have your PC behaving properly again. These carefully thought-out step-by-step guides make solving problems even easier.

covered the low disk space and modems wizards, so you should be quite familiar with the basic principles involved in using these new features.

On the next page we'll be looking at some of the other major troubleshooting wizards and the type of problems that they can help you solve. Of course, they can't cover every conceivable problem that might occur but they should make a significant contribution for most day-to-day queries.

In the detailed step-by-step sequences on pages 26 and 27, we'll look at the troubleshooters designed to handle problems with printers and sound. These can be very complicated, due to the inherent complexity of the matters they are dealing with. But, if you follow the instructions carefully, the wizards should be able to help you solve the problem.

THE AUTOMATIC SKIP DRIVER

Another useful aspect of Windows, which is related to the troubleshooting wizards, is the Automatic Skip Driver (ASD). This feature identifies programs that have caused Windows to crash or fail to load, and automatically stops them from loading. The ASD is activated via a short wizard that checks for previous startup failures, identifies the cause and disables it.

PC TIPS

Professional assistance

If a troubleshooter fails to help, it will suggest contacting a Microsoft technician via email, checking out various Web sites or contacting the maker of a problem application. This is a good approach, as often the program's authors can provide a small program (a 'patch') or a driver as a fix.

Wizards for common problems

There are over a dozen troubleshooting wizards available from the Windows Help window – some of which you may use time and again.

THE FOLLOWING is a list of the more widely used troubleshooting wizards. They can all be accessed from the Windows Help window as described in the following pages. In addition to the troubleshooters itemized below, others you will find particularly useful are the wizards for problems with low disk space (covered in detail in Stage 7, page 26), modems (covered in Stage 7, page 27), and printers and sound (covered on the following pages). There are also several other wizards for dealing with more specialized problems, such as networks and infra-red printing.

● DirectX Troubleshooter

The release of Windows 95 heralded the first appearance of DirectX on PCs. This is a collection of software drivers and routines that allows Windows to run Multimedia tasks faster (the 'X' stands for a variety of software sub-categories, such as DirectDraw, DirectSound, Direct3D and so on). The only problem was that DirectX was slightly unstable and could prove incompatible with some software and hardware combinations. The DirectX Troubleshooter, now much improved, is able to identify problems with compatibility and tell you how to deal with them.

● Display Troubleshooter

Problems with the PC's monitor display are quite common and might occasionally be connected with DirectX incompatibilities. Usually, though, the problems are due to the use of incorrect or old drivers, or a misidentified monitor. Trouble with software drivers are at the root of many problems on the PC, and never more so than with problematic displays.

Monitors can often be a difficult area because many people don't bother to identify them properly to Windows. Your PC finds it hard to distinguish between different monitors automatically, as some don't have much internal hardware and therefore cannot supply much data for Windows to work on. It's better to identify monitors manually; the Display Troubleshooter will show you how and also point out any other possible solutions to your problem.

● Hardware Conflict Troubleshooter

A hardware conflict is another extremely common problem, which will identify itself clearly but can be very difficult to fix. The Hardware Conflict Troubleshooter starts by asking you detailed questions about some very technical aspects of your PC. It provides direct links to dialog boxes and screens that you don't normally see in everyday Windows use, such as the Device Manager.

Despite this, it is actually simpler than the other troubleshooters. As the problem has already been identified, you need only follow the steps given and answer the questions according to the displays on screen. The Troubleshooter takes you through the process slowly and methodically, though, because if you enter an incorrect setting in the Device Manager it can create extra problems.

● Memory Troubleshooter

The Memory Troubleshooter asks a number of important questions (without giving any additional suggestions) before it decides on a course of action. At the end of the process it takes you through the changes you need to make in the usual way, but these will be based upon the questions you have already answered, not on operations carried out as part of the Wizard itself. This makes it one of the quickest and simplest wizards, although the end result can seem more like a tip than a solution.

The Print Troubleshooter

This Wizard covers a fairly small number of symptoms but it's still vital, as printer problems are notoriously tricky. This example simulates a problem printing a given font rather than a complete printer failure (usually due to incorrect drivers or a loose cable).

1 The easiest way to start a troubleshooter is via the Windows Help window. From the Start menu, click on Help and the associated window will immediately appear on your Desktop.

2 From the Index tab, begin to type in 'troubleshooter' and a list of all the various troubleshooters and associated help files will appear.

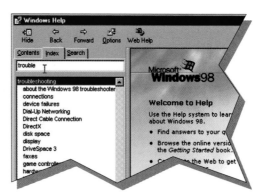

Since they appeared in 1991, TrueType fonts have become the dominant PC font technology for Windows computers. Previously, many fonts were platform-specific (that is, they would work properly only with a particular program or type of printer). TrueType fonts, however, are designed to be used by any type of computer or printer, making printing much easier.

3 Our printer isn't working properly, so scroll down the list until you find the entry named printers. Now click on the Display button to select the Troubleshooter.

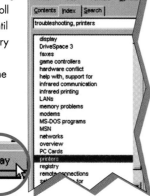

4 To start the Troubleshooter, click on the Click here link. (Before you start you might also want to click the Hide button on the toolbar so that the troubleshooter window is a more manageable size on screen.)

Print Troubleshooter
▸ Click here to start the print troubleshooter.

5 The possible number of problems with a printer is limited, even if the number of solutions is not. In our example, documents are printing out, but some of the fonts are not displaying correctly. Click the third symptom on the list, which describes this problem, and click the Next button.

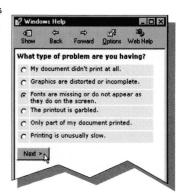

6 The Troubleshooter suspects that there might be a problem with TrueType fonts (see box, top right) and outlines a method of telling your TrueType fonts from your ordinary fonts. In this way we discover that the font we have been trying to print out is not a TrueType font. Answer No, I am not printing TrueType fonts, and click the Next button.

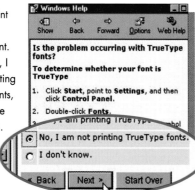

7 A common problem with printing can be that your printer does not have enough memory. With this in mind the Troubleshooter asks you to try printing out a smaller document with the same font.

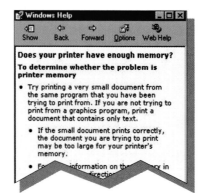

8 In our example this solves the problem, so click on Yes and the Next button. By making these checks, the Troubleshooter has discovered that a lack of printer memory is to blame. This problem can be solved in two ways. The obvious solution is to buy a new printer or more printer memory. However, simply printing documents whose layouts are less complicated is often enough to ensure you do not overtax a memory-deficient printer.

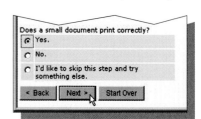

Troubleshooting sound problems

There's a choice of wizards for sound problems: the DirectX or the Sound Troubleshooter. We'll use the latter one, as a DirectX problem is usually identified by an error message.

1 Here we'll be simulating a problem with the sound on our PC. Bring up the Windows Help window (see Step 1, opposite) and type in 'troubleshoot'. Select the sound entry and click on Display.

2 Now, click on Sound Troubleshooter and press Display. If the Sound Troubleshooter doesn't work, we can always come back and run the DirectX one.

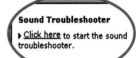

3 Start the Troubleshooter by selecting the Click here link. Remember, at this point you might also want to click the Hide button on the toolbar to reduce the size of the troubleshooter window.

Sound Troubleshooter
▸ Click here to start the sound troubleshooter.

4 Our simulated problem is quite simple: we aren't getting any sound although the software appears to be playing it. The first page of the wizard asks you to describe your problem. The second option – The sound appears to play, but I do not hear anything – describes the problem well, so click on that, then press Next.

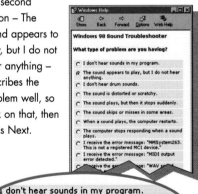

I don't hear sounds in my program.
⊙ The sound appears to play, but I do not hear anything.
I don't hear drum sounds.

5 The first suggestion is to make sure there's nothing wrong with the sound card. Following the advice, open the System icon in Control Panel and check that your sound card is enabled. Verify that your sound card is selected as the preferred device and that Windows is configured to use your sound card's audio features. This doesn't solve our problem, so click on No near the bottom of the page.

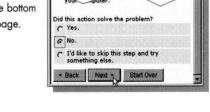

6 The next page suggests checking for problems with the wave audio device and CD audio device. Check the Control Panel to see if these devices are installed and configured properly. If they aren't, the Troubleshooter will show you how to install them. In our example, the devices are fine, so click No again to continue the Troubleshooter.

7 Now you are asked to check that Windows is correctly set up to play MIDI sounds. Follow the steps exactly. In our case this is not the root of the problem, and neither is the next page, which concerns the CD audio drivers. Answer No near the bottom of both these pages to go on to the next page.

8 The next page suggests checking that you have the latest version of your sound card's driver software. To do this you need to visit your manufacturer's Web site and compare the version numbers of the latest drivers available to the ones you are using. To check the age of your current driver, go to the Device Manager. Right-click on the My Computer icon on the Desktop, select Properties from the pop-up menu and then select Device Manager in the dialog box that appears. Click the Driver tab of your sound card's properties window. In our example there is a newer version of the driver and using it will solve our problem.

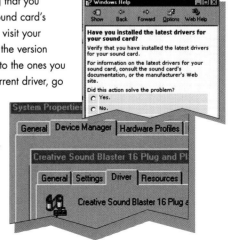

Network Neighborhood

One of the most important Windows applications is networking. Although few home computers will ever use the Network Neighborhood, understanding the principles can prove very useful if you use computers at work.

WHAT IT MEANS

NULL MODEM

This term is used to describe a special cable that can simply – and cheaply – be used to connect two computers together. The name comes from the fact that it's almost identical to the cable employed to connect a computer to a modem; 'null' indicates that a wire inside the cable is connected differently from a normal modem cable. Null modem cables are usually quite short, perhaps two or three metres, but can be suitable if the computers are close together – as in a home office, for example. A null modem connection is simple and straightforward, but it is much slower at transferring information than machines that are on a fully fledged network.

Office PC users will probably find that their computer is part of a network – a number of computers connected together. If so, you can access files and folders that are stored on other PCs that are on the network. You can also share hardware devices such as printers that are connected to the network.

Networks are very seldom found at home, not because they are particularly expensive or difficult to set up, but simply because very few people have more than one PC. Even if there are two machines in a home office, it is still easier and cheaper to set up a null modem connection, rather than creating a network that has just two computers on it. However, networking is an important feature of Windows – with its own icon on the Desktop – and is worth learning about as it is widely used in the working environment.

● The components of a network

A network can consist of anything from three or four computers to literally thousands of PCs. The basic components are a network card, some cable and some software (which comes as part of Windows). A network card costs around £30 and fits in one of the expansion slots inside your PC (see Stage 1, page 90).

Larger networks have special, powerful computers called servers, used to store files in a central location. All the devices are connected via a hub. Smaller networks, with perhaps just four or five computers, often do not use a central server. Instead, the individual computers might share part of their hard disks, thereby allowing other users to work on their documents.

● Advantages of networking

Businesses use networks because it makes collaboration much easier. In addition to enabling communication by email and the easy transfer of work documents, staff can also share folders on their PCs. This helps to increase productivity.

The biggest advantage of a network with a centralized file server for storage is that it's a lot more efficient to back up the business's data. It is unwise to rely on individual computer users to back up important data but

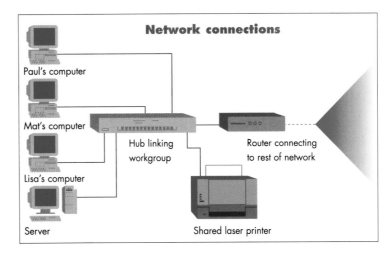

Network connections

Paul's computer

Mat's computer

Hub linking workgroup

Router connecting to rest of network

Lisa's computer

Server

Shared laser printer

a central server can be set to do backups automatically overnight. Another major benefit is that it is a simple matter to share expensive hardware, such as a laser printer. If six people can share one large, £1,500 printer between them, this makes significant savings in cost and space.

The diagram above shows a typical small workgroup that shares a laser printer and a server. The workgroup is also connected to a larger network.

How Windows deals with networks

WHAT IT MEANS

When Windows was developed, it was set up with networking in mind. This is why the Network Neighborhood icon is prominent on the Desktop.

ONE OF THE major features of Windows is its ability to handle networks. This usually happens through the Desktop icon called Network Neighborhood. Double-clicking on this icon allows you to browse through the PCs in your workgroup and other computers on the network.

The Network Neighborhood icon appears on your Desktop, even if you don't have any sort of network connection. It isn't easily removed (see page 16) and if you double-click on it when you are not on a network, it displays an error message.

● Network Neighborhood functions

When a computer is connected to other PCs via a network, the Network Neighborhood icon provides a gateway to them. The pop-up window works in a similar manner to the My Computer window and performs much the same functions, except that it is concerned with network devices instead of local hardware. You will see other computers and any printers shared by the network listed in the Network Neighborhood window. To connect to another computer you simply double-click on it. Windows then does some checking to

see if you have permission to use the other network device. (Most offices use passwords and strict authorization systems to protect confidential information.) This takes just a few moments.

Once you are connected, you'll see a window that shows the shared area of the other computer. This works just like a window on your own computer. You can drag and drop files and folders from window to window, and even open and save files on the remote computer's hard disk.

● Managing files

It is useful to set up special shared folders or drives on each computer on the network so users can keep part of their hard disks for private use and part for shared files that everyone else can see and use.

On page 10, we explore some of these principles. It's unlikely you'll test them at home, but they will help you get the most out of any office network you come across.

WORKGROUP

Large networks are almost always split into smaller sections to reflect the different departments of a business or company. These are called 'workgroups' and have names such as Sales and Marketing or Production Department.

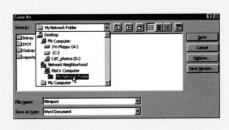

When a computer is part of a network, other PCs can be accessed very easily via Network Neighborhood. In this example, a file created on one PC is being saved on another PC's network folder via the Save As dialog box, which shows the network folder in much the same way as a folder on the first PC.

Exploring Network Neighborhood

If your computer is connected to a network, you can try this process for yourself. Otherwise, just read through the steps to understand the principles.

1 Network Neighborhood is really simple to use. Double-click on its Desktop icon to start. (If you don't have a network connection, you may see an error message, depending on your PC.) This brings up the main Network Neighborhood window, with an icon labelled Entire Network, as well as any other computer in your workgroup.

2 If you double-click on the Entire Network icon you will see all the computers and hardware devices that are on the network. This includes computers, printers, scanners and storage devices.

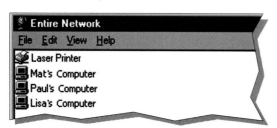

3 Accessing another computer on the network is as simple as double-clicking on its icon. Windows then asks for a password (see Password protection box, below). Type in your name and password and Windows will check it.

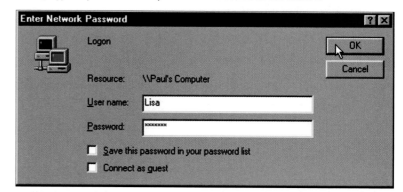

4 A new window pops up. The title bar contains the name of the computer you are connected to and the window shows the shared areas of the computer as one or more folders.

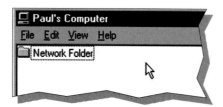

5 Look through the folders to find some documents. Double-click on one of them and it will open up as if it were on your own computer.

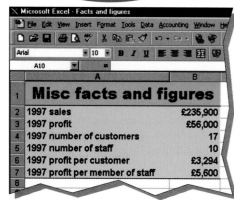

6 You can also copy files and folders between computers, using the same commands and menus as if the data were on your own machine. Here we are copying the company's logo from the remote computer to our own Desktop by simply dragging it onto our Desktop.

PASSWORD PROTECTION

Some network items are protected by passwords – you can connect to them and use their files only if you have permission and you know their password. If you do have permission, you type your name and password when Windows requests it and you will then be given access.

Sometimes, however, the controls on a computer network are not so strict and users can connect to (or log on to) a device as a guest, without needing to type in a name and password. This anonymous method is often used when sharing folders in a small or informal network.

Finding and mapping a computer

Windows enables you to track remote PCs on your network and then explore their contents using the Map Network Drive command.

1 If you can't find a computer on the network, and you are sure that it should be there, you can search for it in much the same way as you might search for a file on your own computer. To begin, click on Computer in the Find folder of the Start menu.

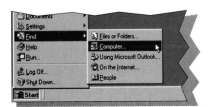

2 Network computers are usually given sensible names like Lisa's Computer, so searching for them is quite easy. Just type in the name, or portion of a name, and click the Find Now button.

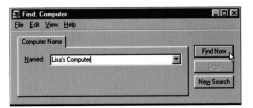

3 If the computer is on the network (see Missing names box, below), you'll find it listed at the bottom of the dialog box. Double-click it and connect to it as usual (see Step 3, page 10).

---

1 Windows has a command called **Map Network Drive**. You can use it to make a folder on a remote computer appear as if it were an extra hard disk on your own computer. Right-click on one of the folders and select the Map Network Drive command.

2 A dialog box appears, asking you to give a letter to this folder. Accept Windows' suggestion by clicking the OK button.

3 Instantly, a window appears with the contents of the folder. The icon at the left of the title bar shows that this window is a network drive (inset).

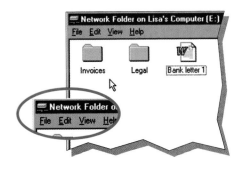

4 You can also see your new drive in the My Computer folder on your Desktop. Notice that its icon and name make its network status obvious.

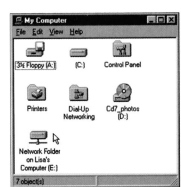

WHAT IT MEANS

MAP NETWORK DRIVE

This is a simple means of using a folder on a remote computer as if it were an extra hard disk on your own PC.

Once you have mapped a network drive, you can refer to it by its drive letter. For example, you will see it appear in the Open and Save As dialog boxes alongside your hard disk (C:) and your floppy disk (A:).

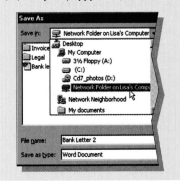

MISSING NAMES

If you use a network a lot, you'll notice that you don't always see the same PCs and devices on it. This is because some other machines might be switched off or someone might have disconnected from the network.

Software

FrontPage Express

Introducing PowerPoint

If you want to produce stylish and persuasive presentations, try enlisting Microsoft's flexible PowerPoint program to help you put across your ideas.

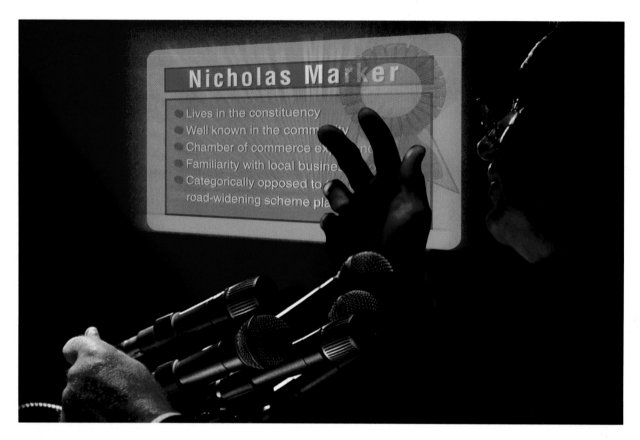

Word processors, spreadsheets and database programs are all essential office software, upon which many computer users in business and at home rely. Completing the set of business programs are presentation programs. The features of such programs are dedicated to helping you communicate information to an audience in a slick and effective way.

● On the approach
All presentation programs have the same basic approach: you create a sequence of slides, which usually contain text (often in bullet-point form) to convey the themes of the presentation. You can also add pictures, charts and graphs to help get the point across.

In many areas of life, the ability to put across a proposal or an idea in a well-presented and convincing way is becoming increasingly important. Anyone from teachers to self-employed business people can benefit from using a presentation program. It's not just a sales tool – it's also useful for training and education.

PowerPoint is by far the most popular presentation program in all these areas. On the following pages we'll show you how to create effective and stylish presentations using this powerful piece of software.

POWERPOINT 2000

PowerPoint 2000 has most of PowerPoint 97's commands, so whichever program you use, future PowerPoint exercises in *PCs made easy* will work in both programs. Where there are any differences, we'll highlight the PowerPoint 2000 method with this type of box.

WHAT IT MEANS

SLIDES

The pages you create with a presentation program are known as slides. This derives from their original application: creating transparent films for display on an overhead transparency projector. The term is used for all types of pages, including paper pages you'll print out and even 'pages' that will only be seen on the computer's screen.

INSTALLING POWERPOINT

If you have Microsoft Office installed on your computer, check on the Start menu to see if PowerPoint has already been installed. If there's no PowerPoint entry, you need to install it. Put the Office CD-ROM into the CD-ROM drive and follow the on-screen instructions that let you add the individual Office programs. If you don't have Microsoft Office, you can buy PowerPoint separately, but be prepared to spend around £280.

● Print and display

There are two ways of using a presentation program: you can create slides with the aim of printing them out, or you can use the computer to display the slides to your audience. Most people will print out the slides and hand out paper copies to their audience. You can also print them on to transparent sheets and use an overhead projector to display them to a larger group of people.

However, for a really slick presentation, many sales people travel with a notebook PC (see Stage 6, pages 108-109) and use PowerPoint to display the slides directly via the screen. Even presentations to larger groups can be done this way, by connecting the notebook to a big external monitor.

One big advantage of giving a presentation directly from the computer is that you can use the computer's Multimedia capabilities in your presentation. Printed slides are static, but slides that are displayed on the computer screen can be dynamic. In addition, you can add sound effects, video clips and animations. Among the most commonly used dynamic effects are special transitions between slides.

This is a special feature of the presentation program and it allows you to make information appear on the screen in attention-grabbing ways. For example, each piece of information on a slide can be made to slide in from the side of the screen – complete with sound effects. Also, when switching to the next slide, you can make it appear as if through vertical blinds. Used with care, these transitions can add professional polish to a good presentation.

Making a start

Each time you start to construct a new presentation using PowerPoint, you will go through these initial steps.

1 The first time you start PowerPoint, you'll see Microsoft's Office Assistant appear to give you general advice. Click on the Start using Microsoft PowerPoint option.

2 In the dialog box that appears, select the fourth option, Blank Presentation, and click on the OK button.

3 PowerPoint asks what slide layout you want to use. Select the first one from the New Slide window and click the OK button.

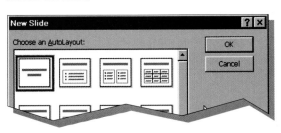

4 You'll now see the first slide in your presentation, ready for you to enter your own text. On page 32, we introduce the features of the PowerPoint workspace.

The PowerPoint workspace

Like any new software, PowerPoint includes some familiar tools and some new features. Here, we introduce the workspace.

ONCE YOU HAVE started the PowerPoint program and chosen the options to set up a new presentation as shown under Making a start, on the previous page, you'll see the window below. At this stage, the Window closely resembles a Word document in landscape form.

There's a typical collection of menus and toolbars and a floating menu box. Explore the menus and you'll find that many are almost identical to those in Word and Excel. By drawing from your experience with one of these programs you'll find it easier to learn PowerPoint.

The page looks spartan at the moment because there are no colours or effects. This lets you concentrate on the task of inserting your information on the page. Any visual elements can be added to the page later, when the text has been positioned.

THE DISAPPEARING WORKSPACE

When using PowerPoint to display the slides directly from the computer screen, the workspace disappears, and the slide occupies the full screen. This helps maximize the impact of the presentation by reducing distractions. Use the Slide Show button at the bottom of the screen to preview this, and press the [Esc] key to return to the editing view.

Formatting toolbar

This toolbar brings together the most common formatting options for text items in your slides.

Title bar

As with all Windows programs, this displays the program and document name, together with the window control buttons.

Menu bar

The nine text menu options provide access to the complete set of commands available in PowerPoint, and the single document icon at the far left lets you minimize and close the document you're currently working on.

Standard toolbar

The top toolbar includes buttons for one-click access to file operations, such as Open and Save, and links to other programs such as Word and Excel.

Common Tasks

This floating box lets you carry out the most common presentation tasks quickly: adding a new slide to your presentation, choosing a different type of slide layout and adding an overall design to the slides.

Click to add title

Click to add sub-title

Document

The document area shows the current slide; here it still contains the original text boxes.

Text boxes

The text in these boxes simply acts as an indication of where to type your own information. You can choose a different slide layout for different arrangements of information (see Step 1, opposite).

Mode buttons

These buttons let you switch between various PowerPoint view modes, including a text-only Outline View and a Slide Show which shows the slides occupying the full screen.

Drawing toolbar

PowerPoint documents can use the same graphical objects as Word and Excel. Using the Drawing toolbar, you can add objects such as WordArt, lines and boxes.

Status bar

Three areas on the Status bar provide confirmation as to which slide you are working on and any design settings you have applied, and also alert you if there are any incorrectly spelt words in your slides.

Editing slides with PowerPoint

The most basic task in PowerPoint is adding your own information to the slide layouts. Here we've started an election candidate's manifesto presentation from a blank slide.

1 Follow the steps shown under Making a start on page 31, but select the second option in the New Slide dialog box. The preview shows that it includes bullet point items.

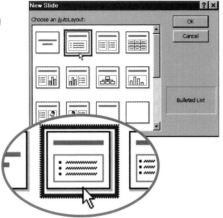

2 The first slide appears; it's not entirely blank, but has placeholder text for the title and for the first bullet point.

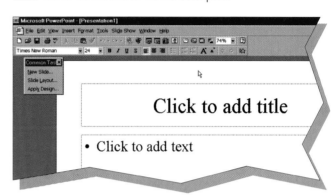

3 Click on the title: you'll see the placeholder text disappear, leaving a flashing text cursor in the centre of the text box.

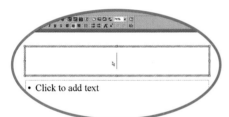

4 Type in your slide title. Here, we've used our election candidate's name – it appears in the same text format as the placeholder.

5 Now click on the second of the text boxes. Again, the text disappears, but a greyed-out bullet point remains so that you don't have to create it yourself.

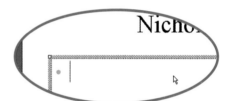

6 Type the first point for this slide of your presentation and press the [Enter] key. A new bullet point appears for the next point.

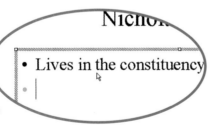

7 Type as many bullet-point notes as you need. Note that if one of the items is too long, it wraps on to the next line with the correct indent, just as in Microsoft Word.

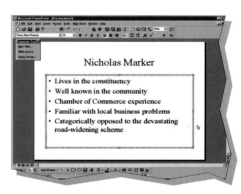

8 Select the Save option from the File menu, give your first presentation a name and save it.

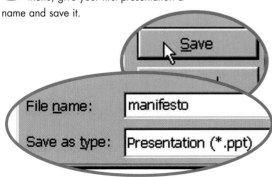

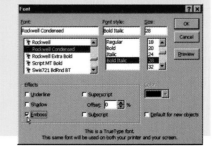

PC TIPS

Formatting basics

Use the text-formatting toolbar to change the typeface, size and alignment of the text in your slides. The Font command in the Format dialog box provides access to other text options, including embossed effects.

The AutoContent Wizard

If you haven't created a presentation before, it's worth spending some time going through PowerPoint's AutoContent Wizard. It contains tips and advice from presentation professionals.

For many people, presenting formal information is hard work, primarily because it's usually an infrequent task compared to using a word processor or spreadsheet. Even before the potentially nerve-racking experience of presenting the information to an audience, the most basic task of getting the information into order can prove to be no easy job. In fact, without logical and easy-to-follow information, any presentation is unlikely to hold the audience's attention for long. However, there's plenty of advice provided by PowerPoint itself.

Even though the individual needs of each presentation are likely to be unique, PowerPoint can help with most presentations through its AutoContent Wizard. This leads you through a series of choices that cover many common types of presentation. This works for many different presentations because the logical sequence of information is often the same, regardless of the specific details.

In explaining a new business project, for example, a slide presentation will introduce the concept, describe its details, cover its competitors and outline its launch schedule. You can use the slides as a reminder or guide as to what to cover in your presentation. You could even spot useful ideas that you might otherwise have missed.

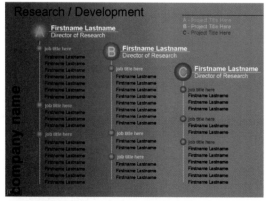

Using AutoContent's Organization Overview option means you don't have to create layouts like this from scratch. You can simply replace the dummy information on the ready-made slide.

● **Options and advice**

PowerPoint's AutoContent Wizard covers a wide range of presentation tasks. At the simplest level, there's the Announcement/ Flyer Wizard, which creates a two-page PowerPoint document that ensures the important elements of an event are fully covered. At the other extreme, the Organization Overview includes slides where the layout of detailed information would be hugely time-consuming to create from scratch. Some AutoContent Wizard options also include advice and tips from American business guru Dale Carnegie's range of business aids.

Once you have used the AutoContent Wizard to create a 'shell' presentation, you can replace the placeholder information and/or pictures with your own.

Creating an announcement presentation

Using the AutoContent Wizard is easy. By choosing from a range of presentation tasks and telling PowerPoint how you'll be making the presentation, you can get your computer to do most of the work.

1 Start PowerPoint and choose the first option, AutoContent wizard, from the three options in the opening dialog box. Click the OK button.

2 Now the AutoContent Wizard dialog box appears. Click the Next button.

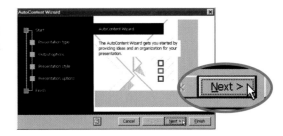

3 In the next screen, click the Personal button and select Announcement/Flyer from the panel before clicking Next.

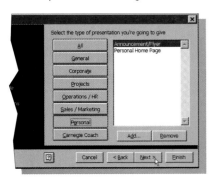

4 In the next two screens, make sure you tell PowerPoint that you're creating a presentation for display on screen.

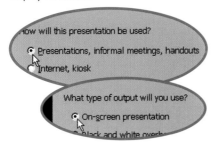

5 The first, or title, slide usually includes some information about the presentation and its author. Type the appropriate text into the three boxes on the next AutoContent Wizard screen. In the final screen click the Finish button.

6 The PowerPoint window changes to show an Outline View of the slides: the slide text is shown on the left (two slides are shown here) and a floating window on the right previews the current slide in colour. Click the Slide Show button at the bottom of the screen.

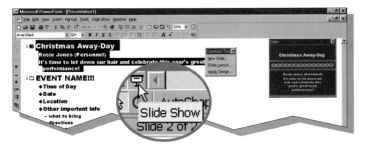

7 You can now see the first slide across the full screen. Check the spelling and information and then press the [Esc] key to return to the Outline View.

8 Now edit the information on the second slide to suit your announcement. Simply highlight and change the text as necessary, using the placeholders as a reminder of points to include. As you add the information, the Color preview window will change.

9 Use the Slide Show button again to see the effects of your changes.

Re-ordering slides

To get your point across, it's vital to present information in a clear, logical order. PowerPoint helps you organize your ideas by making it easy to sort your slides.

When you are setting up any document, it can sometimes be hard to see how to present the information it contains in the best way. As you put your thoughts together while writing a letter, for example, you might need to move some paragraphs around to make the logic easier to follow.

The same principles apply for a presentation. You might discover that certain slides need to be moved to make a point clearer or to keep your audience's attention. Remember that with a letter, readers can re-read earlier sections if they lose track of the thread, but in a live presentation, the audience can't skip back a few slides to remind themselves of what you were saying.

For this reason, it's vital to run through the order of a presentation and ensure that none of the slides is out of place. Fortunately, re-ordering any number of slides is easy, and there are several ways you can do this.

● The wrong way

Importantly, the most obvious way isn't necessarily the easiest. In most Windows programs, if you want to move items from, say, page three to page five, you can select them, use the Cut command (either from the Edit menu or by pressing [Ctrl]+[X]) and then go to page five and use the Paste command.

There are two main reasons why this isn't the best approach in PowerPoint. Firstly, you can easily leave a text box or picture behind by accident. Secondly, there are so many steps involved that the job can become very arduous and time-consuming – especially if you need to re-order several slides to do it.

● The right way

For these reasons, PowerPoint includes an easy-to-use Slide Sorter View mode (see PC Tips box, right), which is designed to let you move complete slides around by dragging and dropping. There's no risk of leaving an object behind, and the task is performed with a single action. Even better, you can select more than one slide, so you can move whole

Microsoft PowerPoint provides the tools to help you get your slides into the optimum order quickly and easily.

sections of your presentation around very quickly. This simply can't be done using Cut and Paste commands in the normal Slide View mode.

You can also move slides around in Outline View mode (see PC Tips box, right). Here, the contents of the slides are shown as an indented array of text bullet points. Even though only the text is shown, by dragging the slide icon that appears on the first line of each slide, all objects on the slide move, too.

In the exercise opposite, we show just how easy it is to use these different views to manage your presentations.

PC TIPS

Switching views

Use the mode buttons at the bottom of the PowerPoint window to switch quickly from one view to another. The Slide Sorter View is the button made of four small rectangles. On its left is the Outline View button. On its right are the Notes Pages and Slide Show View.

How to re-order a presentation

Switching between view modes makes it easy to move slides into whichever new position you want them.

1 Start with a presentation using around half a dozen slides. We've made a short presentation about an imaginary flower show.

2 Press the Slide Sorter View button at the bottom of the PowerPoint screen.

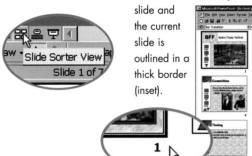

3 The PowerPoint window changes to show the slides together. This gives you an overall feel for how your presentation progresses. The order is shown by a number under each slide and the current slide is outlined in a thick border (inset).

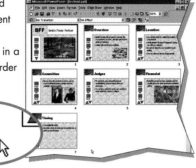

PC TIPS

Space saving

When using the Outline View mode to re-order slides, you will often find it useful to reduce the amount of information on the screen. Press the Collapse All button on the Outlining toolbar (on the left of the screen) to hide the contents of the slides. You'll see just the title of the slides, which makes it easier to move slides around, especially on long presentations. Press the Expand All button below when you want to see the full contents again.

4 In our example, the Timing slide is at the end. It ought to go closer to the front. Click once on the slide to select it and drag the mouse pointer to an earlier position (we've chosen to put it just before Location, slide 3). The thin grey line between slides 2 and 3 indicates where the Timing slide will go.

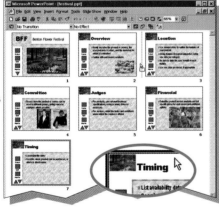

5 The Timing slide appears in its new position and all the subsequent slides are re-sorted and renumbered.

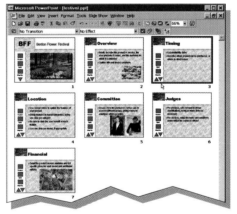

6 You can also move slides using Outline View. Looking at the new order, we now find that we want to move the Financial slide (which is currently last, slide number 7) ahead of the two slides covering personnel (5 and 6). Select the slide and press the Outline View button at the bottom of the screen.

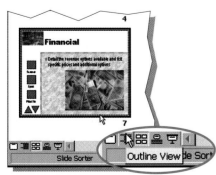

7 In Outline View, the slides appear as text only, with a numbered slide icon to the left of each heading. The current slide is selected (highlighted in black), so simply drag its slide icon up to the right position – in our example it goes before the Committee slide, currently numbered 5 (inset).

8 When you release the mouse, the Outline updates to show your changes, with the Financial slide now at number 5. If you switch back to Slide Sorter View, you can see that all the objects that make up each slide have also moved, including the picture on the Financial slide.

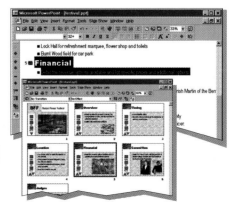

Introducing the Slide Master

PowerPoint's Slide Master provides an easy way to give your presentation a uniform style by adding standard elements to every slide and providing a background template for you to add your own data.

A s well as actually coming up with the most persuasive information for the slides in your presentations, it's important to get the look and feel of the presentation itself right. By choosing a design (colours, typefaces, repeating graphics and so on) that complements the slide information, you can help make the presentation more effective.

Although it is up to you to create a good design, PowerPoint helps by providing a background slide called a Slide Master to save you time and effort. It works in a similar way to Background in Microsoft Publisher (see Stage 6, pages 90-91). When designing, you often want headings, picture boxes and text columns to appear in the same position on every page, and PowerPoint allows you to take the same approach with the slides in your presentation. If you edit the special Slide Master page, adding, removing and altering items as required, these changes will appear on every individual slide.

● **Adding logos and design styles**
If you have a logo which you want to use in the same position on every page, for example, it's much more efficient to add it to the Slide Master than to add it to every slide in your presentation. Firstly, you only have to import the logo once. Secondly, if you add slides later, you don't have to remember to add the logo to them – it appears automatically. Finally, if the logo has to be changed, you only need to go back to the Slide Master and re-import it once to update all the slides automatically.

The overall design of the Slide Master also helps to set the tone of the presentation. For example, it can be sober, with corporate blue shades and a company logo, or lively, with fun graphics, bright colours and unusual typefaces. In fact, you may possibly be using this feature without realizing it when you create a presentation with one of the

Slide Master will help you to approach the design and creation of individual presentation slides in a disciplined way.

PowerPoint templates. Each of these templates is set up so that you overlay your information on a ready-made Slide Master created by Microsoft. This means that whenever you use a template, you can try out different approaches without having to do a lot of extra work. Simply create your presentation and then edit the Slide Master design (see PC Tips box, right, and opposite) to see what it would look like with another design.

PC TIPS

Editing the Slide Master
When editing a slide, if you click on an object that resides on the Slide Master, the Office Assistant automatically gives you more information about the Slide Master and offers to take you to it (see inset left). Click on the second option to edit the Slide Master.

Using the Slide Master

Here's an easy way to set up an effective presentation incorporating colour, formatted text and graphics for a school sponsorship bid.

1 Start up PowerPoint and create a simple text-only presentation, as on pages 31-33. We've set up a few slides about sports sponsorship.

2 Click on the View menu, select the Master option and then select Slide Master from the sub-menu that appears.

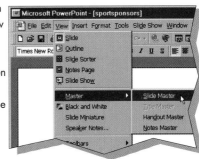

3 The PowerPoint window now shows what lies behind your slide. At the moment, it's merely a collection of text boxes, with little formatting and no colour.

4 Use the mouse to select all the text in the title box and then use the text-formatting list box to choose a new typeface.

5 Now you can format the other text in the slide. Here we've selected the main text and made it bold using the toolbar button.

6 The next step is to add a coloured background and some graphics to the Master Slide: click the Rectangle button on the Drawing toolbar at the bottom of the window and drag a box from the top left corner of the slide to the bottom right. At first, the white box will obscure all the other slide items.

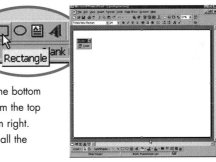

7 Right-click on the box, select Order from the pop-up menu and then Send to Back from the sub-menu. The other boxes reappear. While the box is still selected, use the Fill Color button on the Drawing toolbar to add some colourful formatting.

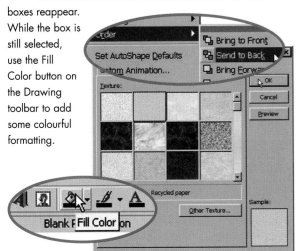

8 Add other graphics objects using the Drawing toolbar. Here we have drawn circles in our school's colours and moved them to overlap only the top left-hand corner of the slide. We have also added a clip-art picture in a black panel.

9 Press the Slide Show button to see how the style of the Slide Master has been applied over the text you set up. As you go from one slide to the next, you will see that the same style applies to all the slides in your presentation.

Microsoft® PowerPoint

Introduction to printing

Every presentation needs to be printed out at some point. Here's how to use PowerPoint's print commands to ensure that you and your audience get the most appropriate type of hard copy.

Slide shows and presentations take many forms and have many different types of audience. A necessary result of this is that presentations often have very different print requirements. Some presentations are intended to be printed and posted or faxed to other people; at the other extreme, others are designed purely for live on-screen slideshows. Many slides have to be created with both types of uses in mind.

● **Flexible printing**

To cover all the choices, the print options in PowerPoint have to be very flexible. One very obvious example is that you don't want a slide show that has been designed to fit a computer screen with a 4:3 width and height ratio to look silly when you print it on A4 paper's 210mm by 297mm dimensions. Fortunately, PowerPoint takes care of this subtle difference so that you can concentrate on the content of your slides, rather than the technicalities.

Even if you always plan to deliver your presentation from the computer screen and never to hand out paper copies, it's still often useful to print it out. Many people find it easier to proof-read their documents on paper, rather than directly from the PC screen. For this reason it is a good idea to print out your presentation, even in text-only form (see PC Tips box, right), as you'll find it easier to spot spelling and grammar errors.

● **Time-saving options**

Some slide shows are best printed with one slide to a page; for others, though, this would be impractical. Imagine that you have designed a 40-slide presentation to be given live from computer screen. If you wanted to hand out a hard copy to every member of a large audience, it would be both time-consuming and wasteful of paper to print and hand out one slide to a page. In

It is incredibly useful to print out the PowerPoint slides you have created. Not only can you carefully check them for errors but you can also hand them out to accompany your presentation.

such circumstances, PowerPoint lets you print two, three or six slides to a page, which is much more manageable. Even at six slides to a page, the text information and graphics in the slides remain perfectly legible. This is because the slides are designed to be easy to read from several metres' distance when giving a presentation. As this distance is obviously greatly reduced for printed pages, your printer's ability to print in detail ensures that the mini-slides on the page are still perfectly readable.

● **Print preview**

PowerPoint differs from Word and Excel in that it doesn't have a Print Preview feature (see Stage 1, page 42 and Stage 2, page 56). It does, however, let you switch quickly from colour to a black and white view, so you can check how your slides will look when printed without colour before committing them to paper.

(see Stage 1, page 42 and Stage 2, page 56).

Printing a slide show

Make use of PowerPoint's flexible printing capabilities to get hard copy printouts of your presentation slides.

1 Open a presentation with a large number of slides. We've used the organization template to generate a slide show of 10 slides quickly. They are shown here in the Slide Sorter View (see page 37).

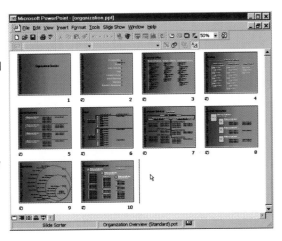

2 Click on the Black and White View button on the toolbar. Your slide show changes to show how it will look when printed.

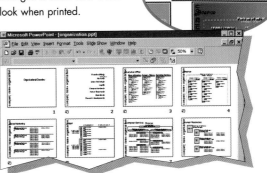

3 Select the second slide by clicking on it once; then press [Ctrl]+[P] to bring up the print dialog box. Make sure the Current slide option is selected from the Print range section and click the OK button.

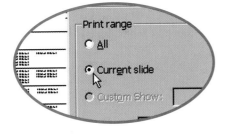

4 The printed page contains the slide's black and white content only, stretched to fit the maximum area of the page, without distortion.

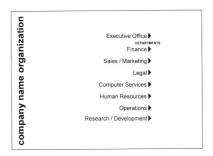

5 Bring up the Print dialog box again. This time select All in the Print range section, and choose the Handouts (6 slides per page) option in the Print what: list box.

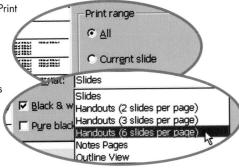

6 Check that PowerPoint has automatically ticked the Frame slides option at the bottom of the dialog box. If not, tick it. Click the OK button.

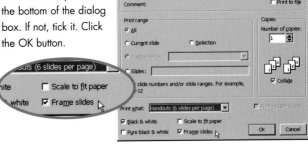

OVERHEAD DISPLAY

If you have a colour inkjet printer, you can buy special transparent film to create slides to display on an overhead projector (OHP). When light from the projector shines through the coloured ink on the film, it produces a coloured image on the white OHP screen. Make sure you buy the right type of film for your printer (check the manual for details) and also select the appropriate print setting (the printer manual will give you the necessary details) so that the computer automatically adjusts the amount of ink deposited on the page to suit the film.

7 The entire slide show fits on two pages, and the large amounts of information included on these slides are still quite readable. (You can choose other Handouts options including two and three slides per page, if necessary.) The frame around the slides makes sure that the text information looks like the slide that the audience sees and isn't just floating on the page.

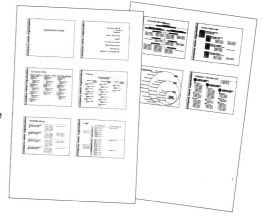

Clip art and charts

Presentations come alive when you include graphics to illustrate the text in your slides. Here we show how to add eye-catching images and useful charts to your slide shows.

If your presentations are made up entirely of text, your audience will probably get bored very quickly. Your slides might contain all the information that's required, but without any images they will be missing a vital and powerful element.

Illustrations can be used in two main ways: you can use them either to catch the audience's attention, or as charts that provide information themselves.

● Art for art's sake

To make your presentations more appealing, you can use the huge amount of themed clip art that comes on the CD-ROM provided with the PowerPoint package. You can also use the clip art supplied with other programs or even buy selections on CD-ROM.

You can adapt existing clip art to make it as large or small as you need, or you can create your own graphics with a program such as CorelDRAW or Paint Shop Pro. In fact, any pictures that you can transfer to your PC can be inserted into your PowerPoint slides. For example, if you want to liven up a presentation about a local club or society event, you can add photos taken with a digital camera.

● Presenting numerical data

Graphics can also help you put across a numerical message but these need much more careful preparation. Suppose you want a slide to show financial data such as the turnover of a home-run business or a breakdown of business expenditure. You could list this information as a table of numbers, perhaps in rows and columns, but you will be missing a very useful presentation tool: the graph or chart.

It's much easier to spot an overall trend at a glance by looking at a simple bar graph than by comparing figures in a table – as you

Your presentations will improve when you add some pictures. You can use just about any form of graphics, from photos to bar charts.

will see in the exercise opposite, where we've used a bar chart to show the growth in club membership numbers for a fictional fossil-hunting society.

● How to add graphics

It takes only a few moments to add graphics to liven up your presentations. PowerPoint comes with ready-made AutoLayout slide templates, where you need only double-click on an existing element to bring up the appropriate dialog box or window. This is one of the program's most popular features.

Graphics can also be combined with other PowerPoint techniques. If you want a graphic such as a clip-art logo to appear on every page, add it to the Slide Master (pages 38-39). You'll then be assured of consistent size and positioning on every slide.

PC TIPS

As well as graphics, you can insert other kinds of objects into your slide shows, depending on your software. Inserting objects works in much the same way as with Excel (see Stage 5, page 59). To see the full range of objects you can insert into your presentation using PowerPoint, click on the Object command in the Insert menu.

Illustrating your presentations

It takes just a few seconds to add a sprinkling of pictures and graphs to your slides and you'll be rewarded with a more effective slide show.

Microsoft®PowerPoint

PC TIPS

If you need to alter the size of a piece of clip art, or a chart, just click on it once and then drag one of the eight tiny handles. A dotted line appears indicating the new size of the object. Release the mouse button and the object is redrawn.

1 Start with a blank presentation and choose the Text & Clip Art slide in the New Slide dialog box.

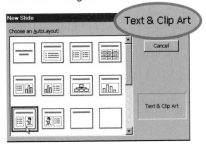

2 You'll see a simple layout appear with placeholders where you add your material. Double-click the clip-art placeholder.

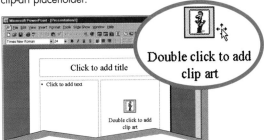

Double click to add clip art

3 The Clip Gallery appears (the pictures you see depend on the Microsoft programs installed on your computer). Select a suitable picture for the presentation and click the Insert button.

4 The picture appears on your slide. Add the text for your slide in the title and text panels provided.

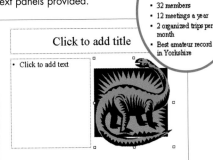

Leigh Amateur

• 32 members
• 12 meetings a year
• 2 organized trips per month
• Best amateur record in Yorkshire

5 Now we'll set up a bar chart on another slide. Select New Slide from the Insert menu. Select the Chart AutoLayout from the New Slide dialog box.

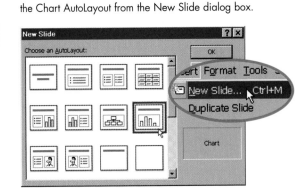

6 When the new slide appears, double-click on the chart placeholder (inset). A spreadsheet-like window pops up, with dummy information.

Presentation1 - Datasheet		A	B	C	D	E
		1st Qtr	2nd Qtr	3rd Qtr	4th Qtr	
1	East	20.4	27.4	90	2	
2	West	30.6	38.6	34.6		
3	North	45.9	46.9	45		
4						

uble click to add

7 Type the information you want to see displayed as a bar chart into the cells in the table and then press the X button to close it.

Presentation1 - Datasheet		A	B	C	D		
		1999	2000	2001	2002		
1	Full members	7	17	14	21		
2	Family members	4	9	7	11		
3							
4							

SHORT CUTS

All you have to do is press [Ctrl]+[M] to insert a new slide. This means you don't have to use the mouse to click on the menus. Instead, you will instantly see the New Slide dialog box, as shown in Step 1.

8 You'll now see the chart in place on your slide. Add suitable text to give it a title.

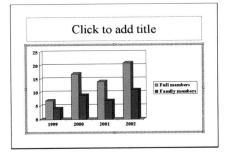

9 Change to Slide Sorter View (see pages 36-37) to view both slides side by side.

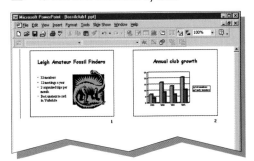

Animated slide shows

When giving a presentation directly from your computer screen, you can make use of extra tricks to hold your audience's attention. Here's how to use animated effects for maximum impact.

When professional presenters give a computer-based slide show, they use several tricks of the trade to make sure that their audiences are both entertained and informed. By adding animation and special effects, it's possible to add sparkle to a presentation and ensure that the information is put across in exactly the right way for maximum impact.

You can take advantage of such professional ideas yourself. Any computer that can run PowerPoint can apply special effects to the slides in a computer-based presentation. These make it look more dynamic and interesting than simply being an on-screen version of a paper-based slide show.

There are two main ways to apply animation in a presentation. The first is by animating the way objects appear on an individual slide; the second way is by making animated transitions from one slide to the next (see Transitions box, opposite).

● Animating objects on a slide

When you're giving a slide show, you'll often find that you don't want to present all the information on a slide at the same time. For example, suppose that you are talking your way through a slide show and you come to a slide that contains five bullet-point items, each of which you want to introduce with a sentence or two.

Normally, PowerPoint will simply show all the information on each slide in one go. But, in a case like this, if your audience sees the complete set of points as soon as the slide appears, they are likely to start reading ahead and might not listen to your argument properly. To avoid this problem, you could put each bullet point on a new slide, but that would be unwieldy and create lots of slides with very little information on each one.

A better, and more simple, solution is to keep all five bullet points on one slide but make them appear one by one, telling PowerPoint when you want the next item to be displayed. This puts you in control so that the presentation, and your audience's attention, follows your lead. This sort of technique mimics the way that most TV news programmes present text summaries during a news story: for example, the main features of a government budget plan are commonly listed on screen as a series of bullet points, which are timed to appear in step with the reporter's narration.

● Synchronizing your animation

With PowerPoint, you don't need to time the appearance of items on screen. You simply tell the program which items on the slide you want to animate and the type of animation to use, and you then trigger the changes with a click of the left mouse button. The next item is revealed with each successive click until there are none left; another click then takes you to the next slide in the presentation. But if

When used properly, animation can dramatically improve your audience's appreciation of your presentation.

Microsoft® PowerPoint

you want a more regular, automatic animation style, you can time the animation instead (see Self-running slide shows box, below right).

● Moving pictures

The need to control when objects appear doesn't just apply to text; you might also want to control other objects in your slides. For example, suppose you have a slide containing text about finance, together with graphs that show past performance and projected figures for the coming year. Your audience might become so distracted by the attractively coloured graphs that they don't fully take in the text that they are meant to read alongside it. However, you can prevent this by making the graphs appear only after you have outlined the other basic data.

Of course, there could also be times when the text relates directly to the graph. In such cases, it makes more sense to show the graph first, let the audience digest it, and then make your text points appear.

● Choosing animation options

PowerPoint makes all these variations easy through its Custom Animation settings (see page 46) and gives you plenty of choices for the way that objects appear on your slides.

One of the most simple ways is one of the most effective – by making each item slide onto the screen from the right-hand side. There are plenty of other options: you can make text appear as if it is being typed one letter at a time, make a graphic drop in from the top of the screen and so on.

Many animations include sound effects as standard – the sound of a typewriter, for example – but these should be used in moderation (see PC Tips box, left).

SELF-RUNNING SLIDE SHOWS

You can use PowerPoint's animation effects to create self-running slide shows, just like those you can see at exhibitions and museums around the world. By adding a transition (see Transitions box, below) and using the time option in the Advance section of the Slide Transition dialog box, a slide show can run without any intervention from you. The only requirement is to give viewers enough time to read the information on the screen.

Advance
☐ On mouse click
☑ Automatically after
30 seconds

Transitions

Animating a transition – where one slide swaps for the next – is a good way to liven up a presentation without detracting from the content.

THE ANIMATION EFFECTS that you apply to text and graphics on your slides can help make your presentations more effective through controlling the way information is presented. But transition animations that change one slide for another simply add sparkle to the visuals. By making the transitions a little more original, you can help make your slide show stand out from the rest.

Usually, each slide in a PowerPoint presentation appears immediately and fills the screen. There's no delay, no sound and no drama. But PowerPoint's built-in transition effects make the changeover of slides more entertaining. Many mimic the way in which TV shows dissolve from one scene to the next, where you might see a scene fade to black and then a new scene blend in from the darkness, or a new scene might slide in from the right of the screen, covering the previous scene.

PowerPoint has plenty of transitions to try out, including some that look like chequerboard patterns, and horizontal and vertical blinds. You can apply transitions to individual slides in your presentation, or to the complete slide show with a few button presses. Each transition can trigger a sound effect, too.

Experimenting with transitions can be fun, but you'll soon realize that too many can become very irritating if used in long presentations. Take a tip from the TV experts: they, too, can add flashy scene transitions at the click of a mouse button, but audience research has shown that these can have a negative effect. In particular, there are some transitions which simply take too long and it's not very helpful to make your audience wait for the next set of information.

Here is PowerPoint's chequerboard transition pattern at work.

Animating text in your slides

Animating the appearance of text items ensures that your audience's attention doesn't wander ahead of what you are saying.

1 Open up a presentation and locate a suitable slide for animation. We've chosen a slide where we want our audience to consider each point in turn, without moving on to later items before we're ready.

2 Click on the Animation Effects button located at the far right of PowerPoint's Formatting toolbar to bring up the small floating toolbar that controls animation.

3 Click once on the text box that contains the list of items you want to animate and then click the Drive-In Effect button on the new toolbar. Note: if you select a non-text object, some of the buttons will be missing, as some effects can't be applied to every sort of object.

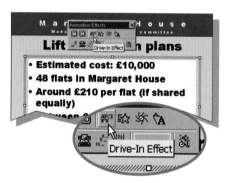

4 To see how this effect works, you need to change to the Slide Show view. The quickest way to do this is to click the Slide Show button at the bottom of the PowerPoint screen.

5 When your slide appears, all the text from the bullet-point list seems to be missing from the slide. Click the left mouse button once.

6 The first item now slides in from the right. If your PC has sound, you'll also hear a tyre-screech sound effect from its speakers – the Drive-In Effect. In a live audience presentation, you could now talk to the audience about this item, safe in the knowledge that they can't yet be thinking about the text that follows.

7 Click the left mouse button again and the next item in the text box slides in.

8 Continue clicking to bring up the remaining points. Once there are no more items left to animate in the text box, the next mouse click will lead to the following slide in the show.

Dynamic slide transitions

When switching scenes in your slide shows, give them a professional look with transitions.

1 Open up a PowerPoint presentation that contains several slides and go to the first slide.

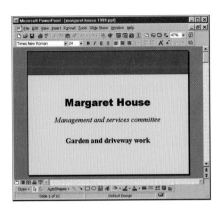

2 Click on the Slide Show menu and select the Slide Transition command. This brings up the Slide Transition dialog box. Initially, No Transition appears in the drop-down list box in the Effect section.

3 Select one of the effects from this drop-down list box. As soon as you choose one – we've opted for a vertical blind effect – the small preview picture shows how the transition works. You'll see the dog picture change to become a key.

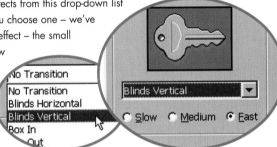

4 Once you have chosen a transition effect, click the Apply to All button to close the dialog box and return to your presentation.

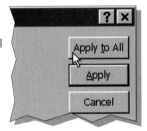

5 Press the Slide Show button at the bottom of the PowerPoint window and your first slide will appear according to the transition you chose in Step 3. This first slide appears from a blank (black) background and you can see the vertical blinds clearly before the transition finishes.

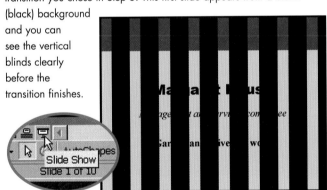

6 Click again and the first slide will turn into the second, with the same transition effect. This time the change is more subtle as the slides are similar. (Note: for clarity, we have darkened the visible parts of the first slide so that you can see the vertical blind pattern clearly.)

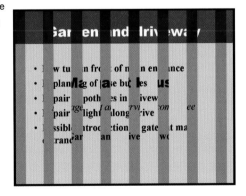

7 After just a second or so, the whole of the second slide becomes visible as the transition finishes.

Garden and driveway

- New turf in front of main entrance
- Replanting of rose bushes
- Repair of potholes in driveway
- Repair of lights along drive
- Possible introduction of gates at main entrance

PC TIPS

Too many transitions

While the transition commands are very useful, you should, wherever possible, choose one type of transition and stick to it. Be very wary of mixing too many eye-catching transitions that could undermine your carefully composed presentation by distracting from its essential content.

Introducing FileMaker Pro

Databases are the way most information is stored and analysed on computers. Here we will show you how simple it is to build your own databases with FileMaker Pro.

FileMaker Pro is a powerful and versatile database. We will show you how to get the most out of this useful program.

Have you ever wondered how the people at directory enquiries are able to find the telephone number you want so quickly, even when you give them just the person's name and town? The secret is that they type those details into a computer, which then searches a huge database for the correct number.

A database is simply a collection of information (data). What makes it so effective is that the information is carefully organized to be as accessible as possible. We all use databases in everyday life, even if we don't realize it. For example, your address book, diary, card file indexes and filing cabinets are all types of database.

Databases stored on computers, however, are especially powerful. You can search for particular items, sort the information and then print it out just the way you want. In many cases, databases consist of one file that

contains all the information you need. For example, an address book might hold all your friends' names, addresses and telephone numbers. Sometimes, though, databases are made up of several files. An example of this might be a database for a leisure centre that has different files for bookings, membership and payments.

A database file typically consists of two parts. The first part contains information about the structure of the database, while the second, much larger, part contains the data itself. This data is split into structured sections called records. Each record is, in turn, split into smaller elements called fields.

In the case of an address book, a record would contain all the information associated with one person – name, address and telephone number. Each one of these smaller elements would be stored in a field. You

SHORT CUTS

Like most other applications, FileMaker Pro makes extensive use of keyboard shortcuts for commands on the menu bar. For example, there are quick ways to open and close a file in FileMaker Pro. The Open command on the File menu can be performed by pressing [Ctrl]+[O] and the Close command by pressing the [Ctrl]+[W] keys.

might even choose to break these fields down into smaller ones. For example, the person's name might be broken down into separate fields for firstname and surname.

FileMaker Pro is one of the most flexible and easy-to-understand database programs on the market. The version we are using is FileMaker Pro 5 from FileMaker Inc (available from www.filemaker.com). Over the next few pages, we'll show you how to create your own database files in FileMaker Pro; how to enter data into those files; and how you can manipulate that information. Here, we'll start with the basics.

● Using FileMaker Pro

Installing FileMaker Pro is a simple matter of inserting the CD-ROM into the computer and following the on-screen instructions. As part of the process, FileMaker Pro will ask for your name, and the program adds this information to databases automatically where relevant (see page 51).

After installation, you can create a new database by choosing New from the File menu. One of the benefits of FileMaker Pro is that it comes with a range of pre-built templates for home, educational and business database files. These templates are ideal for beginners as they avoid the chore of setting up a new database structure from scratch (see Making a start with FileMaker Pro box, below).

You can view your database file in several different ways. These views are known as modes. The one that you'll use most of the

time is called the Browse mode: this is the view that lets you search through records in your database, add new records, edit existing ones and delete unwanted ones. In Browse mode you can view the database as a list of records or as a form. As a list of records, the database looks a little like a spreadsheet (see Stage 3, pages 56-57). Under the form view the database displays the contents of one record at a time on a form that you can design or customize yourself. Most database users prefer to enter data using forms instead of the cramped spreadsheet-style view, as it is easier to see information.

If you want to add a new record to your database, click on the New Record button on the FileMaker toolbar and type information in the boxes that represent the fields. You can click in each box in turn and type in the information, or use the [Tab] key to move from field to field.

● Automatic saving

Unlike most other programs, including Word and Excel, there's no need to save your work as you go along. Each time you add a new record to your database, or change an existing record, FileMaker Pro saves the information automatically. This is a standard procedure in all database programs.

When you've finished working on your database file, close it by going to the File menu and selecting the Close option. You can return to FileMaker Pro and reopen your file at any time in the usual way by using the Open command on the File menu.

MAKING A START WITH FILEMAKER PRO

Once you have installed FileMaker Pro from the CD-ROM, you'll see that a new group of items has been added to your Start menu (below). Click on the FileMaker Pro program and you'll see the New Database screen that lets you choose which database you want to work on (right).

The first option allows you to use one of FileMaker Pro's ready-made, but empty, databases or templates. These cover many popular tasks, from storing an inventory of your home contents to handling business expenses. If you select this option, a panel on the right lists the templates available. However, for those times when none of the templates suits your needs, you can

start with a new, blank database. You can define the fields you want to use to record information and design the layout of the form on which you will insert the information. If you have already created a database, there will be a third option below the two create options (see dialog box below). Choose this option to open an existing database to work on.

FileMaker Pro workspace

Although the work area of the FileMaker Pro window differs from that of a word processor or spreadsheet program, many elements are similar to those in other Windows programs.

START FILEMAKER PRO and when you see the New Database screen, select the Inventory template from the template list and then press OK. A short description of the template will then appear. Click the Form button to see the main database form, as shown

below. Currently, the database is blank, but it is useful for pointing out the different elements of the FileMaker Pro screen.

The first time you open the database, it appears in Browse mode, showing one record per form – as illustrated below.

Title Bar
This confirms the program name and the name of the database file you're working on (it is called Inventory in this example).

Menu Bar
The full range of the FileMaker Pro commands is available through the standard Windows Menu Bar.

Book
This card index icon, together with the record indicator underneath, allows you to move through the database by clicking from one record to another.

Field
Each record in a database is made up of individual elements called fields. Each field contains a specific piece of information relevant to that record. Here, for example, the record for an item in the inventory includes fields for its location, cost and date of purchase.

Toolbar
The toolbar looks and works like the toolbars of other Windows programs, such as Word and Excel.

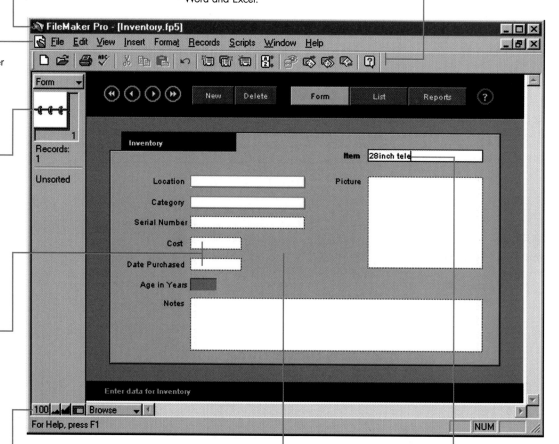

Status Bar
The bar at the bottom of the screen gives useful information, including confirmation of the mode in which you're working and buttons that allow you to zoom in and out of the screen.

Browse Mode
FileMaker Pro has four views (modes) in which you can look at your database file. The one you'll use most frequently is Browse mode, which lets you change the information stored in the database.

Insertion Point
The flashing vertical line shows you where any text you type will be added.

Creating and editing a database

We all have something in our lives that could benefit from better organization. Here we show you how a database can help to keep track of a series of office messages.

1 Start FileMaker Pro and select Messages from the list of templates. Click OK.

2 FileMaker Pro asks you where you want to create your database. Choose a suitable location on your hard disk, type a name for the database and then click Save.

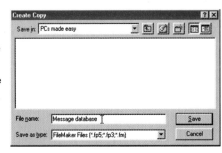

3 At first, a short explanation of the template and database appears. Click the Form button to continue.

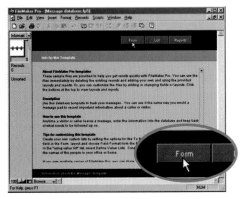

4 FileMaker Pro opens the database with a blank form (this form template, along with the database structure, is stored in the template). Note that the Record indicator on the left of the screen (inset) shows that there are no records in the database.

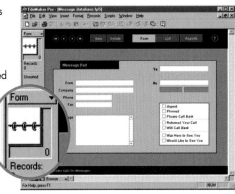

5 To add the first record to your database, press the New button. When the record appears, you'll see that several fields are automatically filled in for you: the date and time are taken from Windows and the By field is filled in with the name of the person to whom FileMaker Pro is registered.

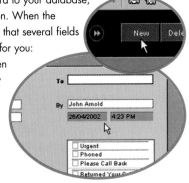

6 Fill in the other fields, using the [Tab] key to move from one to the next.

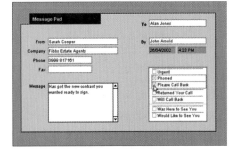

PC TIPS

Spell check
To see if the spelling in the current record is accurate, select Spelling from the Edit menu and click Check Record in the sub-menu. The Spelling dialog box helps you make any corrections required.

7 When you have completed all the fields, press the New button again. The form clears itself, ready for you to type in another message.

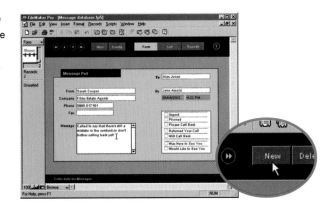

8 When you've finished entering new records, select Close from FileMaker Pro's File menu. Note: there's no Save command as FileMaker Pro automatically saves your work as you go.

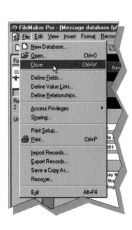

Modifying a database

FileMaker Pro's business, home and educational templates make ideal starting points for building your own database files. Here's how you can customize them.

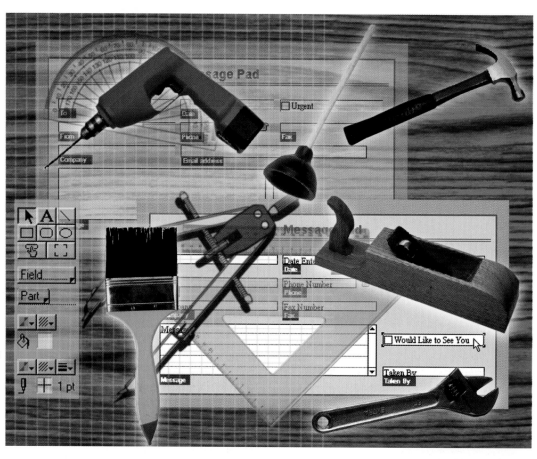

Creating a brand new database file from scratch can take quite a long time. With FileMaker Pro, it is much quicker to make customized alterations to an existing database.

On pages 48-51, we saw how to create a database using one of the ready-made templates provided with FileMaker Pro. But what do you do when none of the Filemaker Pro templates matches your exact needs?

The answer is to create your own database file. One way to do this is to create a brand new database from scratch, but you can save time simply by modifying one of FileMaker Pro's templates to suit your precise needs. If you choose a template that contains most of the fields that you need, this will cut down on the work you have to do.

● Planning your fields

Before you start, it's wise to identify the pieces of information you want to store in each record of your database (you'll usually use one field for each piece of data). Then you will need to choose the right type of field for each separate piece of information.

FileMaker Pro lets you use several types of field. For example, you would use the Text type for a surname field, the Number type for an age field and the Date type for a date-of-birth field. If you try to insert the wrong type of data into a field (text into a date field, for example) FileMaker Pro will ask you for the right type of information.

● Deleting and adding fields

After working out which fields you need, you choose a FileMaker Pro template that is closest to the type of database you want. Then you create a new database file, using the basic template but adding and removing fields to customize it.

Removing fields is a two-stage process. First, you remove the fields from the form that you use to edit records. Then you remove the unwanted fields from the database itself. It's vital to understand that the second action permanently removes data in the deleted fields. To avoid losing data in this way, you should do all your customizing before you type information into the database records.

Adding new fields to your database involves the same two steps as removing fields. You have to add each new field to the database and then add it to the forms you use to edit the records.

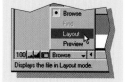

Customizing a database template

Although FileMaker Pro's templates are extremely useful, you may not find one to suit your needs precisely. Here we show you how simple it is to customize a template.

1 Modifying an existing template is the easiest way to create a new database file. Start up FileMaker Pro. On the New Database screen select Create a new file using a template. Then choose Messages from the list of templates. Click the OK button and the Create Copy dialog box will appear.

2 Now use the Create Copy dialog box to save your new database. Here we've saved it as My messages database in a folder called My Databases.

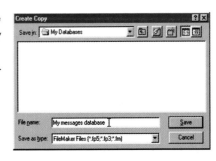

3 When the Template information page appears, click the Form button. Then, select Layout Mode from the View menu.

4 To remove a field from the form, click on it and press the [Del] key. Here we're in the process of deleting six fields that are grouped together at the bottom right of the form.

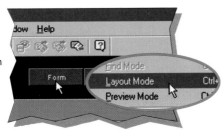

5 You must also remove these fields from the database definition. Otherwise, these unwanted fields will still be present in the database, occupying disk space and slowing the database down unnecessarily. Select Define Fields in the File menu.

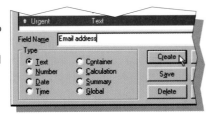

6 This pop-up dialog box lets you add and remove fields. Select each of the fields you have removed from the form in turn and click on the Delete button for each one. Click the Delete button when FileMaker asks you to confirm each deletion.

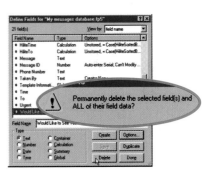

7 You add a field using the same dialog box as in Step 6. Select Text in the Type section, type 'Email address' into the Field Name box and click the Create button. Press the Done button to go back to your form layout.

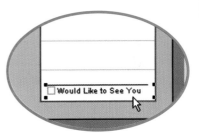

8 The Email address field automatically appears at the bottom of the layout. Use the mouse pointer to drag and drop the Fax field to the right of the Phone field and then drag your new Email address field into position below the Phone and Fax fields.

9 Here's the new database ready for adding and editing records. On page 57, we'll show how to apply formatting to fields to get the look you want.

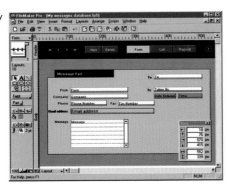

PC TIPS

Different field types

The Type section of the Define Fields dialog box (see Step 7) lets you set up other field types in addition to text fields. We'll show how to add and use other field types on pages 56-57.

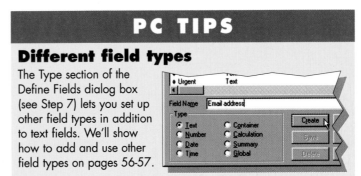

Creating a new database from scratch

Templates provide a quick and easy way to build databases, but they won't cover all your needs. Here's how to create the database you want by building it from scratch.

S o far, we have discovered how to create a database using the templates provided with FileMaker Pro. We found that we could use the templates as they stand or customize them to suit our own purposes. The advantage of customizing is that it's quick and simple to do. However, if you want to build a database file that doesn't bear any resemblance to the built-in templates, FileMaker Pro lets you create database files from scratch to deal with such situations. While this is a more complex process, it does give you far greater freedom to create exactly the sort of database you want.

● Planning makes perfect
The first step in creating a completely new database is to plan what you want. You need to think about the same things as you would if you were customizing a template: what information do you want to store in each database record, and what type of field should you use to hold each item of information?

You'll probably have text information, such as names and addresses, that you can hold in text fields. It's also wise to use text fields rather than number fields to hold data such as telephone numbers because this ensures that zeros at the start of long-distance numbers are displayed and allows for spaces, for example. However, numerical data is best stored in a number field, and FileMaker Pro has special types of fields for items such as dates and times (see FileMaker Pro field types box, opposite).

In addition, you'll need to think about how you want your database's layout to look in Browse mode. When you define your new database, FileMaker Pro will automatically create a very simple layout. However, this is not much more than a list of the field names with a box for each data entry. We'll show how you can change the style of your layout using these fields on pages 58-61.

● Designing a layout
It's a good idea to sketch out on a piece of paper a rough idea of how you want your layout to look. That way, you'll be able to make sure your information is clearly presented and easy to understand. You can add headings and you can also group together fields that hold related information (for example, address and postcode fields).

Creating a database file can seem a little complicated at first, but with some forward planning you can ensure you have a database that is perfectly suited to your needs.

Once you've completed your planning, you're ready to define the fields for your database. The process starts in the same way as creating a new database using a template, except you select the Create a new empty file option in the New Database dialog box.

● **Define your fields**
You define the fields one by one, choosing a name for the field and deciding what type of field it is. Don't worry if you make a mistake – you can always delete fields you don't want and add new ones to replace them. You can even come back later and define new fields if you forget some. When you've finished defining your fields, you can move on to look at the layout. This process is quite similar to rearranging a layout from an existing template (see pages 52-53).

You start with the very basic default layout that FileMaker Pro provides, so this is where your planning on paper will come in handy. You can use the mouse to reposition fields and labels, as well as to add or delete elements such as text headings, to make your layout attractive and its content easier to understand.

FileMaker Pro field types

Choosing the right type of field for each piece of data is the most important task in database design.

IT'S POSSIBLE TO design a database in which every field is a text field, such as in a simple database of first names, last names and dates of birth. But if you do this, you miss out on FileMaker Pro's extra capabilities for dealing with particular types of data. For instance, if date-of-birth information is entered into a text field, it can't be sorted into chronological order properly.

With databases where you want to perform manipulations or calculations, it's essential to look at the various fields that FileMaker Pro provides and choose the most appropriate of the eight different types available.

Text
A field of this type can hold up to 64,000 letters, numbers and symbols used as text.

Number
A field of this type can hold numbers up to 255 digits long. You can perform calculations on data stored in a number field, multiplying a Price field by a Number Required field to get a total cost, for example.

Date
This type of field includes the day and month portion of the date. If you omit the year, FileMaker Pro enters the current year.

Time
A complement to the date field, the time field can store information in the form of hours, minutes and seconds.

Container
This is a special type of field that can be used to store graphics, sounds and other objects. With this type of field you can build up an illustrated database, such as a pictorial guide to plants, for example.

Calculation
This type of field holds the result of a calculation that uses values held in other fields, such as the total cost mentioned in the Number field description, for example.

Summary
In some databases it's useful to add a field that summarizes information from a number of records in the database, rather than just the current record.

Global
This type of field holds data that is the same for every record in the database. You might, for instance, put a company logo into a global field. Another use might be to hold a constant often used in calculations.

Define Fields for "My Jazz CD Collection.fp5"

0 field(s)   View by: creation order

Field Name	Type	Options

Field Name: Artist

Type
- ◉ Text
- ○ Number
- ○ Date
- ○ Time
- ○ Container
- ○ Calculation
- ○ Summary
- ○ Global

Create Options...
Save Duplicate
Delete Done

Defining a new database

It can take a while to define fields because you have to create them one at a time, but once you have them set up, they are ready to use. Here we show you how to create a simple database for a collection of jazz CDs.

1 With FileMaker Pro running, bring up the New Database dialog box by selecting New from the File menu. Select the Create a new empty file option and click on OK.

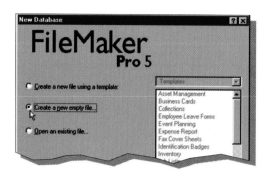

2 Type a suitable name for your new database file and select the folder where you want to save it. Then click the Save button.

3 The Define Fields dialog box opens automatically. Type the name of the first field (Artist) in the Field Name text box. Select the Text Type option and click on Create.

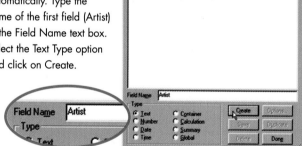

4 The field appears in the list at the top of the dialog box. Follow the procedure in Step 3 to add each of the extra text fields shown right.

5 Now add a number field to hold the duration of the first track. Type Duration 1 into the Field Name text box, choose the Number option and click on the Create button. Now repeat the process seven more times until you have number fields to hold the duration of each track.

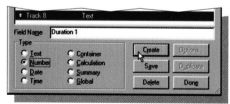

6 Create a date field and call it Recording Date. Select the Date field type and click on the Create button, as before. Now all the fields for our database are defined, so click on the Done button to finish.

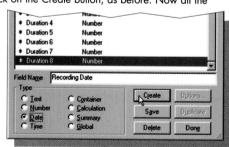

7 FileMaker Pro automatically creates an empty, basic layout for your database. You can now switch to Browse mode to start adding information (see pages 48-51), or tweak the design a little first (see opposite).

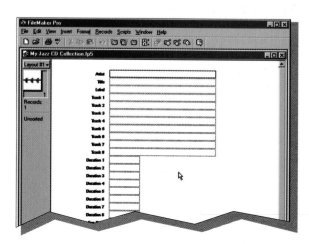

PC TIPS

Re-ordering fields

If you need to change the order of the fields you have added to your database, you can simply move them up and down the list in the Define Fields dialog box. Click and hold the small double-headed arrow just next to the field name and then drag the field to the right position.

Changing your new database's layout

**Now you've gone to the trouble of defining your database, it's time to improve its appearance.
Here we alter the layout of the jazz CD database from the previous page and add headings for clarity.**

1 Follow the exercise on the previous page to get to the basic layout that FileMaker Pro provides. Switch to Layout mode by selecting Layout Mode from the View menu.

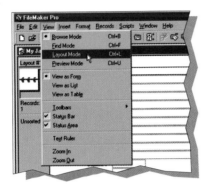

2 Use the mouse to drag and drop the fields and labels to new positions (see pages 52-53). Start with the Duration 1 field: click and drag it beside Track 1. FileMaker Pro shows you a dotted outline as you drag the mouse.

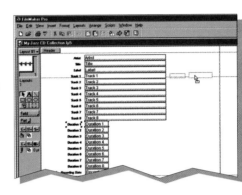

3 Continue to rearrange the fields and their labels to make the layout easier to understand. Here we've moved the duration fields alongside their corresponding track fields. We've also made room for some headings.

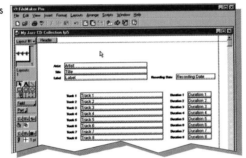

4 You can remove text labels from the layout without affecting the definition of the database itself. In this case, we don't need labels for each duration field. Click on each of the duration labels and press the [Del] key to remove it.

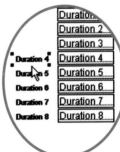

5 Click the Text button on the status area to the left of the screen to add a heading above the list of tracks. Click just above the column of track fields and type a label, Track Names. Use the same method to add a Track Times label above the column of track durations.

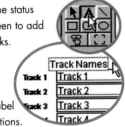

6 Add an overall heading, My Jazz CD Collection, at the top of the layout and right-click on it. Select the Text Format option from the pop-up menu that appears, and use the Text Format dialog box to choose the font, size, style and colour you want. Click OK when you've finished.

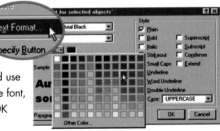

7 To make sure that the fields are clearly visible on the page when you come to enter information, you need to add a border to each. Right-click on the first field and select Field Borders from the menu that appears.

8 Tick the Top, Bottom, Left and Right boxes in the Field Borders dialog box and click on OK. Now repeat the process for all fields – you can select several fields at once by pressing the [Shift] key while you click.

9 Switch to Browse mode by selecting Browse from the pop-up menu on the Status Bar. You can now see the modified layout: it's already easier to find your way around. On pages 64-65, we'll show you how to tweak layouts even further.

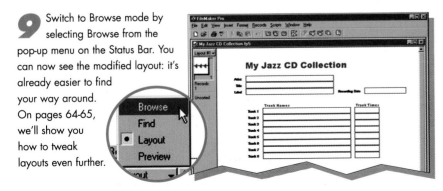

FIELD ORDER

FileMaker Pro looks at the field positions on your database form to work out the order in which it will move from field to field when you enter data in Browse mode. Generally, it assumes that you want to enter data from top to bottom and from left to right, and so this is how you are requested to insert the data.

Adding more layouts

Layouts are flexible tools and they allow you to view the information in your FileMaker Pro database in many different ways. Here's how easy it is to add more layouts when you need them.

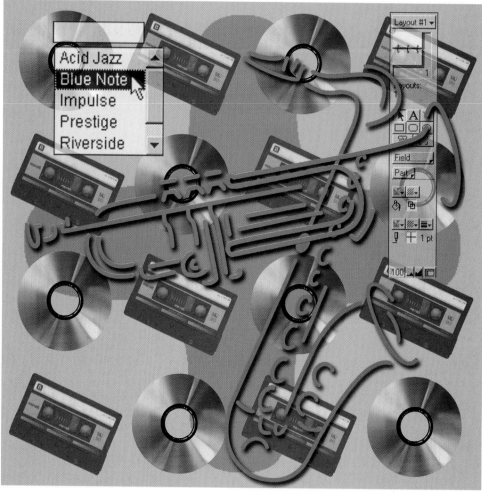

W e have seen that setting up a simple layout for data entry is part of the process of creating a new database file from scratch (see pages 54-57). However, there's much more to layouts than simply entering data: for example, you can use them to find information in your database and to set up mailing labels ready for printing.

The important thing to remember is that a layout itself does not store information – it simply provides a way of looking at it. The information is stored as the main part of the database file.

● More tools

You can have as many layouts associated with your database file as you like. For example, you might have set up an address-book database that includes fields for name, address, postcode, telephone number and email address. The layout you use to browse these contact details might include all these fields, but the layout you use to print out envelopes will include only the name, address and postcode fields.

Adding a new layout to your database is almost as easy as modifying an existing one (see pages 52-53). Already included with FileMaker Pro are several pre-defined layouts that cover various common uses. These are the Standard layout (which is the one created automatically when you define a new

database), a columnar report, an extended columnar report, a single-page form, labels, envelopes and a completely blank layout. The single-page form and blank layouts are good for both browsing and data entry. With a blank layout you can create a customized browser or a data entry screen to suit your needs.

● Choose a name

FileMaker Pro will always ask you to choose a name for your layout. Pick a name that will remind you of the purpose of your layout: Envelopes and Labels, for instance. That way you'll be able to quickly find the layout you want when you come back to use your database again later. Don't worry if you decide you want to change the name – FileMaker Pro allows you to rename, copy and delete layouts at any stage.

You can either create layouts to your own specifications, or use the ones that are provided in FileMaker Pro.

● Starting afresh

If none of the pre-defined layouts suit your needs, it's best to start with a blank layout (see page 60). This allows you to position fields and other objects, such as text and graphics, exactly where you like. All the tools you need to add objects to your layout are in the status bar at the left of the FileMaker Pro window (see The status area in Layout mode box, right).

Additional formatting tools are available either from the Format menu or simply by right-clicking on an object. You aren't limited to displaying fields as simple text boxes in your layouts. You can change their colour, size and text style, as well as adding borders. You can also change the style of the field itself (see page 61). For example, you can use special commands while you are in Layout mode to make it easier and faster to enter information when you are in Browse mode. If your database includes a field that must always contain one of a small number of options, you can tell FileMaker Pro in advance which information is acceptable. When entering data, you need only select an option from the list instead of typing it.

The status area in Layout mode

A FileMaker Pro layout presents the data contained in a database. To decide exactly how information is presented both on screen and in printouts, use Layout mode.

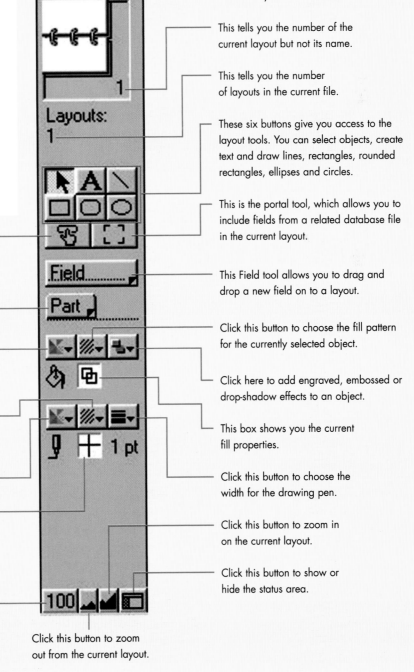

Click here to switch to a different layout.

This tells you the number of the current layout but not its name.

This tells you the number of layouts in the current file.

These six buttons give you access to the layout tools. You can select objects, create text and draw lines, rectangles, rounded rectangles, ellipses and circles.

This is the portal tool, which allows you to include fields from a related database file in the current layout.

This Field tool allows you to drag and drop a new field on to a layout.

Click this button to choose the fill pattern for the currently selected object.

Click here to add engraved, embossed or drop-shadow effects to an object.

This box shows you the current fill properties.

Click this button to choose the width for the drawing pen.

Click this button to zoom in on the current layout.

Click this button to show or hide the status area.

This button tool allows you to add a new button to your layout.

This Part tool allows you to drag and drop a new part into your layout.

Click this button to choose the fill colour for the currently selected object.

Click this button to choose the pattern for the drawing pen.

This button allows you to choose the colour for the drawing pen.

This box shows the current drawing pen properties.

This tells you the current magnification percentage for viewing the current layout.

Click this button to zoom out from the current layout.

Adding a new layout

Here we show you how easy it is to create an additional layout for an existing database. We use the Blank layout option to create one completely from scratch.

1 When we created our new jazz CD database (pages 56-57), we also set up the initial layout. Luckily, you can have more than one layout per database file because we also need one for making cassette labels for those jazz recordings that are on tape. Let's start by switching to Layout mode by choosing Layout Mode from the View menu.

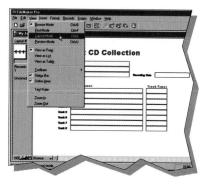

2 Now we're ready to begin building our cassette label layout. Choose New Layout/Report from the Layouts menu.

3 Type the name of your layout in the Layout Name box in this New Layout/Report dialog box. We've chosen the descriptive name Cassette Label. Make sure that you select the Blank layout option from the list and then click on the Finish button to continue.

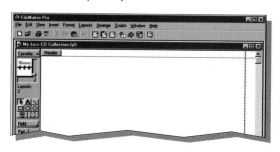

4 The screen will show a blank layout like the one below. This is the type to choose if you want to build a custom layout of your own.

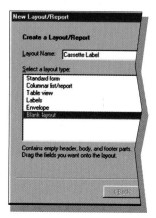

PC TIPS

Alternative layouts

When working on a database with several alternative layouts, use the pop-up list of layouts located at the top of the status area to allow you to switch between them.

5 Now we can add the fields from our database that we want to include in the layout. Position the pointer on the Field button in the status area and drag the field to the position where you want it to appear.

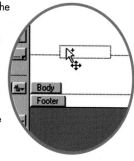

6 Now FileMaker Pro will open the Specify Field dialog box for you to choose the field you want in this position. Select Artist in the list of fields and untick the Create field label box because we don't want text labels in this layout. Finish by clicking on the OK button.

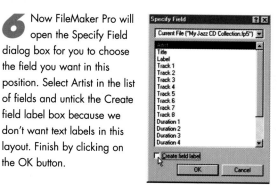

7 The Artist field appears in place on your layout.

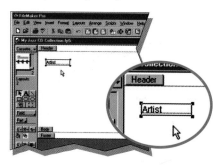

8 Here we've continued to use the same drag-and-drop technique to add ten more fields to our cassette label layout. We've placed them in roughly the right positions to start with but we can always come back later to move them, change their dimensions or apply formatting to them so that they print out neatly and fit on the cassette.

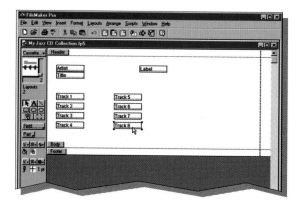

Formatting pop-up list fields

Make your new database layout easier to use by adding ready-made lists to enable speedier data entry in the future.

FileMaker Pro

1 Here's the cassette label layout created on the previous page. At the moment, all the fields are plain text boxes but we want to modify the Label field to work like a pop-up list so that whoever enters information can choose a record label from the list instead of having to type it in.

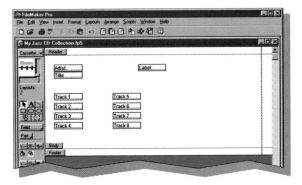

2 Start by clicking on the Label field to select it, then choose the Field Format option from the Format menu.

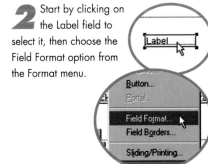

3 FileMaker Pro will now open a Field Format dialog box like this. Select the second option from the Style section and then select Pop-up list from the list box.

4 Now set up the choices for the Label field. To do this, click on the using value list box and select the Define Value Lists option.

5 The Define Value Lists dialog box opens. Click the New button at the bottom of the box. Type a name for your list in the Value List Name text box of the Edit Value List dialog box.

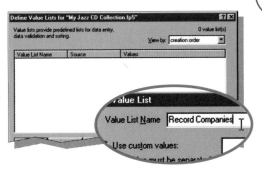

6 The large text box in the Edit Value List dialog box is now ready for your list of choices. Remember to press the [Enter] key after every entry so that each one is on a separate line. Click the OK button to continue.

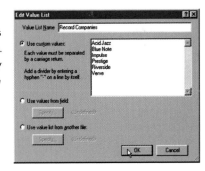

POP-UP LISTS IN FILEMAKER PRO

Most Windows programs use features called drop-down list boxes. These let you choose from a list of options. FileMaker Pro lets you add list boxes to your database layouts. That way, people entering data into your database can choose from a list of options rather than having to type the information into a text box.

There's nothing to distinguish a pop-up list from a normal text box until you click on it. When you do this, the list of available options appears and you choose one in exactly the same way as you would if you were using a more conventional drop-down list box.

7 Click the Done button to return to the Field Format dialog box. Make sure there's a tick in both boxes of the Behavior section of this dialog box and then click on the OK button.

8 Switch to Browse mode to see how the finished pop-up list works on the Label field. All you have to do is click on the Label field and the list of choices will appear. Then you can select the one you want from the list.

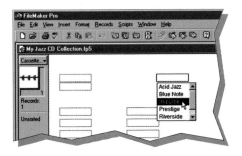

Finding and printing database information

A database file can hold lots of information, but you may well want to locate and print particular bits of information. Here we show you how to print data from FileMaker Pro.

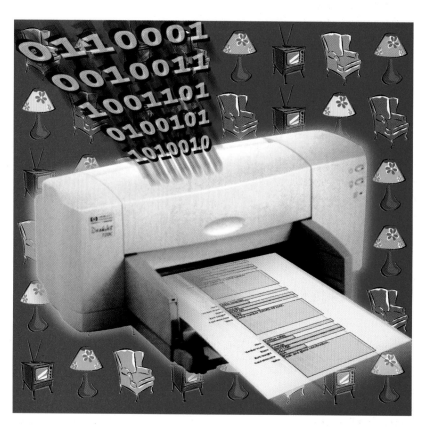

For a physical record of data stored in your database, search for the records you want and print them out.

So far we've concentrated on setting up database files and organizing how the information can be laid out on screen. However, there are many occasions when you'll need to find information in the database and also times when you will want to print out some of that information. For example, you might want to produce a set of mailing labels for a sub-set of people in an address book database.

As you'd expect, FileMaker Pro includes tools to enable you to find and print out information from your database. First, you use Find Mode to tell FileMaker Pro which records you want, and then you choose how you want the document to look by selecting a layout before clicking the Print command.

The layout follows the same pattern that you have created on the screen. If you haven't already got a suitable layout, you can always add a new one especially for printing (see pages 58-61).

● Finding records

Find Mode lets you choose a sub-set of records to work on or print-out. You are presented with a blank layout: type the information you want to find into the relevant fields and press the Find button. FileMaker Pro then searches the database for records that match your entry.

For example, if you want to print an envelope for a specific person in your address book database, you could type 'Blake' into the surname field and 'Sarah' into the first name field. After the search, FileMaker Pro shows only the matching records – almost certainly just one person. With this technique you can easily choose sub-sets of information: for example, choosing CDs from a particular record company in our jazz CD database (see pages 56-57). FileMaker Pro also lets you search for records with numerical and date information, such as all records in a home contents insurance database where the value is over, say, £200.

● Before printing

It's a good idea to check that all the fields fit inside the page by viewing the position of the margins (see To the edge of the page box, right). Another sensible precaution is to preview on screen what your printout will look like before you commit it to paper. You can do this by using Preview Mode, which you can switch to easily by choosing this option from the View menu.

Printing specific records in a database

Here we show you how to print just those items of information that you want from a database, instead of printing the entire contents.

1 Here's a simple home contents database, containing basic text and numerical fields. We want to print only those records that cover items in the lounge. Select the Find Mode command from the View menu.

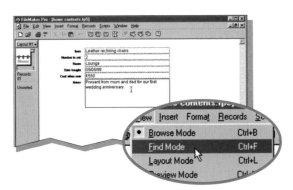

2 FileMaker Pro presents what looks like a blank record: type in the information you want to find. In this case, we've typed 'Lounge' into the Room field. Click the Find button in the status area on the left-hand side of the screen.

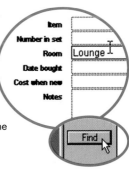

3 FileMaker Pro switches to Browse Mode and shows the first matching record. To indicate that you have selected a sub-set of the 82 records in the database, the status area shows the number of records found – 21 in this case.

4 Now check how the fields fit on the print area of the page. To do this, switch to Layout Mode, then select Page Margins from the View menu. In this example, all the fields appear safely within the white rectangle inside the margins.

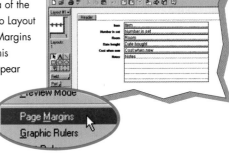

5 It's also wise to see exactly how the records will print on the page. Click on the Mode button in the bar at the bottom of the FileMaker Pro window and choose Preview from the menu that appears.

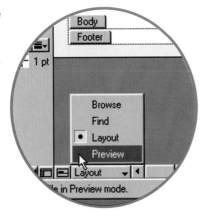

6 You can now see how the records matching the 'Lounge' search appear on the printed page. In this case, there are three records printed per page. If there's a problem, you can return to Layout Mode and adjust the layout without wasting paper.

7 When everything's OK, choose Print from the File menu. The Print dialog box works much like those of Word and Excel. In most cases you'll want to print the records you're browsing – as shown here. Click the OK button to print the pages.

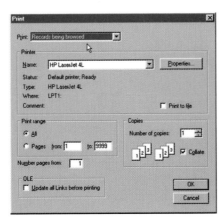

PC TIPS

Using all records

Once you have finished working on a sub-set of records, you can undo the effects of a Find command by selecting the Show All Records command from the Records menu. FileMaker Pro reverts to the complete database again.

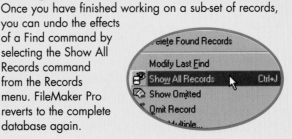

Adding graphics to database layouts

Graphics will brighten up your layouts and can make them easier to work with. Here are some tips for mastering FileMaker Pro's drawing tools.

M odifying layouts in FileMaker Pro is a simple job and on pages 54-57, we show how you can even create new layouts to suit your own purposes. You can also arrange and format the fields and text labels to make your layouts much easier to work with. However, you can create an even greater impact by adding graphics to your FileMaker Pro layouts.

If it's done properly, adding some graphical elements to your layouts will enhance them considerably. Graphics can actually make your layouts simpler to understand, as well as improving their overall look.

Layout Mode provides several drawing tools which are accessed by buttons in the grey status area on the left side of the FileMaker Pro window. These work much like the drawing tools in Paint (see Stage 1, pages 74-75) and those in Word (see Stage 3, pages 46-49). You can draw straight lines, rectangles (including squares), ellipses (and circles) and rectangles with rounded corners. You have considerable control over the properties of these items, and you can, for example, change the colour and thickness of lines and outlines, as well as the type of shading used.

While these tools sound rather basic, when combined and used with different colours, they can help you to create really effective layouts.

● The whole story
Being able to create graphics is only half the story, though. FileMaker Pro includes several features that make it easy to manipulate graphics and position them accurately in a layout. All graphics objects can be modified

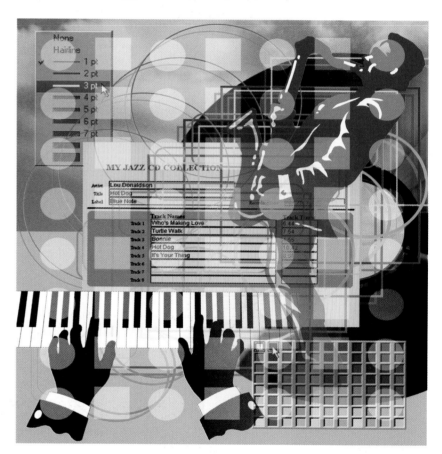

By using lines and simple shapes in combination you can quickly create effective layouts for your databases.

after they've been drawn, so you can change any of their properties, move them to a new position, or even resize them. You can also place them on top of or behind each other or other objects in the layout. This facility can be used to create backgrounds for your layouts, as shown in the example opposite. The backgrounds will make the database much easier to read.

It can be difficult to position graphics accurately by eye, but help is available from FileMaker Pro. You can use tools such as rulers, positioning grids and guidelines and, if they get in the way later, you can remove them from view, see Drawing guides box, page 65.

see Drawing guides box, page 65.

PC TIPS

Grouping objects
Sometimes it's convenient to group several graphics objects together and treat them as one item. In Layout Mode, hold down the [Shift] key and click on all the objects you want to group together. Finally, select the Group option from the Arrange menu.

Inserting graphics in a layout

Improve the look of an existing FileMaker Pro layout by adding a colourful background and some neat dividing lines.

1 Here's the jazz CD collection database we've already created (see pages 56-57). To make the layout more appealing and easier to use, we'll start by adding a line to divide it into sections.

2 In Layout Mode, click on the Pen Color button in the status area and choose the drawing colour you want from the palette. Then click on the Pen Width button and select the thickness of line you want.

3 Select the Line tool (marked with a diagonal black line) and drag a horizontal line across the layout.

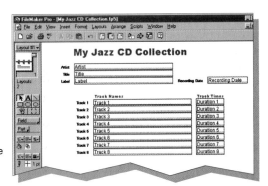

4 If you put the line in the wrong place, simply drag and drop it into the right position.

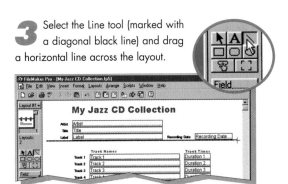

5 Next, set the Pen Width to None, click on the Fill Color button and choose another colour from the palette. Click on the Fill Pattern button again and choose the one you want. We've opted for a solid fill.

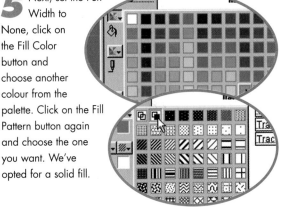

6 Click the Rounded Rectangle tool and drag a large rectangle around the fields at the bottom of the layout.

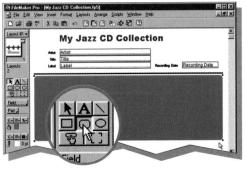

PC TIPS

Drawing guides

You can use the Show menu to switch on several aids to help you position objects accurately in a layout. Select Graphic Rulers to display rulers for measurement; choose Ruler Lines to make a positioning grid visible; or pick T-Squares to bring up horizontal and vertical moveable guidelines.

7 The rectangle obscures some of the fields in our layout. To fix this, select the rectangle and choose the Send to Back command from the Arrange menu.

8 Finish the layout by setting the fill colour for the fields to white. Select all the fields and choose white from the Fill Color palette.

Working with records

The records in your databases are stored in the order you enter them, but you can re-order your records to view them any way you like.

Creating databases, entering data and designing layouts to make them easy to use is only a small part of what FileMaker Pro is capable of achieving. When it comes to working with records, it is likely that you'll spend time performing such activities as looking through the database for specific records and deleting, duplicating and editing them as necessary. FileMaker Pro's Browse Mode contains a selection of useful tools to make this type of work easy.

● Manipulating records

For example, a club membership database will need to be regularly updated to reflect the fact that some members might not want to renew their subscriptions. The person using the database might decide simply to delete the records of all members who do not renew. This would be a straightforward task of locating the records of lapsed members and choosing the Delete Record command from the Mode menu.

Duplicating a record creates an exact replica of it. While exact duplicate records are rarely needed, this feature can be useful when you want to add a record which duplicates most of the information from an existing record. Select the Duplicate Record command and then edit the new record by clicking on the relevant fields and retyping the information. Don't

forget that any changes you make will be saved automatically – you don't have to save the file yourself. It is especially important to remember this when deleting records, as, unlike in Word or Excel, there's no going back a step if you change your mind.

● Databases with many records

Searching through a database to delete, duplicate and edit records is no problem when your database contains just a handful of records. However, most databases grow quickly – there can be hundreds or thousands of records, even in simple databases – and browsing through a big database looking for records can be an arduous task.

You can get FileMaker Pro to do the work for you by looking for the records you want. By using the Find command (see pages 62-63),

FileMaker Pro's facility for sorting records into any particular order is both quick and easy, and extremely useful.

OMITTING RECORDS

There might be times when you want to exclude a particular record from the set that you can see in Browse Mode. You can do this by displaying the record you want to hide, then choosing Omit Record from the Records menu. You can use the Omit Multiple option in the Select menu to hide several consecutive records.

Show All Records
Show Omitted
Omit Record
Omit Multiple...
Sort...

together with the Sort command, you can quickly locate and concentrate on the relevant records. This is important, as it's not only business databases that grow to include large numbers of records. For example, if you list the contents of your home in an insurance inventory, it might stretch to well over 100 records. An avid collector creating a database of stamps will quickly surpass even that.

● The Sort command

When looking through your databases in Browse Mode, you will see the records in the order that they were entered. FileMaker Pro provides several ways for you to browse through these (see Quick ways to browse box, below). For information which needs to be presented chronologically – for example, in a club-membership database where it's necessary to see who has been a member of the club the longest – viewing entries in date order is fine. Imagine, however, that there are several categories of member – Standard, Premium and Associate – and that the database reflects this with a Category field for each record. By using the Sort command, you can view the records by any category you want.

● Sorting different types of data

FileMaker Pro can sort the database by almost any kind of field. Text information is simplest: by default you'll see an ascending alphabetical sort (A to Z) but you can choose descending order (Z to A). You can also create a custom sort order if ascending and descending are inconvenient (see page 69).

Numerical fields can also be sorted, so re-sorting a customer-order database based on the value of the order is easy. Similarly, date and time sorting is simple. However, some types of fields, such as Container and Global, cannot be sorted although it's unlikely that you'd want to order records by such fields.

● Planning for a sort

You'll soon find the Sort command indispensable for browsing and manipulating records. With experience, you'll discover that predicting the types of sort you will want to do on a database helps you plan the fields in your database. For example, if you use a single field to hold both first and last names in a database, it's complicated to sort them by last name. For this reason it's better to use two fields so that you can sort easily by last name or first name.

Quick ways to browse

IN BROWSE MODE, the grey status area on the left side of the FileMaker Pro window gives you three ways to browse through records. Each method is useful for a particular purpose.

The first way is to use the two Rolodex-style index card icons at the top of the status area. Click on the bottom index card to move forward one record or click on the top index card to move backwards by one record. The number of the current record is shown below and to the right of the bottom index card. This method is useful if you want to move through a small number of records.

The next method is to use the small tab just to the right of the two index cards. You can use the mouse to drag this up and down – the number of the record you've scrolled to is shown in the same place as before. This method is useful if you want to browse between records that are a long way apart.

Finally, if you know the number of the record you want to see, you can actually click on the record number below the index cards and type the new number in. When you press the [Enter] key, FileMaker Pro will display the record you want to see.

Just click on the bottom index card to move forwards, or the top index card to move backwards, through the records.

You can use the tab at the side of the index cards to move quickly through a large number of records. To do this, click on it with the mouse pointer and drag it up or down.

It is also possible to click on the record number and then, in the box next to it, type in the number of the record you want to go straight to.

Sorting in a database

Here we start re-ordering records in a typical FileMaker Pro database. In this example, we've used a child's school reports.

1 Here's a simple database to store information about children's school reports. Each record can hold information on one subject from a child's school report for each year. Let's see how we can sort the records in the database in order of highest marks attained.

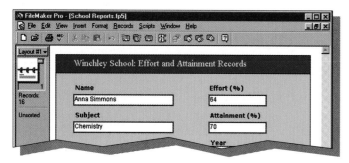

2 While working in Browse Mode, go to the Records menu and select the Sort command.

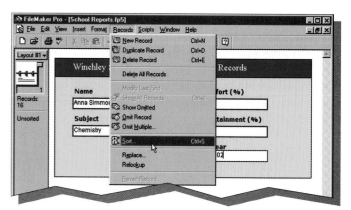

3 The Sort Records dialog box appears. Click on Attainment in the list box of fields on the left and press the Move button.

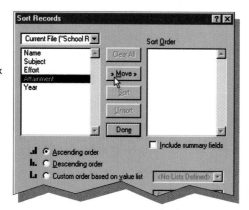

4 Attainment appears in the Sort Order panel on the right. Click on it to select it and then choose Descending order (inset) from the options at the bottom of the dialog box. Instruct FileMaker Pro to sort the records in the database by clicking on the Sort button.

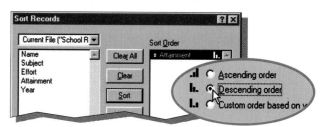

5 The indicator in the status area tells you that the records have been sorted. The first record is now the one with the highest attainment score. Click on the cards in the status area to browse through the database.

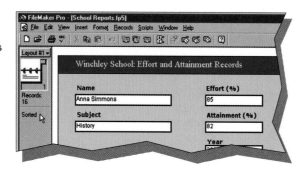

6 FileMaker Pro lets you undo sorts after you've done them. The first step is to re-open the Sort Records dialog box and click on Unsort.

7 Now the current record is number 2 out of 16. The message in the status area changes to remind you that the records are unsorted.

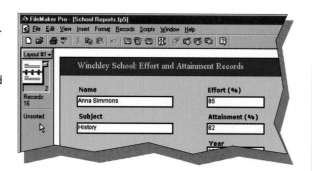

MULTI-FIELD SORTS

By adding more than one field to the Sort Order panel (Steps 3 and 4), you can sort by several fields. For a phone listing in an address database, for example, you can sort records by last name and then by first name.

SHORTCUTS

FileMaker Pro includes many keyboard shortcuts to make working with databases much quicker. For example, to bring up the Sort Records dialog box, just press the [Ctrl]+[S] keys together.

Sorting records into a custom order

Simple ascending or descending sorts aren't always the answer to your needs: by using FileMaker Pro's custom order lists, you can sort in any way you like.

1 In this database of people involved in an amateur dramatics production (right), we need to do a sort that shows the records in order of the importance of the roles played by everyone, from producer and director to actors and technical crew.

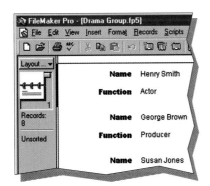

2 To begin, select Sort from the Records menu.

3 The Sort Records dialog box appears, with the two fields in this simple database listed (below left). Select the Function field, then the Custom order based on value list option.

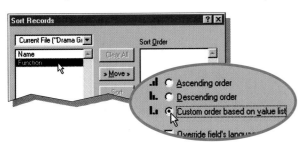

4 The next job is to tell FileMaker Pro the order in which to sort the records. Click on the list box at the bottom right of the dialog box and choose Define Value Lists.

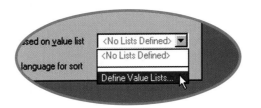

5 A new dialog box opens. Click the New button and then type in a name for the value list in the Value List Name box (we've chosen Roles).

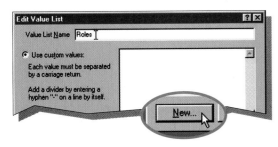

6 Now type the functions in the large text panel on the right, putting them in the order that you want the drama group members to appear. Press the [Enter] key after each one so that each entry is on a new line. Next, click on the OK button and then the Done button on the next screen.

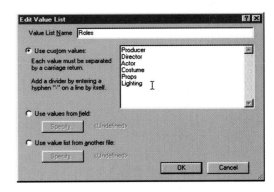

7 Once the Sort Records dialog box reappears, make sure that the Function field is still highlighted and press the Move button to add it to the Sort Order list on the right. Now you can tell FileMaker Pro to carry out your custom sort by clicking on the Sort button.

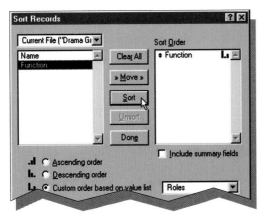

8 Your custom sort appears. The people involved have now been sorted into an order that reflects the importance of their roles in the production. The producer and director are at the top of the list.

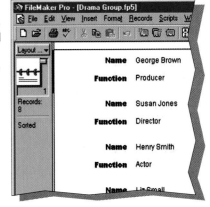

Saving space when printing

Learn how to use FileMaker Pro's special printing features and you can make your printouts look better, and save wastage by using paper more efficiently.

Printing from FileMaker Pro is simple (see pages 62-63). However, when you're printing several records, you'll often find that there's a large amount of wasted space – and paper – if some of the fields are blank.

For instance, perhaps your database has seven fields to handle long addresses, such as Suite 17, Unit 7, Madison Industrial Estate, Long Lane, Cricklewood, London NW2 9ZZ. If so, you'll find that records with much shorter addresses, such as 79 Acacia Avenue, London N3 2TW, will print with four lines of blank space within them. At best this creates ugly areas of white space, and at worst it wastes many sheets of paper.

A similar problem affects fields placed side by side on a layout. For example, it's common practice to use two fields for names: the first name and last name. If you place these fields side by side, those records with short first names will leave large gaps before the last name. You could shorten the first name field box and drag the last name field closer, but long first names will then be truncated. However, with a little preparation, you can avoid all these problems.

● Sliding fields

By using a technique called sliding, you can tell FileMaker Pro to conserve space when printing such layouts. The program checks for empty space (completely blank fields and/or fields with little data) and slides other fields to close the gaps.

Fields can slide horizontally (left) or vertically (up) or in both directions at once. Horizontal sliding is especially useful for closing up space between related fields, such as the first and last name, or between fields set within the main text of a letter and the actual text of the letter. Vertical sliding means records with many blank fields take up less space down the page.

Fields aren't the only items you can slide on a layout – almost any object can be slid. When you slide a non-field object, it doesn't shrink but simply moves closer to the data contained in the field towards which it slides.

Dip into some of FileMaker Pro's user-friendly commands to make your data printouts look more professional. Saving space on the printed page also means you'll waste less paper.

Client list				
Name				
Mr	Jim	F.		Brown
Mr	Hector			Chrome
Ms	Phylida	P.		Dunthorne
Dr	Sylvester	K.		McGee
Mrs	Catherine	B.		Plows
Mr	A.	V.		Swifton

Client list
Name
Mr Jim F. Brown
Mr Hector Chrome
Ms Phylida P. Dunthorne
Dr Sylvester K. McGee
Mrs Catherine B. Plows
Mr A. V. Swifton

The printout on the left is what you get if you print without sliding fields to occupy empty space. Sliding fields reduce the gaps between the names to fit them into the space provided (above right).

Sliding fields on layouts

Making fields slide to conserve space is a simple matter of ticking boxes in the appropriate dialog box. Here we show you how to slide fields both horizontally and vertically.

1 This FileMaker Pro file holds details of playgroup attendees. It has fields for Child name, Parent first name, parent surname, Address and Postcode. Select Preview from the button at the bottom of the screen.

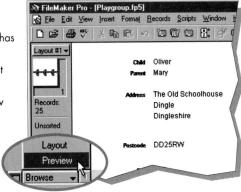

2 The Preview shows how the records will print on the page, unless instructed otherwise. In this example, there's a lot of wasted space between the Parent First name and Surname fields, and between the Address and Postcode fields.

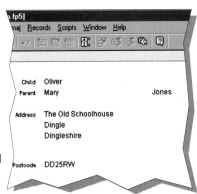

3 Switch to Layout Mode and then click on the Surname field. Select Sliding/Printing from the Format menu. In the dialog box that appears, tick the Sliding left box and click the OK button. Do the same for the Parent field.

4 Sliding fields are indicated by small arrows on the field borders which show the slide direction. If you can't see them on your screen, click Show on the View menu and select Sliding Objects from the Show sub-menu.

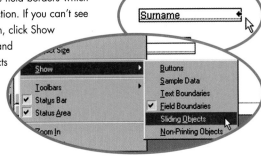

5 To minimize vertical white space, select the Address field, bring up the Set Sliding/Printing dialog box (Step 3), then tick the Sliding up based on: box. Click on the OK button and repeat the exercise for the Postcode field.

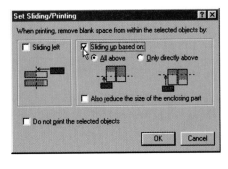

6 It's also important for field labels to slide with the field. In this example, we need to set up the Postcode label to slide. Select the label, and repeat the same process as for the Postcode field.

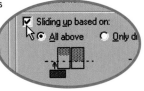

7 Now switch to Preview mode again. You can see how the gaps between the addresses and postcodes have closed up and also how the Parent First name and Surname fields have closed together.

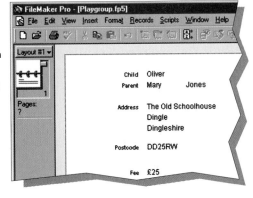

PC TIPS

Preventing objects from printing

You can save space and paper by setting some layout objects as non-printing. Bring up the Set Sliding/Printing dialog box for the object and tick the Do not print the selected objects box. The object will appear on screen, but not on the printed page.

Introducing fields for special purposes

Not all the information you want to store in a database will fit neatly in a text or number field. We show you how to solve this problem using FileMaker Pro field types.

Many databases are created from simple text and number fields. However, some data is neither text nor numbers. For example, you might need to store dates, images and values calculated from fields. For this sort of data, using the right field type is important.

Dates, for example, are the next most common type of field after text and numbers. Using a proper date field instead of simply typing 25 November 2002 into a text field allows FileMaker to carry out searches and calculations based on simple chronological functions (see pages 66-67).

There are also many other types of information that you might want to store in a database. Examples could range from everyday items such as fixed figures and regular calculations, to more exotic things, such as sounds, pictures and even video clips. FileMaker Pro has been designed to deal with this kind of material. And by choosing the right type of field you can create a more effective database.

● Container fields

As an example of non-numerical, non-text data, consider a register of every car owned by the members of a Lancia enthusiasts' club. This is likely to include names and addresses in text fields, date of joining in a date field, and details about the cars in more text fields. But what would really make the database useful is if it could hold a picture of each car.

This is a perfect use for Filemaker Pro's Container fields, which can be set up so that as you move from one member record to the next, the picture of the car changes

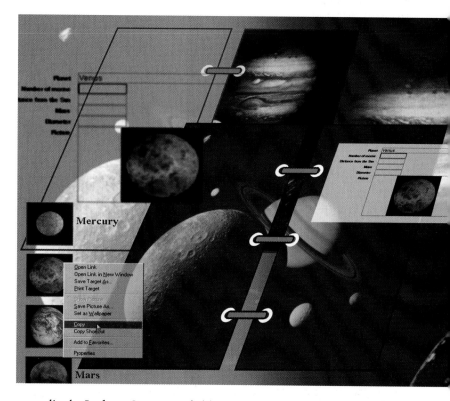

Databases of astronomical material can hold images, calculated orbits, dates and other types of data.

accordingly. In fact, Container fields are designed to hold just about any type of object, including Windows sound recordings (see Stage 5, pages 22-23) and even movie clips. For example, you could create a single database that stores photos, sounds and video clips of your children as they grow up.

● Global fields

There are also special fields to help you to solve other problems. For example, a company creating a database for a price list might need to add VAT to each item. The database could be set up with a number field called VAT, but then someone would have to type the data (17.5%) into every record in the database. This also means that if the VAT rate changes, someone would have to go through the database changing the information in every record. There's also a risk of records being missed and some prices being wrong.

By using a Global field to store the VAT rate, the problem is solved in one go: a Global

PC TIPS

Account and phone numbers

Although phone numbers and account codes are obviously made up of numbers, they both often have text characters, such as hyphens, so it's better to treat these types of numbers as text rather than numeric data. If you use a number field for phone numbers, 0999895734 would be stored as 999895734 because the leading zero is dropped for numeric data.

field ensures that the information is the same for every record, so typing the information once adds it to every other record. If the VAT rate does change, typing the new figure into one record updates it for all of them.

Global fields aren't just limited to numbers. You can also use them to store text, date, time and even Container data. Of course, since all the fields contain the same information, you can't use a Global field for searching or sorting the records in a database.

● Calculating with a database

In the example above, it's very likely that the VAT for each item in the database needs to be worked out and added to the cost of the item to produce the overall figure that will appear in the price list. The Calculation field is designed for exactly such a purpose.

When you create a Calculation field, you tell FileMaker what calculation you want carried out. It will then put the result in the field. The VAT example is simple: the extra amount to charge is the price multiplied by the VAT rate (which is already stored in the Global field discussed above). By typing in a simple

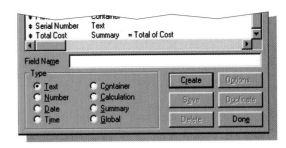

When you are creating a database, or modifying an existing one, you can insert any of these different types of fields by simply selecting the appropriate one from the Define Fields dialog box.

formula, similar to that used in an Excel spreadsheet, you can ensure that FileMaker does the calculation for every record in the database. This prevents repetitive data entry and helps avoid mistakes being made.

● Versatile fields

Calculation fields are very versatile, as they can deal with more than just numbers. For example, you can get FileMaker to work out the day of the week automatically from day, month and year information which is held in a date field.

Summary fields

Summary fields are a special type of field used to collate information from several records in the database file. Used properly, such fields can save lots of time and effort.

WHEN IT COMES to getting accurate analyses or summaries of information contained in the database, Summary fields are ideal.

For example, a home inventory might contain number fields to store the value of each item in the database, with one item per record.

As you buy and dispose of household items and update the database, it's important to keep track of the overall value of your home contents for insurance purposes.

As items change in a household inventory database, FileMaker can automatically maintain a total value.

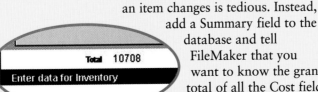

You could simply print the records out and tot up the values with a calculator, but doing this every time an item changes is tedious. Instead, add a Summary field to the database and tell FileMaker that you want to know the grand total of all the Cost fields in the database. As soon as

There are several different types of Summary field, including Total, Average and Maximum, each selected by a simple button press.

you make a change to the database, the Summary will automatically update to show the new figure.

● Flexible summaries

The total figure might be the most common type of Summary field used in a database, but FileMaker can provide others, too, including an average value, a maximum or minimum figure, or a count of the number of fields. These can all be used in a variety of different ways when working with everyday data. More advanced options for the Summary Field include Standard Deviation, which is useful for statisticians.

Putting pictures in Container fields

If you want to incorporate items other than text in a FileMaker Pro layout, such as pictures or even sound, you will have to use a Container field.

1 The Container field is ideal for holding unusual sorts of data, such as pictures. Here we'll create a bank of information about the planets in the Solar System. Start by creating an empty database.

2 Use the Define Fields dialog box to add a text field for Planet, and number fields for each of the following: Number of moons, Distance from the Sun, Mass and Diameter.

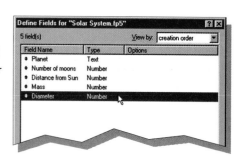

3 Now type Picture into the Field Name box, select the Container option from the Type list and click the Create button. Then click the Done button.

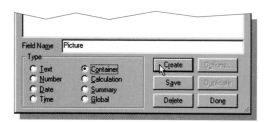

4 When the database layout appears, switch to Layout Mode. Right-click on the Picture field and select the Graphic Format from the pop-up menu.

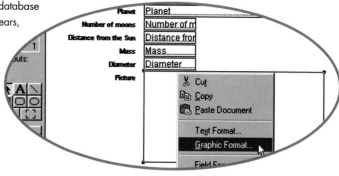

5 The Graphic Format dialog box opens to let you decide how pictures should appear in the field on the layout. Choose the Reduce or Enlarge option so that FileMaker will adjust the picture to fit as much of the box as possible. Click the OK button to continue.

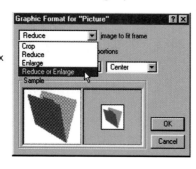

6 Now you need the pictures. The NASA Web site at http://photojournal.jpl.nasa.gov contains many excellent space images. Find a suitable picture (we've chosen Venus) and copy it to the Windows Clipboard by right-clicking on it and selecting Copy from the menu that appears.

7 Return to the database and switch to Browse Mode to enter information. Right-click on the Picture field and select Paste from the pop-up menu (inset, top). Type text and number data about Venus into the other fields (inset, bottom).

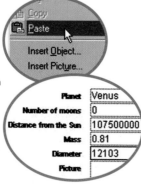

8 Here's the record for the planet Venus, complete with all its data and its picture in place. You can add pictures, numbers and text to the records for other planets in exactly the same way.

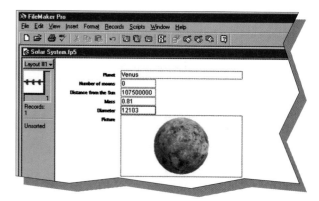

Using Global and Calculation fields

A great way of making the most of FileMaker's useful functions is to enter constant data only once and have several calculations done for you automatically by FileMaker. Here's how to calculate the retail price mark-up on every item of a shop's stock.

1 Start FileMaker Pro and create a new empty database. When the Define Fields dialog box appears, add three simple fields: Item and Description as text fields, and Cost as a number field.

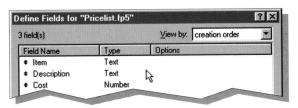

2 Add a new field called Markup and select the Global option from the Type list before pressing the Create button.

3 FileMaker Pro asks you what type of global field you want. Make sure the Number option is selected before clicking OK.

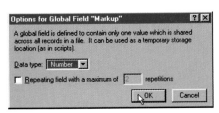

4 The Markup field appears in the top part of the dialog box as normal. Now add a Price field, selecting the Calculation field type before pressing the Create button.

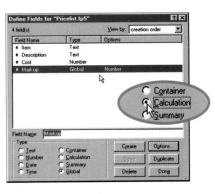

FileMaker Pro

5 FileMaker needs to know what to calculate. In the Price = panel in the lower part of the dialog box, type: 'Cost*(100+Markup)/100' and press the OK button. This adds a percentage profit margin (mark-up) to the cost of the item.

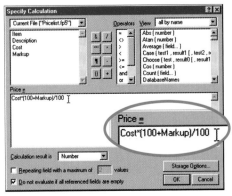

6 The Price field now appears in the Define Fields dialog box. Press the Done button to create the database.

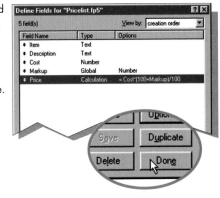

7 Now you can use the database (we've added some simple colour to make the database layout clear, as on pages 64-65). Start by typing some Item, Description and Cost information.

8 Type in a Markup percentage (we used 65%) and press the [Tab] key. FileMaker does the calculation for you and displays the result next to Price.

9 Press [Ctrl]+[N] to add another record. Notice how the Markup field, being Global, is already filled in. As soon as you type a Cost figure and move to the next field, FileMaker works out the price for this new item.

Calculations and functions

Calculation fields make calculations simple. They work with many types of data in a variety of documents – not just with simple sums, but also with a wide range of calculations involving numbers, text and other functions.

The beauty of calculation fields is that they allow you to make calculations on data in all types of fields (see pages 72-75) – without the bother of keying all of it into a calculator.

To make them work, you need formulae that tell FileMaker Pro how to perform the calculation. You create these formulae by combining basic existing formulae called functions. Each of these functions performs a particular calculation to produce a single, specific value.

With Calculation fields you can easily create useful summaries of complex sets of figures. On the next page, we show you how to calculate batting averages.

● Types of function

FileMaker Pro has 13 groups of functions: text, number, date, time, aggregate, summary, repeating, financial, trigonometric, logical, status, design and external.

Number functions are the most widely used of all. They are used, for example, to calculate quickly the square and square roots of any number, or to round a decimal number to the nearest whole number, or to generate random numbers.

Surprisingly, perhaps, text functions are also widely used. These let you make calculations and manipulations with text fields. You might wonder what calculations you could possibly do on text, but text functions are remarkably useful. You might, for example, accidentally design a database that has a text field for numeric information. This is where a text function comes in, enabling you to convert 'text numbers' into real numeric data that you can use in calculations. You can also use text functions to split a text phrase into individual words (which is useful if you want to split a single name field into separate first and other

names). You can even work out the number of characters or words in any text, and replace one section of text with another.

● Time and date functions

Time and date functions, of course, give values based on times and dates. Using these, you can, for example, split dates into day, month and year or times by second, minute and hour. A time and date function might help you set up a database that automatically tells you when accounts are overdue, for example.

Aggregate functions produce results by performing calculations on several fields at once. For example, the Average function works out the average of several fields. Other aggregate functions can work out the highest and lowest values in a set of fields. Logical functions provide true/false information on relationships in data.

As with simple Calculation fields (see page 75), functions are added through the Specify Calculation dialog box. The functions are listed, and you add them to formulae that you build with the field names.

OTHER FUNCTIONS

It's worth exploring other functions to see how they can help you design your databases.

Financial functions work like numerical functions, allowing you to work out values for interest payments, for example. For school work, trigonometric functions give you sines, cosines, tangents and so on.

Status and design functions are there to perform advanced calculations that will provide information about the state and structure of your database.

Using a function to calculate averages

One of the most commonly used functions calculates an average for a set of figures. In this example, we'll calculate average batting scores for cricketers in a five-way cricket tournament.

FileMaker Pro

1 Start by choosing New Database from the File menu and use the Create New File dialog box to store the file.

2 Create a text field for Name and then five number fields for Innings1 to Innings5 as shown here. These fields will store the individual scores from each game.

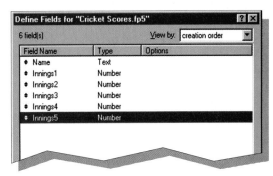

3 Add a calculation field called Average Score and click on the Create button to bring up the Specify Calculation dialog box.

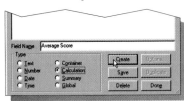

4 Scroll through the list of functions on the right of the dialog box to find Int [number]; this rounds a number to the nearest whole number. Double-click on it to add it to the formula being built in the Average Score = panel. The word 'number' is highlighted in the formula, so any other functions added will replace it.

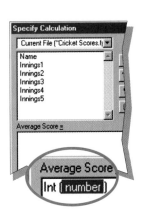

5 Find the Average function, and double-click on it to add it to the formula. The field text is highlighted ready for replacement.

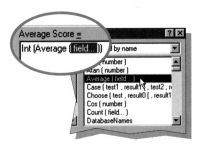

6 Double-click on Innings1 in the list of fields on the left of the dialog box and type a comma after the Innings1 field in the formula.

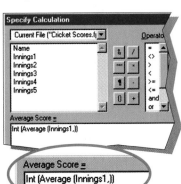

7 Repeat Step 6 for the Innings2, Innings3 and Innings4 fields. Add Innings5, but since this is the last in the list, don't add a comma after it. Click on the OK button and then click the Done button in the Define Fields dialog box.

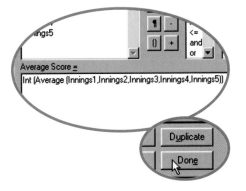

8 FileMaker Pro shows the database in Browse Mode and you can start typing in the information for the first record. The Average Score field is then updated automatically as you type in the scores for each of the five innings.

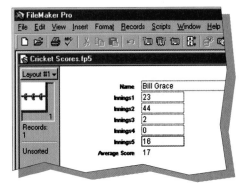

Introducing FrontPage Express

If you want to start making your own Web site, or just try Web editing for fun, Windows 98 includes an easy-to-use Web editor: FrontPage Express.

Many different types of program can be used to create Web pages, but it pays to be choosy. For example, the Notepad program supplied with Windows lets you save text files in the HTML format used for all Web pages (see Stage 3, pages 154-157). This is a great free program, but the downside of its approach is that you need to know the HTML language to be able to key in the HTML code before you start. And, although HTML is one of the easier programming languages to learn, creating Web pages by typing HTML is hard work.

● Why not use Word?
If you have Microsoft Word on your PC, you can use it as a simple Web-editing program. You can create your page using Word's familiar commands and then save the page in HTML format (.htm) instead of Word's normal document format (.doc).

However, while Word makes creating a simple Web page easy, it lacks the more advanced commands that make multi-page Web sites possible. It's better to use a tool that is dedicated to this task.

● Choosing a Web editor
Not surprisingly, almost all professional and home-enthusiast Web authors use special Web-editing programs to create the HTML code. These programs are designed to be easy-to-use: you create your Web pages as easily as you'd create a leaflet in Microsoft Word, for

Microsoft's FrontPage Express will guide you through the process of designing a Web site, from concept stage to attractively realized pages that'll have visitors flocking to your site.

example. It's a simple matter of pointing and clicking to add pictures, add colour to text, or link pages together. The Web editor automatically creates the necessary HTML code, leaving the Web author free to get on with the design. These dedicated programs are packed with toolbar buttons and menu commands that are solely aimed at Web page design. However, if you use Windows 98, you already have a suitable Web editor on your PC: FrontPage Express, a cut down version of Microsoft FrontPage. It's simple to use and has many features that help you create interesting and visually appealing Web pages.

FrontPage Express

INSTALLATION

If you have Windows 98, you should find that FrontPage Express is already installed on your PC. To find out if you have this program installed on your computer, check in the Start menu for the Internet Explorer group and you should see an entry for FrontPage Express. If you can't see it there, you can use the Add/Remove Programs icon in the Control Panel to install it from the CD-ROM. Click the Windows Setup tab of the dialog box and then select the Internet Tools option. Click the Details button to see the components that are available. Tick the Microsoft FrontPage Express item (right) and then click the OK button to install it from your Windows CD-ROM.

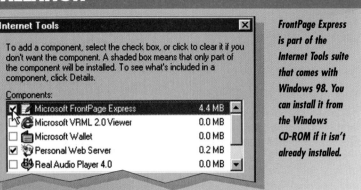

FrontPage Express is part of the Internet Tools suite that comes with Windows 98. You can install it from the Windows CD-ROM if it isn't already installed.

The FrontPage Express workspace

The FrontPage Express workspace looks much like a word-processor window, helping to make the task of creating Web pages as easy as typing a letter.

START FRONTPAGE EXPRESS by clicking on the Start menu, then Programs, then Internet Explorer and finally the FrontPage Express entry. In a few moments the window shown below will appear. It's a good idea to take time to explore FrontPage Express's menus and toolbars. The similarity with other Windows programs – Microsoft Word in particular – means that you probably already know many of the commands you will need when you use FrontPage Express for Web editing. You'll find you'll be creating Web pages within a few minutes.

Menu bar

The 10 menus provide access to the full set of FrontPage commands, from file opening and closing to adding links to other Web sites.

Forms toolbar

This toolbar makes it easy to add buttons and list-boxes to a Web page to create a form.

Text insertion point

The text you type, and the pictures and objects you insert into a Web page, appear at the position of the flashing vertical line in the document area.

Title bar

Like all Windows programs, a Title bar across the top of the window shows the program name. If the document window is maximized, its name also appears in this Title bar.

Standard toolbar

The buttons on this toolbar give one-click access to file opening, printing and saving commands and also make it easy to add pictures and hypertext links to a Web page.

Document window

The work space for your Web page. You can work on several Web pages at a time, copying material from one to another to save time, for example.

Status bar

Indicators for CapsLock and NumLock appear here, together with a useful estimate of the amount of time it would take other Internet users to download your page.

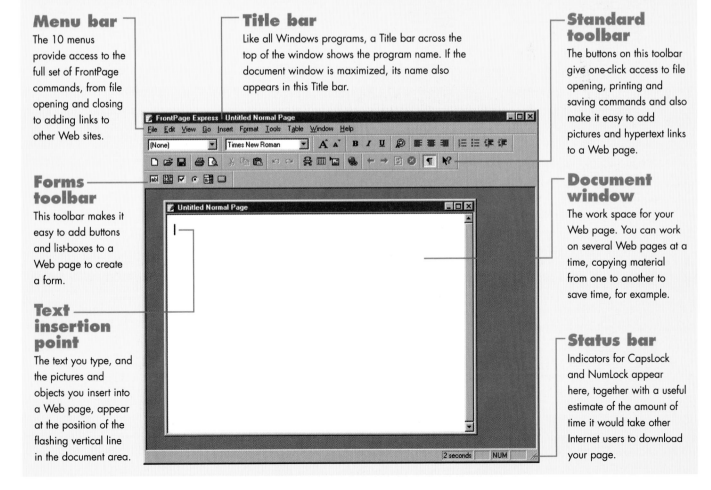

Creating a simple Web page

FrontPage's point-and-click approach means that you don't have to bother with the intricacies of the HTML language. Here's how to create a Web page in five minutes.

1 Start FrontPage and begin typing the text for your Web page into the document area. In this example, we're creating a short and simple **home page** to let our friends know we're on the World Wide Web. Type your text and use the buttons on the Format toolbar to format it.

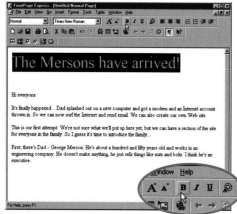

2 You can separate the different sections of a Web page by adding a thin line across the page. First position the text insertion point on a blank line, and then select Horizontal Line from FrontPage's Insert menu.

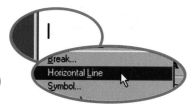

WHAT IT MEANS

HOME PAGE

The term 'home page' refers to the main page of a Web site. It's usually the one that displays first when someone visits your site. It must be named carefully (see Step 7) so that Web-browser programs can find it automatically.

3 The line appears as a very thin horizontal rectangle extending almost all the way across the page. This is the default for the lines in HTML, so it's very common on Web pages.

4 You don't have to accept the line's default appearance, however. To fine-tune the line's look, right-click on it and select Horizontal Line Properties from the pop-up menu.

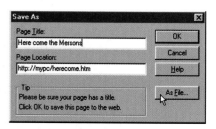

5 When the Horizontal Line Properties dialog box pops up, set the figure in the Width box to 80. This restricts the line to 80 per cent of the Web page's width. As the Center option is already selected, it'll be equally indented from both left and right sides of the page. Click on OK.

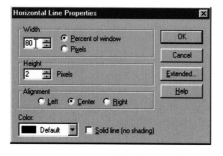

6 Finish editing your text and select Save from the File menu. First, you need to give this page a title; this will appear in the Title bar of the Web browser whenever the page is viewed. We want to save this page as a file on our PC's hard disk, so click the As File button.

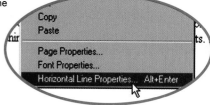

7 Now use the Save As File dialog box to choose a folder for your Web page and then give the file the name index.htm. This name is essential for a home page because Web browsers always look for the file called index.htm (or index.html) when they visit a Web site.

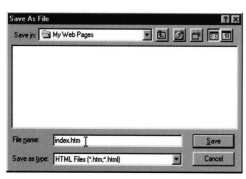

8 To view your page as it will be seen by other Internet users, locate the folder where you stored the index.htm file and double click on its icon. Windows will start your Web browser program and display your page. It's good practice always to check your Web pages on your own PC before uploading them to the Internet. That way you can avoid any embarrassing spelling mistakes or inconsistent formatting.

Add graphics to a Web page

Without graphics, the Web would be a dull place. Use pictures to liven up and illustrate your Web page.

1 Start FrontPage and open the index.htm Web page you created on the previous page. To add a background image, select Background from the Format menu. Tick the Background Image box when the Page Properties dialog appears, and then click the Browse button.

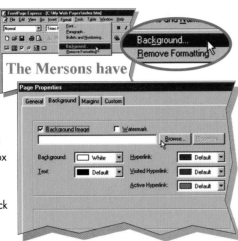

2 Click the Browse button in the next window and then locate and open a background image or texture for your page (see Finding Web graphics box, below). Click the Open and OK buttons to return to your page.

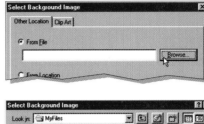

3 The background image is repeated to fill the page. This one looks like the edge of an airmail letter against a wooden desk surface. However, the text on the page overlaps the coloured part of the image, making it hard to read.

4 You can fix this by indenting the text on your page. Select the text and then click the Increase Indent button (you may have to do this twice, depending on your background image). This command indents text on both left and right sides to keep the text in the central white area where it's easy to read.

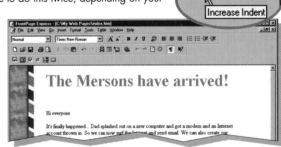

5 You can also insert pictures into the main part of the page. Move the text insertion point to the position where you'd like your picture to be, and select Image from the Insert menu. Click the Browse button in the Image dialog box.

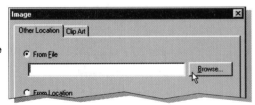

6 Select your image. It could be a scan, one taken with a digital camera or one downloaded from the Web. Click on Open to return to the page.

7 Your picture appears in the document. You can centre it by selecting it and then clicking the Center button on FrontPage's Format toolbar. Save your changes and check the appearance of your Web page in your Web browser.

FINDING WEB GRAPHICS

You can create your own Web graphics with a graphics program such as CorelDRAW or even Windows' Paint program, or you can use photos captured by digital camera or a scanner. However, for many Web graphics, such as background images, textures, buttons and icons, it's worth searching the Internet. Use a search engine to look for royalty-free Web graphics (see Stage 7, pages 140-143). You will soon find that there are many Web sites that offer graphics and many provide a wide range, with thousands from which to choose.

FrontPage Express

Uploading your Web pages

Use Web Publishing Wizard, the companion program to FrontPage Express, to make your Web site pages available to Internet users around the world.

Once you have finished creating your first Web pages with Microsoft's FrontPage Express, you're ready to upload them to your Web space. As soon as you have done that, anyone who types the address of your Web site into their Web browser will be able to see your Web page.

● Before you start
Uploading your Web pages isn't a difficult task in itself – it should take no more than a few mouse clicks and a minute or two. However, you need to ensure that all the necessary files are transferred. If you accidentally overlook a graphics file, for example, you might find that the background image that makes your Web page look great is missing when viewed by other Internet users.

There are, fortunately, some very simple precautions you can take to minimize this possibility. Consider these when you create your Web page so that no files get left behind in the upload process (see Copying all files box, opposite).

The exact process for uploading your Web page files depends on your Internet service provider (ISP). Most ISPs have set up their Web server computers so that uploading is a simple matter of copying the files to an area of the computer that includes your user name, members.firstmail.com/~fredsmith, for example.

Make sure that you know this address before you start. You'll need this address, together with your user name and password, to start the copying process. This is the same

Before anyone can see your Web pages, you have to upload them to your Internet service provider (ISP). This might seem like a complex task, but FrontPage Express and the Web Publishing Wizard make it easy.

user name and password you use to log on to your ISP and also to collect your email. Your user name and password data is required for security reasons, so that only you can upload files to your Web space.

● Web Publishing Wizard
FrontPage doesn't have the necessary features to copy files to the Internet, so you have to use the Web Publishing Wizard from the Windows Internet Tool suite (see PC Tips box, right). By following an easy step-by-step process, this identifies the files and folders you want to upload and copies them.

Once you've finished copying your files, check the Web pages before telling everyone the Web site address. This helps to avoid embarrassing errors and omissions.

You can also register your site with the most popular search engines. These special Web sites are perfect for helping you to publicize your Web site and get more visitors.

Uploading a Web site

Let the Web Publishing Wizard guide you through the task of copying your Web page files to the Internet.

1 Click on the Start menu, then the Programs folder, and then the Internet Explorer folder. Click on the Web Publishing Wizard program. If it's not visible, you can install it from the Windows CD-ROM (see PC Tips box, opposite). When the Web Publishing Wizard appears, click the Next button.

2 Tell the Wizard which folder contains your Web pages. Click the Browse Folders button and then locate and select the folder from the list shown in the Browse for Folder dialog box.

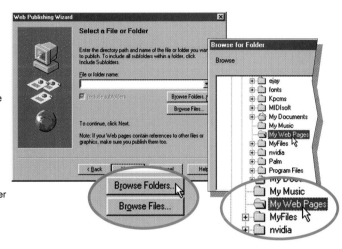

3 The Wizard lets you give your ISP Web site a descriptive name. This can be anything you want, and, unlike Web page names, can include spaces.

4 Next you must tell the Wizard the precise address of your Web site; if you're not sure what this is, check with your ISP (the information is usually contained in the Help or Frequently Asked Questions (FAQ) section of an ISP's Web site).

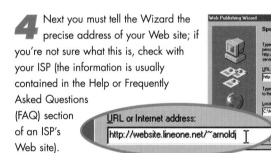

5 When you click the Next button again, the Wizard prompts you to connect to the Internet. Click the Connect button to continue.

6 If the Wizard prompts you for your User name and Password, just type in the same data you use to connect to the Internet.

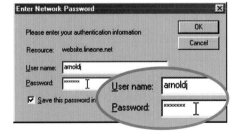

COPYING ALL FILES

For your Web pages to appear correctly to other Internet users, all the files you have used in your design must be copied to your Web space. The easiest way to ensure that this happens is to keep all your .htm and image files within one folder. For example, if you store your .htm files in a WebPages folder and store your graphics files in an Images folder within this folder, the Web Publishing Wizard will copy them at the same time as the .htm files. You also need to make sure that the Include subfolders box is ticked in Step 2.

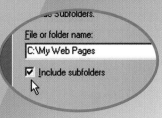

7 When the Wizard has all the information it needs, click the Finish button. The files for your Web pages are now copied one by one from your hard disk to your Web space.

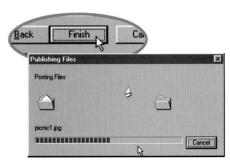

8 When the copying process has finished, click on OK. Next, start your Web browser and type the address for your Web site into the Address box. Check your layout to ensure there are no missing pictures (see Copying all files box, right). If you have any links on your Web page, check that these work properly too.

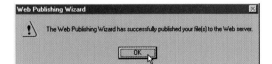

Link your Web pages

By linking Web pages together with hyperlinks, visitors to your site can jump directly to the topics that interest them. Such 'hot' links are the essence of the Internet.

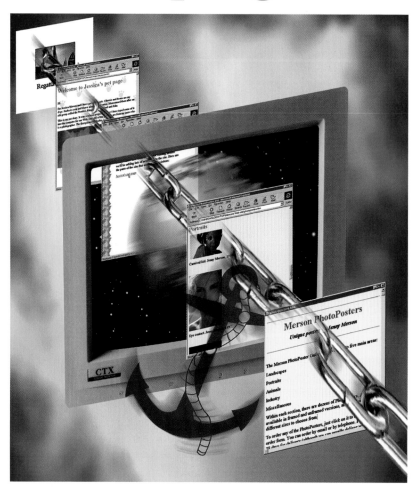

Without links, a Web site is limited, but connections are easy to set up with FrontPage.

While a simple page uploaded to your ISP's Web server is a good start, it is the creation and linking together of several interesting Web pages that produces a fully fledged Web site. A Web site may consist of anything from half a dozen to several hundred Web pages. Visitors to your site should be able to move easily and quickly from one page to another via hypertext links.

First, you need to create the new Web pages to link to and from. The number of pages you have to design will depend on the type and amount of material you plan to put on your Web site. One aimed at dog lovers, for example, might have one page devoted to each single breed of dog, with the page displaying information on size, temperament, grooming and so on. A commercial site aimed at promoting a self-employed person's business might have pages providing services, pricing, recommendations and contact details.

● Creating extra pages
Using FrontPage Express, it is just as simple to create these pages as it was to create the initial index.htm file (see pages 80-81). All you do is add the appropriate text and pictures by using exactly the same commands.

As you create these Web pages, you also add links between them. These links provide the objects – text or pictures – that visitors click on to move to another page (or a different part of the same page). For example, a commercial Web site listing vehicles for sale would almost certainly have a set of links on the home page to connect to individual pages for cars, vans, motorbikes and so on. The page for cars might then include links to further pages – one for each manufacturer, then one for each model. There is no limit to the number or arrangement of links in your

Web pages. Some Web sites simply link pages in a single series, while others use pages that have links to every other page on the Web site. But while the choice is yours, you should spend a little time planning on paper how your site will be organized to keep things manageable (see Site organization box, opposite). Most sites are set up so that the home page acts as the hub of the Web site which allows a visitor to find every page on the site by following the links that start there. To make sure your site works properly, you need to edit your home page – the index.htm file – to add links to new pages so visitors to your Web site can follow the clickable links from your home page to all the other pages on your Web site.

● Types of link
There are several different types of link. The most common are those that transfer visitors to another page on your site (see page 86).

(see page 86).

WHAT IT MEANS

HYPERTEXT
The HT in HTML, hypertext is the general term used for text documents where you click on hot spots in one document to see another document. The information you see when you look through many programs' Help files is also arranged as a series of hypertext documents.

PC TIPS

Always make sure you add a link back to your Web site's home page on all your other Web pages. This makes it easy for visitors to return to the start of the Web site if they want to refer back to the home page. A common place for such a link is at the bottom of each page.

Back to home page

Another type is the Anchor link, which looks just like a normal link but works slightly differently, taking visitors to a particular part of a Web page instead of the top of the page. Anchor links are particularly useful for helping visitors get around long Web pages. They are often used in long and detailed FAQs, the frequently asked question pages that you find on many Web sites.

● Exploring more links

When you gain more experience of using FrontPage Express, you can add other links to help make your Web pages more interactive. For example, you can add a mailto link that automatically starts up the visitor's email program so they can email you quickly and easily for feedback on your site, and you can also add links that allow people to download files from your Web site.

Site organization

Carefully planning at an early stage how the pages on your site link together could save you work later on.

TO MAKE THE BEST of your presence on the Web, you should use several pages and add links to join them together with point-and-click connections. These links make your Web site efficient and easy for visitors to use.

Sites of just half a dozen or so pages are quite easy to organize in your head, but as your plans get more ambitious, it pays to do some preparation on paper first. If you don't plan well, you run the risk of creating a site that contains all the right information, but is very difficult for visitors to browse around.

Remember, if people can't find something of interest quickly, they're likely to move on to someone else's site. This is important for commercially orientated Web sites, but it also applies to personal-interest sites.

● Planning your Web site

Start by taking a sheet of paper and drawing a box in the centre to represent your home page. Now draw extra boxes, one each to represent the other pages you wish to add to your site. Starting with the home page, draw arrows between the boxes to indicate the links that will connect the pages together. As the pages and lines grow outward, the Web site's interlinking boxes start to resemble a spider's web, and you can see where the term 'Web' came from.

Once all the connections have been made, try to look at the site from the visitors' point of view. First, they will see the home page, so ask yourself if it makes the content of the site perfectly clear. Are there too many intermediate pages before you reach the really interesting

ones? Can some closely related pages be combined into one? Is part of the site completely cut off from other parts, requiring visitors to back-track?

Some of these questions you'll be able to answer only after you have actually created the site. However, the idea of the exercise is to consider any potential problems first before going to the considerable effort of creating the Web pages themselves. While you can, if you want, start making your pages straight away without considering the links, remember that it's a lot easier to redraw a site on paper than it is to change dozens of Web pages once you've set them up.

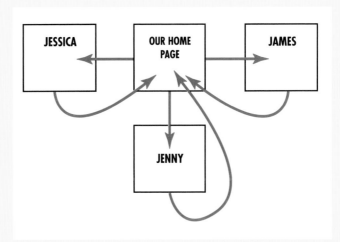

This is the plan for a very simple Web site, yet with just four pages there are already six links: three from the home page to each of the other pages, and three back.

Adding a link

You can set up hypertext links between the Web pages you create with FrontPage in seconds. Here's how to link pages on a family Web site.

1 Open FrontPage Express and create another page for your Web site. Use the formatting commands to style the text and the Insert menu to add pictures as before (see pages 80-81). In this example, we've created a Web page for one of the family members.

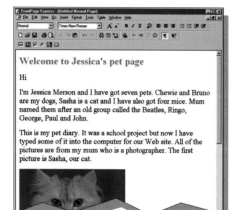

2 Save this Web page, but do not close it. Give the page a descriptive title and then save it in the same folder as the index.htm home page you created on page 80. When you name the file, be careful not to use any spaces or special characters (see File names box, below).

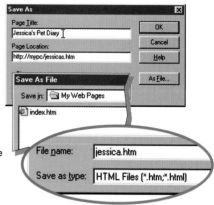

3 To add a link from the index.htm page to the new page, you must edit the index.htm page. Open this file in FrontPage Express and move the flashing bar that indicates the text-insertion point to the position where you want this link to appear. Select Hyperlink from the Insert menu.

4 When the Create Hyperlink dialog box appears, click on the Open Pages tab and you can see the pages you are working on. Select the page you just created and click the OK button.

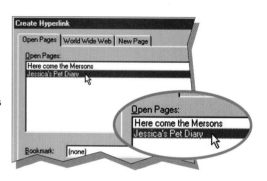

5 FrontPage Express may alert you to the fact that this page is not yet available to other Internet users. Click the Yes button to proceed.

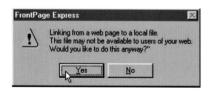

6 You can now see the hypertext link, underlined in blue in the index.htm page. Notice how the link given is the page's title – this is a lot more user-friendly than a file name, because you can use spaces and special characters in a title.

Here are the parts

Jessica's Pet Diary

FILE NAMES

Although titles can include spaces and special characters (see Steps 2 and 6), it's not a good idea to include either in the actual file name. Although Windows lets you use spaces and some special characters in file names, other Web server computers may not understand them. This can prevent links from working.

7 Now you can test this link. Save the changes and open the index.htm file in your Web browser. Then click on the link you have just created.

8 Your Web browser now switches to the new page. You can use this technique to add links from your home page to other pages on your site.

PC TIPS

Picture links

Most Web authors like to use picture links as well as the text links shown in Step 6. The process is the same, except that instead of moving the text-insertion point to where you want the link (see Step 3), just click on the picture. Once you have told FrontPage which Web page you wish to link to, it will make the picture a clickable link.

Adding an anchor

By using and specifying an anchor you can make your links point to any part of a Web page, which is perfect for long Web pages.

1 Start by opening the Web page to which you want to add anchors. Usually this will be a page that is divided into several sections. In this case, a page is divided into types of photoposter. Anchor links will make it easy to move from one part of the page to the start of any other part.

2 Scroll down the document so that the text-insertion point is just in front of the first category. Select Bookmark on the Edit menu. (Note: FrontPage Express calls an anchor a bookmark.)

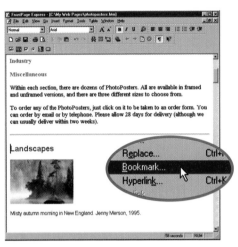

3 Type a name for this anchor into the Bookmark Name box. Click on the OK button. FrontPage Express adds a tiny bookmark icon – underlined with a blue dotted line – at the position of the anchor. Don't worry – this won't be visible when the page is viewed with a Web browser. Repeat the process for all of the other anchors you want on the page, making sure to give each anchor a unique name.

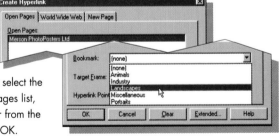

4 Once the anchors are in place, you need to add the links that will jump to them. At the end of the first section of the page, add a new line listing the categories for which you have added anchors. In this example, we've used a hyphen to separate each category of photograph so that it looks more like a list than a line of text.

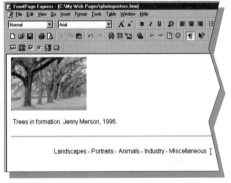

5 Highlight the first category in the line – the word 'Landscapes' – and use the Hyperlink command on the Insert menu. In the Create Hyperlink dialog box, ensure you select the current Web page in the Open Pages list, then select the Landscapes anchor from the Bookmark list-box before clicking OK.

6 Once again, the hyperlink text is underlined in blue to indicate to your Web visitors that it is a link. Note that because you had first selected some text in the Web page (the word 'Landscapes'), it is this text that is hyperlinked instead of the title of the page.

Landscapes - Portraits

7 Repeat the process for the other anchors in your Web page. To make your page as visitor-friendly as possible, use the Edit menu's Copy and Paste commands to repeat this line of hyperlinks after each section in the Web page.

Landscapes - Portraits - Animals - Industry - Miscellaneous

8 Now preview your Web page using your Web browser. You can test out all your anchor links: each time you click on one, the Web browser takes you to the invisible anchor.

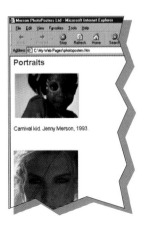

PC TIPS

For long Web pages, it's worth adding a 'Back to the top of page' link at the bottom. A visitor who's browsed to the end of the page can get back to the top with a single click – instead of having to use the scroll bars.

FrontPage Express

Formatting text

Just as formatting text in a word-processed letter helps to make its message clear, so formatting text on an Internet Web page makes information on your Web site easier to understand.

In the complex world of the Internet, your Web site will stand out if its words are clear and well laid out.

Thanks to FrontPage's 'what you see is what you get' (WYSIWYG) approach, if you can use a word processor then you can transfer the same skills to creating Web pages. Typing text and inserting pictures on a Web page, for example, use almost the same processes as Word. The same is true for formatting your text to make it clear and easy to read.

It helps that the FrontPage toolbars include buttons for many of the formatting options that can be found in a word processor. Open up FrontPage next to Microsoft Word on your screen and you'll see that some of the buttons are identical. Adding bold and italics, and making paragraphs of text line up on the left and right margins, are easy. There are also buttons to add indents, make bullet lists and add colour to text (see page 90).

● Fonts and the Web

However, although some commands appear in both programs, there are differences in the way they work. The most important is the use of fonts.

Although you can use different fonts in your Web pages, just as you can in Word documents, you need to think through the effects. The pages that Web authors create with FrontPage will be displayed on hundreds of different computers: not just Windows PCs, but also Apple Macintosh machines or hand-held computers. The Web page creation and publishing process includes a tricky and easy-to-overlook problem. While the words and the formatting in your Web site will appear exactly as you see them in your Web author, you cannot be sure that a visitor's computer has the same typefaces as yours. If the

SHORT CUTS

FrontPage shares many of the quick and easy text formatting keyboard shortcut commands of other Windows programs. You can use [Ctrl]+[B] for bold; [Ctrl]+[I] for italics; and [Ctrl]+[U] for underline.

typeface isn't present, and on some Web browsing devices such as Internet TV there are few fonts, another one will be substituted.

Sometimes these differences will be slight, with just a minor variation in line length for the main text on the page. But the more you have used fonts in your design, the more likely it is that the differences will make a more substantial alteration to the way the page looks. For instance, if you have used several typefaces to make different parts of your page visually distinct, any such distinctions may disappear altogether when viewed by a visitor.

● **Popular typefaces**
The safe option when choosing fonts is to stick to the handful of common typefaces. Mostly these fall into two categories: serif

and sans serif. Good examples of these, which are found on almost all PCs, are Times (serif) and Arial or Helvetica (sans serif). Even experienced Web designers often stick to these fonts because they can be assured of what people visiting their sites will see. Some experts even prefer to design Web sites without typeface commands so that they look fine for those few visitors who use old Web browsing programs which don't show multiple typefaces at all.

If you really must use an unusual font for an element of your design, such as a heading or logo, you can use a graphics program such as Paint Shop Pro to create a graphic of the text. That way, you can use it safe in the knowledge that no matter what fonts are available on visitors' computers, it will appear as you want it.

Web page widths

No matter how narrow the Frontpage Express window is when creating your Web page, the visitor's Web browser controls the paragraph widths.

YOU MIGHT NOT notice it but there's one crucial difference between the FrontPage window and a word processor window: there is no ruler in FrontPage. This is because in a word processor you must ensure your text fits inside the printed page, while on a Web page an author cannot know how wide the page will be on visitors' screens.

A Web browser wraps text from one line to the next according to the width of the Web browser window. Open up one of your Web pages – or visit any Web site – and resize the window to make it narrower and then wider. You will see the text reflow, but the width of paragraphs depends entirely on the width of the Web browser window. If someone with a 21-inch monitor views a Web site that you've created on a 14-inch screen, what they see will look very different from your original creation. The most annoying problem is that they will see long lines of text that are quite hard for the visitor to read from one line to the next.

You can estimate the effect that different widths of Web browser window will have on

your Web page by changing the size of the FrontPage window itself. If you are using a high resolution screen, for example, drag the right edge of the FrontPage window inwards to see how the text reflows. This will help you to spot potential problems, but it still can't solve them since the HTML that FrontPage produces is exactly the same. The ideal solution is to specify the precise width of your paragraphs.

Different Web browser window widths can make the same Web pages appear very different.

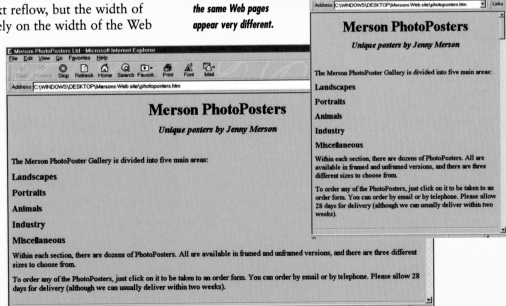

HTML heading styles

HTML includes a set of ready-made text styles. With a few clicks you can add several formatting effects at once to any text in your Web page.

1 Start FrontPage and open up one of your Web pages. In this example, we've opened an unformatted page that's looking a little too plain. While we could simply use the Format toolbar to change type size, emphasis and so on, using headings is quicker and maintains consistency.

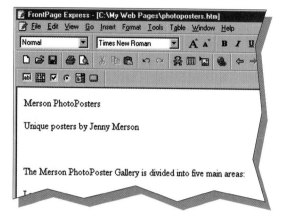

2 Start by selecting the major heading in the Web page. Now click on the arrow next to the Change Style box on the Format toolbar. FrontPage lists the ready-made set of related formats that are part of HTML. Click on the Heading 1 entry.

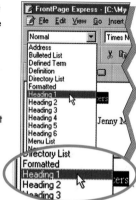

3 Your heading is now much bigger and in bold. Because this heading style is part of the HTML standard, you can be sure that the same effect will be visible to everyone using other Web browsers.

4 Now select a sub-heading and apply a different Heading from the Format menu. You might want to experiment with various headings until you get the right size and weight compared to other text sizes in your document (the smallest headings might even prove smaller than your main text).

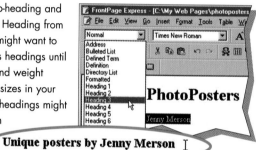

5 You can also use some of the other text formatting commands in combination with the heading. Select the major heading and click the Center button on the FrontPage Format toolbar. Note that while the Bold button has no effect – because the Heading styles already include bold emphasis – you can still add Italics if you need them. We've done this for the sub-heading here.

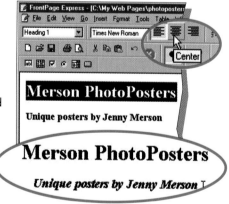

6 You can also use FrontPage's Text Color button (inset) to add suitable colours to your headings and sub-headings. Choose colours that give contrast against the background of the Web page, but don't make the colours too jarring, or the text will become difficult to read. If necessary, change the background (see Background colours box, below).

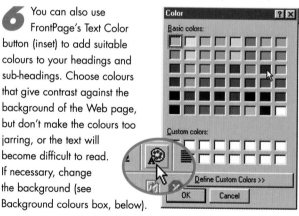

7 As usual, the real test is what the page looks like in a Web browser. Save your changes and then open the page in your Web browser to see the effect.

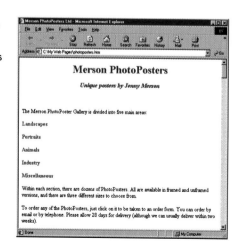

Using fonts in your pages

A careful choice of fonts can help to make your Web page stand out from the rest while remaining easy to read.

1 Open up your Web page in FrontPage Express. In this example, we want to change the typeface used for most of the page from the default – Times New Roman – to something more modern. Start by selecting all the page contents: choose Select All from the Edit menu or press [Ctrl]+[A].

2 Now choose a different typeface from the Change Font list box. This lists all the fonts installed on your computer, but it's a good idea to avoid unusual and uncommon fonts (see pages 88-89). If you choose a font that's supplied with Windows, such as Arial, most Web visitors will have it.

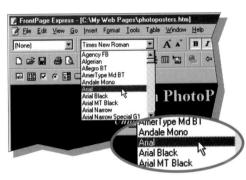

3 You can now see the effects of your font choice. Notice that the two headings keep the same emphasis settings that you selected when you chose Headings for them.

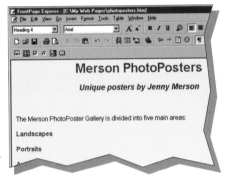

4 Just as with a word processor, choosing contrasting fonts for different parts of your Web page helps to make the page look more stylish – and, with careful font selection, easier to browse. We've changed the headings typeface to the Verdana font that's supplied with Windows. It's a modern sans serif typeface that has more impact than Arial.

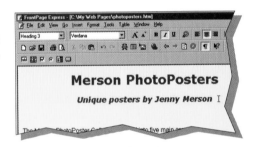

5 Changing the type size can also help to make the structure of your Web page easier to follow. Select the text and use the Increase Text Size and Decrease Text Size buttons to make these changes.

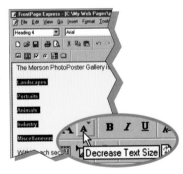

6 In this example, reducing the size of the five categories of poster has made the list stand out much better against the main part of the text.

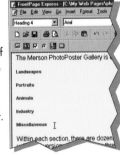

7 To make the list really stand out to Web visitors, you can highlight it with bullet points. Select the text and click the Bulleted List button on the Format toolbar.

8 The bullets appear and the list is indented. These two effects really make it stand out, and you can be sure that the combination of font sizes and formatting makes your page quick to understand and easy to follow for Web visitors.

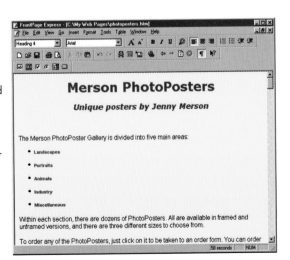

REMOVE FORMATS

If you find that you want to remove the formatting for some or all of your text, select the text and then click on the Remove Formatting command on the Format menu. This is particularly useful when you can't remember all of the text changes you have made; the text instantly reverts to the default Times New Roman font. If you also want to remove the styles, select the text and then choose Normal from the Change Style list box.

Backgrounds and colours

The Web would be a very dull place indeed if every site used the same colours and backgrounds. Employ the tricks and techniques of the Web design experts to make your site stand out from the crowd.

When you're planning your Web site, it's natural to spend a lot of time working out how to structure it, what text and graphics you're going to use, and how you're going to divide the site up into separate pages and then link them all together. However, it's also important to consider the look and feel of your Web site.

While there's nothing wrong with accepting FrontPage's default suggestions for colours of background, text and links, for example, it's likely that you can do better yourself. Moreover, there may be times when the default suggestions don't really suit your site. Unlike typefaces (see pages 88-91), where it is advisable to stick to the handful that can be found on almost all computers, colours and backgrounds are very diverse and offer almost unlimited choices.

● Planning ahead
If you want your site to really stand out, it pays to spend some time considering the colour and background options open to you. By default, the Web pages that FrontPage Express creates are all black text on a white background. As we've already seen (see page 90), by choosing a different colour scheme, you can rapidly give your site a striking look.

It's also a quick and easy procedure to add a background picture or pattern to your Web pages (see pages 94-95). FrontPage itself doesn't come with any sample background

With FrontPage Express, you can make use of a whole palette of colours to brighten up your Web pages.

graphics, but there are thousands of royalty-free images of all types available for free download from the Internet (see Stage 7, pages 140-143). You can drop these straight on to your page, or use a graphics program such as Corel PHOTO-PAINT (see Stages 3, pages 74-89) to edit them first.

● The importance of links
One area that needs special attention is the colour of the links on your Web pages. The standard approach is that when someone visits your Web site for the first time, text links appear in bright blue. If they click on the link to visit another page, then return to the original page, the link changes to a darker, bluish-purple colour. This allows people to see where they have been as they browse around an unfamiliar site.

Although it's a good idea to adopt the above practice, you don't have to keep these particular colours. This is important, because you might choose a background colour or picture that makes the blue and/or purple hard to read when viewed on the computer screen.

● Download issues

When adding this colourful polish to your Web site, you need to bear in mind the impact that your choices will have on the length of time it takes visitors to download your pages to their computers.

The good news is that the choice of colours for text, backgrounds and links makes absolutely no difference to download times. Each colour choice is stored as just six code characters (such as CCFF77, DE6A00 and so on) in the HTML that FrontPage Express generates, and since a 56K modem can download around 6,000 characters per

second, you'd have to make thousands of colour choices in a page to add more than a second or so to the download time.

Backgrounds require more thought, however. A background picture is just like every other picture you use in a Web page, in that it's a separate file that must be downloaded along with the Web page. Most background images used on the Web are in the range 2–10KB (equivalent of around 2,000–10,000 characters), and each one would add approximately a second or two to the download time. Pictures are also tiled on a Web page in much the same way that Windows tiles the Desktop background. This means that you should avoid patterns which have distracting, uneven joins – the ideal background is continuous and seamless.

Colours and the Web

Find out how to extend the range of colours you can use on your pages with FrontPage Express.

WHEN YOU FIRST start working with colours in FrontPage Express, you might be a little disappointed to find that there seems to be only a handful of colours available. These 16 colours, bearing names such as Fuchsia, Olive and Aqua, have been used since the earliest days of colour computing. When HTML was devised, these commonly available but rather basic colours were also specified.

In today's Web world, relying on just this limited palette of colours to make your Web site look good would be impossible. It doesn't help that the 16 colours themselves are either too dull or too bright and this means that text often looks garish against these backgrounds.

Fortunately, since the early days of HTML, extra facilities for specifying any of 16 million colours have become available for Web designers. Since most Web surfers now have computers that can display all these colours, it's well worth exploiting the full range when picking colours for your site. As this range is far wider than the human eye can distinguish, you are bound to find one that is suitable.

However, Microsoft's programmers still list only the 16 basic colours in FrontPage Express. If you want to use the full range, you must first specify the colour by using the Custom entry at the bottom of the list. You can then choose from one of Windows' 48 colours, or select a completely different tone from the colour picker panel that you'll find on the right of the Color dialog box.

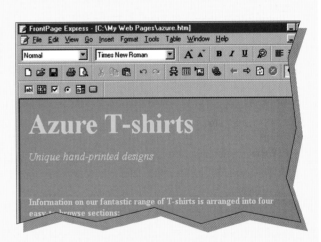

The set of 16 colours provided by FrontPage Express makes for dazzling, eye-watering colour combinations that aren't always visitor-friendly.

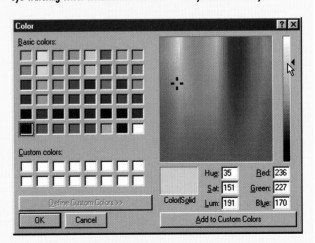

After you have clicked on the Custom option in the FrontPage Express list of colours, you can see the Color dialog box with Windows' 48 colours and the colour picker panel. This allows you to create virtually any colour you want.

At first glance, FrontPage seems to offer just 16 colours for your text and background, but many others are available.

Customizing link colours

Here's how to change the default link colours of blue and purple so that they match or contrast with other colours on your site.

1 Here is a simple home page with links to several other pages. The links show up as blue in the FrontPage document window – the Web's default colour scheme. However, this can cause problems with certain Web page designs.

Azure T-shirts

Unique hand-printed designs

Information on our fantastic range of T-shirts is easy-to-browse sections:

- Size and colours
- Pricing and group discounts
- Ordering (by Web and by post)
- Delivery

2 For example, try changing this Web page's background to a mid-blue. First, select Background from the Format menu. On the Background tab of the dialog box that appears, there are several settings that let you select different colours for parts of your Web page. Click the colour box next to the Background option to see the available colours. Although FrontPage lists only a handful of basic colours, many are too garish, so select the Custom option.

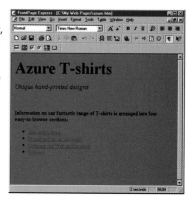

3 On the right side of the Color dialog box is a smoothly shaded spectrum of colours. Click the mouse in this box to choose your colour and then click the Add to Custom Colors button. It then appears as a coloured rectangle in the Custom colors section at the bottom left of the dialog box. Select this rectangle and click OK.

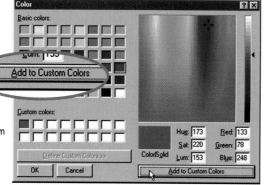

4 This colour looks great, but the set of text links have all but disappeared. The blue background is too close in colour to the default blue of the links.

Azure T-shirts

Unique hand-printed designs

5 To fix this problem, select Background from the Format menu once again. The Background tab of the dialog box also has settings for the text link colours. Change both the Hyperlink and Visited Hyperlink, choosing two colours that are easy to tell apart and that contrast well with the blue Web page background. Press the OK button when you've finished.

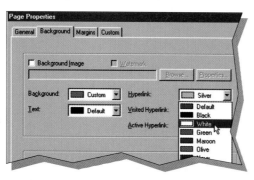

6 Save your Web page and open it up in your Web browser. When the page first loads, all the links appear in the colour you chose for the Hyperlink setting – white in this case. Click one of the links to visit another page.

7 Immediately press the Back button on your browser to return to the previous page. Now you can see how well the colour you chose for the Visited Hyperlink works against the background, and check that the difference between the two link colours is easy for Web visitors to tell apart.

Customizing backgrounds

With thousands of background images available free on the Internet, there's plenty of material to help you design your Web pages. Images can also be edited in a graphics program.

1 Open a page in FrontPage. Here we've decided to change the solid blue background added in the exercise on page 94 to a more textured background. Choose Background from the Format menu.

2 Under the Background tab of the Page Properties dialog box that appears, tick the Background Image box and click the Browse button. When the Select Background Image dialog box appears, click the Browse button again to locate and select an image. Click the OK button.

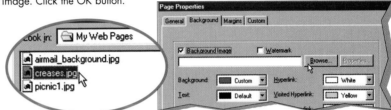

3 Your Web page background is now tiled with the image you chose. However, in this case, the effect of the creased cloth looks fine, but the page looks grey and rather lifeless.

4 To fix this, you can change the colour with a graphics program. We've used Paint Shop Pro, but most image editing programs will be suitable. Use the program's colour adjustment commands to achieve a better result. Here, by increasing the amount of blue and decreasing the amount of red and green in the grey tile, the colour has completely changed.

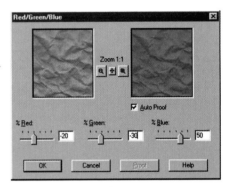

5 Once you have created an image with a more attractive colour, save the image, making sure to give it a different name. (That way you can still use the original picture at a later date without having to undo your changes.)

6 Now you need to choose your revised background image. Bring up the Page Properties dialog box again (see Step 1), and locate and select your new graphic.

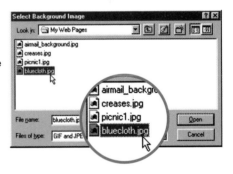

7 You can now see the effect of the change. The Web page looks a lot more appealing than it would with either a plain white background or a dull textured one. By using the colour controls in a graphics program, you can add to the number of background images available for use in your Web pages.

PC TIPS

Non-printing backgrounds

The printing of Web pages is often an overlooked part of the Web design process. Although Web authors may ignore it, they do so at their peril as many Web site visitors print out pages for reading offline. Although Web page backgrounds are great for setting the tone of your Web site, on many Web browsers, the background images themselves don't print out. Even for those Web browsers that can print background colours and images – such as Internet Explorer v5 – unless the Web visitor has made a point of turning on the ability to print backgrounds, they too will see a blank background. Always do a text print-out of pages to make sure that the absence of the background doesn't adversely affect them.

Hardware

Exploring virtual reality

Virtual reality (VR) is much talked about as a way to escape into a world of fantasy and indulge your wildest dreams. So what can virtual reality offer for the home computer user?

Virtual reality (VR) captures the imagination in a way few other computer applications have managed before. Being able to wander around a make-believe world, encountering realistic objects and feeling as though you are manipulating them with your own hands, makes the world of 3D far more accessible and much more fun than any other form of activity.

WHAT IT MEANS

HMD

This stands for Head Mounted Display – the technical name for a virtual reality helmet. These helmets track your responses as you view a computer-generated virtual world through tiny monitors encased in the front of the helmet. The shape of Head Mounted Displays varies from product to product, but they usually look like a cross between a bicycle helmet and an over-sized pair of sunglasses.

● A whole new world

The best definition of virtual reality is that it's an artificial world, created with computer hardware and software, presented to the user in such a way that it appears and feels like a real environment. For the past few years, the first thing that came to mind when VR was mentioned was the virtual reality helmet (or HMD, as the technology is also known). This is still the most familiar face of virtual reality, but there is now hardware available that can be connected to a home PC.

Although the hardware and software which give the best virtual reality experience still remain within the confines of military development, the technology is moving into the mainstream. High-street games arcades already feature virtual reality headsets and specially written 3D games. While they can be expensive, virtual reality hardware and software are becoming more readily available to home computer users. PC add-ons,

The virtual reality helmet – a headset equipped with motion sensors, stereo display screens and speakers – is the classic representation of VR. In fact, there is much more to the technology than just this.

such as joysticks that push back against your hand movements and lightweight helmets that reveal a convincing 3D world, are now much more affordable.

Over the next few years, this hardware and its associated software is going to make it possible for home computer users to enter virtual worlds that will astonish users with the vividness and intensity of their simulation.

● Game software experience

Even if you don't have access to VR hardware, you can still sample the experience on your existing PC by playing a state-of-the-art computer game, such as *Quake III*. In a game such as this, the amazing 3D graphics really do give the illusion of entering and participating in a virtual world.

In another field, Internet-based worlds called MUDs (multi-user dungeons) give a different kind of virtual experience that's less action-oriented, where your strategy builds upon the convincing 3D computer graphics.

● Greater involvement

But even the best of these games is still quite a long way from true VR. Looking at your monitor and hearing sound through your PC's speakers involves only two senses, sight and sound, so this gives something of an incomplete experience. Being able to see and hear the real world outside can also be a distraction.

Special hardware has therefore been developed which fulfills the need for a more complete sensory involvement with the artificial environment of VR.

There have been some experiments with the sense of smell, but this and the sense of taste have been largely ignored by the VR pioneers. Instead, technologists have concentrated not only on making the simulations of sight and sound more realistic but also on adding the sense of touch to the experience.

VR hardware mostly aims to improve the 3D visual effect and add an element of touch that far surpasses what can be achieved via the conventional mouse and keyboard.

The items described here are usually dedicated to stimulating one particular sense as vividly as possible. Although some of these items are currently so expensive as to be beyond the reach of the home user, it's almost certain that prices will steadily fall. After all, it was only 20 years ago that a computer with the power of today's average home PC would have cost several years' salary and would therefore have been out of reach of most ordinary people.

● Home computers and VR

Until very recently, most virtual reality helmets have been far too expensive for home computer users. Those that have been more reasonably priced (although still costing a few hundred pounds) have tended to be of such poor quality as to be ineffective. But recent advances in miniaturization have started to make it possible for some affordable, high-resolution headsets to become available.

VR technology is bound to become more important in the near future. But an HMD isn't the only hardware that is available for your virtual excursions, and here we shall be taking a look at other current equipment, from affordable games controllers to sophisticated tools.

● Force feedback devices

Starting at the bottom, force feedback devices, such as the Microsoft *SideWinder Force Feedback 2*, are down-to-earth and

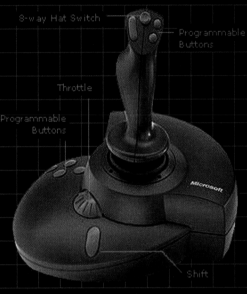

The force feedback joystick (above) is the affordable face of virtual reality. An increasing amount of software, such as MechWarrior 4 (top) is force feedback-ready.

affordable inventions (at around £60). This technology is becoming ever more popular as a component in ordinary joysticks and other games input devices, such as steering wheels and throttle controls.

All force feedback devices work via hardware and software standards established by Microsoft. Their exact function varies from product to product, but basically they allow you

Virtual reality accessories, such as the VR helmet, help to enhance the feeling of actually being part of the game that you're playing. Such technology, which was once extremely expensive, is now rapidly coming within the price range of the average home computer user.

WHERE TO GET VR HARDWARE

Force feedback joysticks and simple devices can be bought from computer stores, but most other VR equipment can be rather tricky to find, especially anything other than the cheapest HMDs. One company, Cybermind UK Ltd, specializes in such objects and can be contacted on 0116 260 4310 or www.cyberminduk.com/

to interact with the controller (such as the throttle), to provide a realistic experience of what's going on in the game or VR world you are in. For example, if you are playing a racing game and drive the car over some gravel, the controller might start vibrating to simulate a bumpy ride. Then, if the car gets damaged and you try to perform a change of direction, it might offer some resistance to your movement. This makes the game-playing experience a lot more realistic, and support for force feedback is now being added to an increasing number of titles.

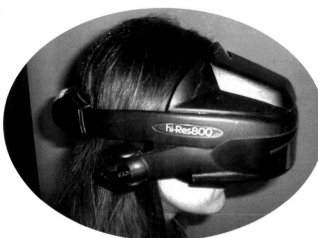

Cybermind's Hi-Res 800 HMD costs £2,650 and includes a motion tracker. VR helmets such as this are light and don't restrict the user's movements. Heavy helmets tend both to hinder your enjoyment and to disorient you, leading to feelings of dizziness.

● HMD – the options

An HMD is the core component of any virtual reality hardware setup and most designs are already in regular use in industry and the military. However, making an affordable home version has been difficult, as cutting corners usually results in a less than satisfactory virtual device. Perhaps the most successful home HMD is Cybermind's Hi-Res 800. Sadly, such systems are still extremely expensive: the Hi-Res 800 costs around £2,650. This headset runs along the same principles as most other HMD devices. It fits around your head so that it completely covers your eyes, and inside it are two small monitors, one for each eye, and speakers for stereo sound. What makes the experience interactive is the HMD's motion-tracking device. This works by monitoring your head movements, so that when you look up, for example, the headset calculates the degree of movement to ensure that your view in the 'virtual world' will

move up by exactly the same amount. The result is that you are able to move your head quite naturally and to use these normal responses as a way to navigate the virtual world. Wearing the headset for too long can lead to disorientation, but the monitors are specially made to prevent eye strain and dizziness.

● System compatibility

Futuristic hardware isn't much use, however, if you do not have the software needed to run it properly. Owing to the current expense of the hardware and the lack of a clear market leader, most of the Multimedia software companies don't, in fact, offer support for any type of true VR hardware.

However, Cybermind has ensured that its particular make of headset doesn't need any extra patches or software at all. By simply selecting the mouse option within an existing game, the Cybermind headset will interpret the movement of your head in exactly the same way that the PC will interpret a movement of the mouse in a normal game.

● Software simulations

This method of hardware support is called 'dumb', because it doesn't know whether the movements it is conveying actually mean anything useful. As a result, it doesn't make much sense for you to buy a headset

for use with a strategy game, where the purpose of the mouse is only to move a cursor.

However, for action games that you play with a first-person view, the simulation works extremely well. A good example is the *Quake* series of first-person perspective battle-style games. In *Quake* you already view the action as if from the eyes of the lead character, so adding a VR headset makes very little difference to the gameplay but it does immerse you thoroughly in the action. Expect to see this type of VR-style involvement in more PC games in the near future.

● Virtual reality gloves

The second most common piece of VR equipment is the glove. But for the average home computer user, its extremely high price (thousands of pounds) is likely to ensure that it remains of academic interest only for some time to come.

Worn on the writing hand, a VR glove is dotted with motion sensors on each of the fingers and around the wrist. These sensors measure the position and movement of your hand and relay information about these measurements to your computer. This

ADDING VR HARDWARE

Installing VR hardware devices on your computer isn't as hard as you might think. Cybermind's headset, for example, simply plugs straight into the monitor and joystick ports, with no further hardware connections necessary. Other VR hardware might appear to be more complicated, but the installation is still via a simple plug-in connection at the back of the PC.

information is then used to create a virtual hand in the 3D world.

The virtual hand is usually displayed on screen, and you interact with it in much the same way as the headset, as it relays movements from the real world to the virtual scene and allows you to pick up 3D objects as if they were real. This piece of hardware isn't as central to the VR

Feel your way around the world of virtual reality with Immersion Corp's Cyberglove, shown above.

experience as the helmet, but it does go a long way towards helping to create a convincing and interactive virtual world.

● 3D manipulators

A 3D glove might be extremely good at giving you a chance to manipulate virtual objects, but neither this nor the HMD are particularly useful as navigational devices. Although you might be able to look anywhere in the virtual world, and pick up objects in it, you often can't move around by any means other than the keyboard or joystick (although a VR glove can

frequently be used like a mouse, where you point forward and press an internal button to move). A 3D manipulator, however, is a more affordable device, and one that gives you a much more intuitive method of navigating in three dimensions. The most simple are usually the cheapest and such devices look like joysticks without a base, which you tilt to move in the required direction. More sophisticated manipulators are shaped like balls and can be held in your hand.

The ball allows for movement in any direction. A number of buttons around the handle of the device give you access to specific features, such as zooming or shifting your viewpoint. Devices like this cost hundreds of pounds, but look set to become much cheaper in the future.

● Touch-simulation interfaces

For the virtual reality fan who wants everything, a haptic interface is a must. These devices are hugely expensive, but do enable the ultimate experience in simulation of the sense of touch.

The easiest way to describe how a haptic device works is to imagine inserting each of your fingers into a thimble and using these as a way of interacting with the computer and 3D world. The 'thimbles' contain tiny

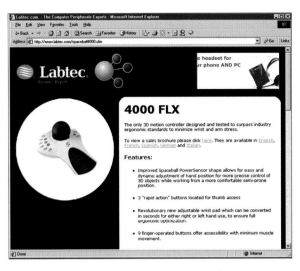

The Spaceball 4000 FLX is one of several hi-tech controllers currently available to help you navigate your way through the world of virtual reality.

pressure points that simulate the texture of the virtual object that you are 'touching' by moving against the surfaces of your fingers.

The more expensive systems, which can cost several thousands of pounds, work with all five fingers and measure the position and rotation of your hand, combining the capabilities of the VR glove with the haptic interface, to create a realistic sensation when you touch virtual items.

Although these high-end virtual reality add-ons are too expensive for most home computer users, the companies that develop them are slowly, but surely, bringing prices down. It may not be too long before you can actually feel folders and files as you move them around a virtual 3D desktop.

CHEAP VR ON A CONSOLE

A cheap alternative to VR on your computer is a home games console, such as the Dreamcast or Sony PlayStation. These are specifically created for playing games and for featuring state-of-the-art graphics. Although when first released they tended to beat the PC on graphics power, they can't be upgraded and so will not be able to keep up as new technology appears for your home computer.

At present, they are still widely used and titles such as *Tomb Raider* and *Gran Turismo* are some of the best examples of current 3D graphics and gameplay. Most of these consoles include basic force feedback controllers, which tremble in your hand as you fire a shot or drive over rough terrain.

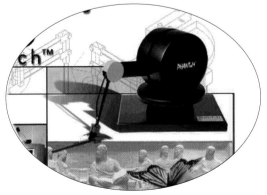

The dictionary definition of Haptic is 'related to the sense of touch'. The bizarre device shown above is a haptic interface. It's designed to recreate the texture and feel of an object appearing on your computer screen or in a VR environment.

Seeing your PC on TV

A large percentage of the purchase price of your computer is taken up by the monitor. But there is an alternative to paying for a PC screen, provided you have a TV.

You might have wondered why it is that you pay a hefty sum for a standard-sized PC monitor – and much more for anything larger – when you've probably got a perfectly good TV screen taking pride of place in your sitting room. This is an important point, especially as it's generally the monitor that takes up so much desktop space and makes the computer a relatively fixed item. Your desktop system unit is probably quite portable and not at all hard to move from one room to another, but the surprisingly heavy monitor makes moving it around a chore.

● PC to TV

You'll be pleased to know that numerous firms now offer a solution in the shape of devices that allow you to display your PC image on a television screen, and this practice is likely to become more common.

Microsoft and Sony, for example, are working together to produce products that create a common platform between computers and home electronics, such as televisions.

Sony already make TVs that accept a signal from a computer without any intermediate devices at all. You attach a cable to your graphics card output at the back of your PC and plug the other end into an appropriate socket at the front of the television. Of course, as they are currently a cutting edge product, these special televisions cost considerably more than the conventional televisions.

Philips also produce a range of 'smart card' televisions, which can do much the same thing, but these are not currently available for the European television system. However, if the technology takes off, the trend will doubtless spread and prices will subsequently fall. The fact that HDTV is changing the face of TV could also help to make combination TV and PC monitors much more common.

It can be very useful to be able to output your computer signal to a large television screen for serious business presentations, or just for fun.

● Conversion devices

A much more affordable alternative to buying an expensive, dedicated television, is to go for one of the devices that convert the signal from your PC into one that can be displayed by your TV. Some of these devices are designed specifically for laptops and are marketed as business presentation devices, which allow you to plug a laptop into an on-site television and play presentations on it. These plug into a laptop slot, but others are suited for home use.

● PC displays on TV

The RealVision Technology uTV-2000 is a personal-stereo sized device that plugs into your PC's USB port and allows you to view PC screens at resolutions from 640x480 to 1600x1200 pixels. Thanks to USB's plug-and-play feature, connection is a lot easier than with alternative devices, where you need to unplug the monitor from the PC to plug a cable into the graphics card output. There is also a PCMCIA version that you can use with notebook PCs that lack USB ports.

Within a few minutes of plugging the USB cable into the PC and connecting the uTV-2000's video output to your TV's video output, you can be watching DVD movies on your TV or enjoying an action game on your wide-screen TV. There's a credit-card sized remote control that lets you position the Windows Desktop on the TV screen and then adjust the colour and brightness settings. You can even zoom in on different areas of the screen.

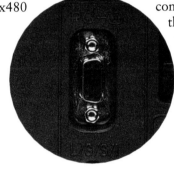

A VGA socket like this on the rear of a TV means that it will accept signals from a PC.

● No wires

Another option available is the wireless approach, using a device such as the PC/TV Airlink from US company AITech (www.aitech.com). The AITech PC/TV Airlink provides a wireless connection between the computer and the TV with a maximum resolution of 800x600 pixels. It can even relay the signal up to 30m through walls, depending on their density, so you can operate the PC in one room, while other people are watching the picture on a television in another.

A special set-top receiver relays signals from the infra-red keyboard back to the PC (infra-red signals can't travel through walls). It also means you can monitor the computer picture from the other room – this can be handy if you want to see what your children are looking at on the computer, for example. You can even buy additional receivers so that you

You can display the contents of your PC to others much more easily by using a big TV as a PC screen. Some TVs – including the top of the range Sony WEGA models – have VGA sockets, and so are simple to connect to your PC.

can see your PC signal on several televisions at the same time. There are other manufacturers that produce similar devices that work within the home on a wireless basis.

● Getting a good picture

There are drawbacks, of course. Regardless of the manufacturers' claims, be aware that you won't get as good a picture on a TV as on a PC monitor, although it can still be impressive and, of course, bigger. The picture will certainly be much better and a lot cheaper than the technology of a few years ago.

On the positive side, such devices will allow you to video your PC output, which could be handy for business presentations. If your PC has a DVD drive (see Stage 4, pages 100-101), you can also watch DVD movies on your TV, without having to buy a separate DVD player.

The uTV-2000 system allows simple connection of your PC to a wide-screen television.

CONTACT POINTS

uTV-2000
RealVision
In the UK contact:
Holdan Ltd
Tel: 0845 130 4445
Price: £150 inc VAT*
www.holdan.co.uk

Wega FD Trinitron TVs
Sony
Tel: 01932 816 000
Price: £2,300-£3,000*
www.sony-europe.com/

*UK prices

Adding a TV tuner

If you plug a TV tuner into your PC, you can view your favourite television programmes on your computer instead of on your TV.

Installing a TV tuner (either as a card or as a USB peripheral) enables you to watch TV on your PC. Depending on the device you buy, you can also access TV text services, such as Teletext, and radio as well. They can all be controlled by on-screen software.

While many extra computer devices can be added without opening up the computer, some useful add-ons need to be fitted inside the case. Adding extra memory is usually the reason why most computer users open the casing on their computers (see Stage 3, pages 94-95) but fitting a TV tuner card can be another reason for doing this.

● How expansion cards work

Expansion cards, such as the TV tuner card, have a connector which fits into a slot on the computer's motherboard. Once fitted and set up correctly, the expansion card works as if it were a part of the motherboard, sending signals to and fro. With a TV

tuner card, these signals include the television picture in digital form.

● Fitting an expansion card

When fitting an expansion card, you first have to ensure that your PC has a slot that can accept it. There are three types of slot in a modern PC: Industry

It's easy to add a TV tuner card to your PC, but it may involve opening up the computer's case. If you're worried about doing this, consider paying a bit more for a USB tuner which can simply be plugged in.

Standard Architecture (ISA), Peripheral Component Interconnect (PCI) and Accelerated Graphics Port (AGP). ISA slots are suitable for simple cards, such as internal modems that don't need a fast connection to the motherboard. PCI slots are faster and better for high-speed devices, such as graphics cards. An AGP slot is a special form of PCI slot intended for the fastest 3D graphics cards.

A typical PC usually has three ISA slots and two or three PCI slots. Most PCs also have a single AGP slot. So when buying any expansion card, remember to check that your PC has the right slot for it – most are designed to plug into a PCI slot.

WHAT KIND OF CARD?

The cheapest way to get TV on your PC is to fit an internal card (about £40), as we show opposite. But that's far from being your only choice; the market leader, Hauppauge, has no less than six different PC TV tuners in its WinTV range. If you don't want to bother delving inside your PC, then a USB (Universal Serial Bus) tuner is ideal. One cable plugs into your USB port, another into your sound card and then you connect your TV aerial. This costs

about £70. For £60 or so, you can get an internal card that adds FM radio. The equivalent USB tuner costs around £90. At about £80, there is yet another tuner/FM card, but this one gives Nicam stereo. Top of the range is the WinTV Theater, which costs £100. This includes a Dolby Pro Logic audio decoder, five-speaker surround sound and FM stereo radio. You can check out the Hauppauge range and any TV tuner developments at www.hauppauge.co.uk.

Fitting a TV tuner card to your PC

Although it might seem a daunting task to fit a card, if you take some simple precautions neither you nor your PC should come to any harm (see Before you start box, right).

1 In your computer's manual find the section which shows the location of the screws that secure the system unit's lid. Unscrew the relevant screws (there might be as few as one or as many as six).

2 Once all the screws are out, the lid will slide forwards and/or upwards to reveal the motherboard and internal components.

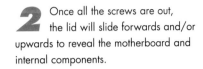

3 At the back of the computer there's an array of slots – large ISA slots and smaller PCI slots. Each slot is aligned with a vertical blanking plate on the back of the PC. Check the PC tuner manual to find the right slot for your TV tuner card and remove the screw that fixes the slot's blanking plate to the PC case (inset).

4 Before removing the TV tuner card from its protective bag, touch the computer case with your hand – this ensures that any static build-up is discharged safely. Then push the card's edge into the slot so the card's metal backplate slips down just inside the back edge of the case.

5 The hole on the top edge of the card's backplate aligns with the hole that secured the blanking plate that you removed in Step 3. Fix the card into place by refixing the screw that you removed in Step 3. Replace the computer's cover.

6 Plug the aerial cable into the aerial input on the card's backplate. Plug the connecting cable from the audio out on the TV card into the audio input of the sound card.

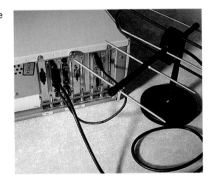

7 Turn on the mains supply and switch the computer on as normal. Follow the TV tuner card's software installation instructions to copy the appropriate driver and program files to your computer. The tuner card automatically scans the signal from the aerial for TV channels.

Adding a second hard disk drive

Although upgrading the hard disk is a complicated process best left to the experts, a grasp of the factors involved will help you buy the right hard disk and understand the changes to Windows that follow.

If your computer has been bought in the past six months or so, it's likely to have a large hard disk – anywhere between 10 and 40 Gigabytes (GB). That's more than 2,000 times as much as the first business PCs sold in the early 1980s!

With each new software program you install and with each new document you create, you fill up the available space. For older PCs, with hard disks of 5GB or less, space might already be tight, but the problem can affect every keen computer user eventually. Even a 20GB hard disk will eventually fill up as software becomes more advanced and consumes ever-increasing amounts of hard disk space.

● **Solving the space problem**
Although Windows does have its own special disk compression feature, a better solution is to add more hard disk space. Hard disks are relatively inexpensive, after all. You can either replace your existing hard disk or add a second one. As replacing the existing disk involves reinstalling every program, folder and file from the old

The inside of a Seagate hard disk drive. Adding a hard disk is a job often best left to your local computer store.

hard disk to the new one, most people leave the original in place and add another.

However, there are complicating factors. First of all, some new add-ons are easier to install than others. There's no denying the fact that adding a second hard disk is one of the most difficult hardware upgrades

you can make. While adding a TV tuner card (see pages 104-105) is easy, even for a PC novice, adding a second hard disk is not to be undertaken lightly.

To start with, it's important to choose the right type of hard disk to work alongside your existing one. Most home computers use a hard disk standard called EIDE. Buying a second EIDE hard disk means that you won't require any extra hardware to add it to your existing PC. The alternative, known as SCSI, needs a special card to work with most PCs.

Although you can mix the two hard disk types inside a single computer, you may find that an extra controller card is required. It is much more straightforward to choose the same type of hard disk as you already have.

Choosing a new hard disk

WHEN IT COMES to size, larger hard drives tend to be much better value. Spin speed indicates how fast the hard disk rotates – usually 5,400-15,000rpm. The higher the figure the better, since it means that data can be read from and written to the disk surface faster.

Seek and access times refer to how quickly the read/write head in the hard disk can locate data on the

disk's surface. Typical figures are 5-10 milliseconds (thousandths of a second). The lower the figure, the better. Throughput measures the maximum rate at which data can be transferred from the hard disk surface in a second. A rate of 40MB per second is typical.

Always buy a reliable brand of hard disk and get as much capacity as you can afford.

● Physical considerations

Adding a hard disk is also a physically complicated procedure. Unlike the TV tuner card, it doesn't simply slip into an empty expansion slot. There are two cables that need connecting inside the computer. Once that's done, the technical issues are more involved, too. To prepare a hard disk for use, you will need to run several complicated utility programs. These utility programs run under MS-DOS, and there are no step-by-step wizards to

help you. The utilities involve wiping all computer data from the new hard disk. This introduces a serious risk of accidentally deleting all the information that is stored on your original hard disk.

● To DIY or not to DIY

For these reasons, most home computer users should seriously consider finding a professional to do the job for them. Due to the large number of variables involved, it's not possible to create a universal

step-by-step guide that works for all computers. The guide below provides pointers, rather than explicit instructions on the procedure for installing a second hard disk. All but the most advanced users should seek expert help. The best option by far is to buy the second hard disk locally. If possible, check the model you intend to purchase in operation, as the fastest hard disk drives can be quite noisy for home use. Then take the computer to the local computer shop to have the new disk installed.

Technical issues when adding a hard disk

Adding a second hard disk to a computer is a multi-stage process. The following guide is intended to give you an insight into the complex process that your computer shop will go through to complete it successfully.

Checking inside the PC:

1 Shut down your PC, switch off the power supply at the mains socket and open up the case.
2 Is there a spare bay for the drive to fit into? If so, is it the right size for the hard disk you want: either 3.5in or 5.25in?
3 Is there a spare connector on the EIDE cable that connects to the motherboard? If so, does it reach to the drive bay where the new hard disk will go?
4 Is there a spare power supply lead for the new hard disk?

Fitting and connecting the new drive:

1 Check the drive documentation for any necessary special adjustments to the drive before fitting.
2 Check the EIDE socket on the new hard disk to find which end has the number 1 pin.
3 Fit the hard disk, fixing it into place with the screws supplied.
4 Connect the EIDE cable to the hard disk, making sure that the side of the cable closest to the number 1 pin also leads to the number 1 pin on the EIDE socket on the motherboard.
5 Connect the power supply lead to the new drive.

After the new drive is fitted in place:

1 Start up the PC and listen for any beeps which indicate that the drive is incorrectly installed.
2 If the PC doesn't start correctly, recheck all the previous steps.

If the original hard disk starts correctly:

1 Go into your computer's BIOS setup screen (your computer manual will tell you how).
2 Find the part of the BIOS setup screen that handles hard disks. The first disk covers your original hard disk; to add the new disk, use the Auto-detect command on the second disk.
3 Save these changes and exit the BIOS setup screen. Your PC will restart.
4 Switch the computer to MS-DOS mode.
5 Run the FDISK utility to create partitions on the new drive.
6 Run the FORMAT utility to get the drive ready for storing data.
7 Restart the computer. Windows should restart as usual.

After Windows has started:

1 Open the My Computer window. You will now see one or more new hard disk icons.
2 The old hard disk's first partition is C:. The first partition on the new hard disk is D:. Other partitions on the old hard disk follow in alphabetical order after the letter assigned to the new disk's first partition and would be E:, F: and so on. Any additional partitions on the new disk follow after the letters assigned to partitions on the old disk and would be G:, H: and so on.
3 Spend some time getting used to this new assignment of drive letters to minimize the risk of misplacing files and programs.

 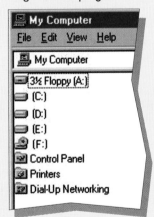

After a second hard drive has been added (right), your My Computer folder will have an icon for each extra partition, and the CD-ROM drive will also have a different name.

Note: software originally installed on the second partition on the original hard disk (for example, when it was assigned the drive letter D:) may no longer work. This is because this partition is now assigned the letter E. Windows can easily lose track of such software. If this happens to any of your software, you will probably need to reinstall it.

Uninterruptible power supplies

The electricity supply to your house does sometimes fail, so an uninterruptible power supply for your PC protects it from loss of data in the event of an emergency.

You're calmly working away at your PC, putting the finishing touches to that long, complicated and vital business presentation in Microsoft Word. You've got the final version of your Excel figures open with quite a few substantial additions. In the background, you've nearly finished a 45-minute download of the graphics you need to create the final impressive effect. And you haven't yet saved any of this afternoon's intensive work. Then there's a power cut, your PC crashes and all your hard work is lost. There's nothing for it but to shout, shrug it off and then work through the night trying to repeat everything you did in the day. This is a worst-case scenario, but it could – and does – happen.

● Be prepared for the worst

If you had an uninterruptible power supply (UPS), a power cut wouldn't matter at all; the UPS would keep your PC going long enough for you to save to disk all your valuable data in RAM. Basically, a UPS is simply a power supply with a battery that runs your PC for a short time in the event of any problem with the mains power supply. There are several varieties of UPS suited to different potential problems and levels of security and, naturally, they vary in price.

● Types of UPS

There are two main types of UPS: simple devices designed to protect a single PC, and the more sophisticated boxes which can cope with major crises in large PC installations.

An off-line, or stand-by, UPS is the simplest, offering protection for a single PC. The device contains a

Home computers can cope with ordinary domestic power fluctuations but not a total failure, or surges caused by lightning. That's when a UPS comes into its own.

battery and power-conversion circuit, together with a switch that detects power cuts. When the off-line UPS senses that the mains power supply is low enough to be considered a power cut, it supplies the PC's power from the UPS's battery-powered 'inverter' instead. This gives you the time to save any data in RAM and to power down the PC in the correct, and safe, manner.

Off-line UPSs are cheap, at around £60–£70, use little power and don't take up much desk space. But switching to battery power when a voltage problem is detected can take several milliseconds, during which time your PC is not receiving any power. It's still possible that this brief interruption could damage the PC or endanger data that has not been saved. So where absolute security is required, an off-line UPS is not recommended.

The line-interactive UPS is an enhanced variant of the off-line UPS. In this case, the UPS has a battery and inverter that come into action immediately a power cut is sensed.

● Online UPS

For the highest level of protection, you need an online UPS. As the name suggests, this type of UPS is in constant operation – even when the mains supply is functioning normally – and the battery charger, battery and inverter are always online. The AC mains supply is converted to DC and then back to AC again before it reaches the computer. This means that any disturbance in the power supply – caused, for instance, by the operation of large machinery or even a stroke of lightning – is ironed out before it reaches the computer.

Because an online UPS is constantly in use, it guarantees the supply of 'clean power'. For this kind of peace of mind you pay more; online UPSs start at around £80–£100, and the price increases with the number of computers you need to protect. UPS protection for a network of, say, 10 PCs could cost in excess of £1,000.

● Power problems and your PC

If you've never experienced a major power cut while working on your computer, you may wonder why

Liebert's Powersure Line Interactive is geared towards supporting groups of PCs. Sealed, maintenance-free batteries are a feature of the models in this range.

anyone would need a UPS at all. The answer is that even if power cuts are rare (at least, in the developed world), the mains power supply can be unstable enough to pose a threat to your PC. If your PC is engaged in 'mission-critical' work, such as carrying out transactions on the Internet or managing your office network and telephone systems, then even that small threat can be worrying enough to make installing a UPS essential.

There are many ways in which the power supply can damage your PC, from spikes to brownouts to sags and surges (see Power problems box, below).

● Do you need a UPS?

Whether you need a UPS depends on how 'mission-critical' your work on the PC is. If you are in the habit of: saving early and saving often; saving work to the hard disk; setting your applications to save frequently; and keeping regular back-ups of important work, you shouldn't need to worry about this type of problem. Big businesses, however, cannot afford the risk of a crucial network server going down, so £50,000 or more spent on protecting computer and telecommunications equipment is good value if it guarantees power and prevents work loss.

The Liebert UPStation provides continuous cleaned-up power for servers and other large computers. It comes in a floor-standing cabinet and has similar alarms to the Patriot 280.

The Patriot 280 has maintenance-free batteries and audible and visible power-failure and low-battery alarms.

POWER PROBLEMS

Some people claim that as much as 80 per cent of all computer and electronic malfunctions are caused by disturbances of one kind or another in the power supply. These disturbances come in a variety of guises, complete with their own rich vocabulary. The main types you will hear about are explained here.

'Spikes' are short bursts of high voltage in the mains supply, sometimes caused by lightning, which can, at worst, fuse circuits in your PC.

'Sags' and 'surges' are, respectively, under- and over-voltage fluctuations in the supply, caused by other electricity-hungry equipment in your home. 'Brownouts' are reductions in mains voltage caused by increased demand. These usually occur at peak times (such as half-time in the televised showing of the World Cup Final when everyone puts the kettle on) and could cause your PC to crash if the power supply falls to a very low level.

'Power failure' is a term that speaks for itself, and is the worst case. The damage this causes can be considerable, such as lost or corrupted data and/or even damage to the system itself.

ADSL superhighway

An Internet connection around 10 times faster than a 56Kbps modem is now available in most parts of Britain and other countries. But broadband isn't an option for everyone.

In 1998–99 British Telecom carried out trials in London of a technology that promised a brave new world of high-speed, permanently switched-on Internet access for both home consumers and businesses. The trials of ADSL (Asymmetric Digital Subscriber Line) were successful, and consumers were delighted with the prospect of a permanent 512Kbps connection (around 10 times faster than current 56Kbps modems), allowing almost instant download of Web sites, not to mention access to movies and other content-rich Multimedia. However, by 2001, the actual implementation of ADSL was proving slow, leaving BT the object of criticism from other Internet service providers (ISPs) and consumers alike.

● The technology

ADSL is one of a number of digital technologies that transform the existing copper phone wires into high-speed digital lines for fast Internet access. It's known as 'asymmetric' because it transfers data at different rates 'downstream' (from a site to your PC) and 'upstream' (from your PC). ADSL uses special compression techniques and the unused frequencies of copper wire to get as much as 99 per cent more capacity out of the telephone line.

This allows you to surf the Net or download a large file at the same time as having a voice call, and all on just one telephone line. ADSL is potentially incredibly fast, with speeds

A car repairer sends pictures of crashed vehicles to insurance companies via ADSL links to speed up work-authorization orders.

of up to 6.1Mbps downstream (around 200 times faster than a 56Kbps modem) and 640Kbps upstream. In practice, however, these speeds are not currently attainable, with 512Kbps upstream the quoted rate for consumer services.

Naturally this immensely faster speed offers all sorts of possibilities for the consumer user and for Web businesses. It allows easy delivery of video and Multimedia content, so enabling you to buy or rent and then download all your business and games software, as well as movies, via the Web. It offers consumers choice and convenience, and for businesses, considerable savings in both time and money (in terms of physical outlets, packaging, post and so on). And, since the connection is permanently on, you can download enormous files overnight, and email becomes an instant service, as does messaging. The possibilities of high-speed access are virtually limitless.

PRICES IN THE UK

The basic ADSL consumer service from both BTopenworld and Freeserve involves a £150 installation fee, including the ADSL modem, and a monthly fee of £39.99 including VAT. You have to sign a one-year contract, and you're unlikely to get a refund if you move house after a few months. Most other ISPs are expected to set a very similar price point.

Businesses have a wider range of options, with speeds from 512Kbps up to 2Mbps. BT's business 1000Plus, for example, offers a maximum speed of 1Mbps for an installation fee of £260 and a quarterly ex-VAT rental of £389.97.

● The hardware

In terms of hardware, ADSL installation requires first of all a reasonable PC with a speed above 400MHz, and a few megabytes of free disk space. You then need a special ADSL modem, which has to be fitted by a BT engineer who also tests your line for suitability. The modem splits your phone line into two bands, one for data and the other for voice.

But not everyone can get ADSL. In the UK, the first hurdle is distance from the local telephone exchange; if you're more than 3.5–4km away, the signals won't travel. So ADSL will initially be an urban phenomenon, as there are more exchanges in towns and cities than there are in rural areas. You can easily find out if you are in range by using the Availability Checker area of the BTopenworld site, the sector of BT responsible for ADSL development and installation, on www.btopenworld.com. Just enter your phone number to find out.

On the other hand, even if you do live in an ADSL-enabled area you won't necessarily be able to receive the service. The installation engineer has to test your line to make sure it does not lose too much of the carrier signal when carrying ADSL. BT believes that only around one per cent of lines actually fail this test.

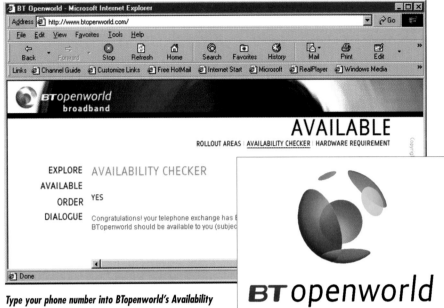

Type your phone number into BTopenworld's Availability Checker to find out if ADSL is available in your area.

● The local loop

For years BT jealously guarded its monopoly of the local loop – the last few kilometres of phone line that reaches your home from the exchange – but these days it is obliged to open access to other ISPs. For your own ISP to supply you with ADSL, it has to gain access to the telephone exchange and install its own equipment.

For many, this simply hasn't happened fast enough. Large ISPs such as Freeserve and AOL became

so angry that they threatened to sue BT, who countered by saying that some exchanges may be over 50 years old and have very limited space for any additional equipment.

Whatever the rights and wrongs of the case, the rollout is at least 18 months behind the schedule envisaged several years ago. While you can sign up for ADSL Internet access online, the process doesn't let you ask questions about likely waiting times. If you're keen to get ADSL's benefits as soon as possible, it may be better to contact the companies directly by telephone and ask about current waiting times before committing yourself to an order that may be months away from delivery.

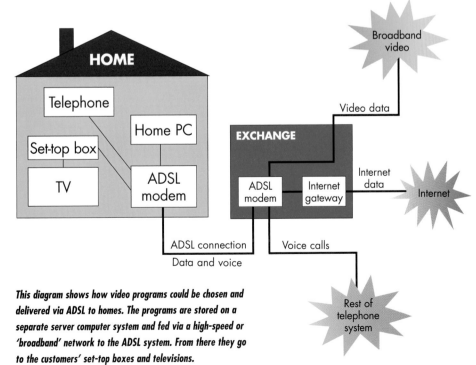

This diagram shows how video programs could be chosen and delivered via ADSL to homes. The programs are stored on a separate server computer system and fed via a high-speed or 'broadband' network to the ADSL system. From there they go to the customers' set-top boxes and televisions.

ALTERNATIVES

If you don't meet the ADSL criteria there may be other options. First of all, if you live in a cabled area you may be able to get cable modem access from the supplier. Cable modems don't offer quite the speed of ADSL, but they can sometimes reach 512Kbps.

Second, BT has trialled 'rate adaptive' ADSL modems. These are capable of supplying a modified (slower) ADSL service to people living more than four kilometres from an exchange. The upstream speed will vary between 64Kbps and 288Kbps, but it's thought that you should be able to download at speeds of up to 512Kbps.

The limits of PC power

Most computer buyers will have noticed that PCs are not only becoming more and more powerful, they are getting cheaper all the time. It may surprise you to know that the computer industry has come up with a theory to explain this phenomenon – the so-called 'Moore's Law'.

Intel's very first microprocessor, the 4004, was introduced in 1971 and featured a mere 2,300 transistors. The 1997 Intel Pentium II has 7.5 million of them; the Pentium III, which powers most modern PCs, has 28 million; and the Pentium 4, released late in 2000 has a staggering 42 million – an increase of 18,260 times in 29 years.

You might think that such an astonishing increase in power would have taken everyone, including the experts, by surprise. Yet as early as

1965 (six years before Intel had even built a marketable microprocessor) one man had predicted the pace of change with an accuracy that still holds true today. His prediction has long been enshrined in the law that bears his name – Moore's Law.

Intel's Pentium 4 processor, shown here with the chipset, has an amazing 42 million transistors – a triumphant example of Moore's law in action (see box, below left).

● **Discovering Moore's Law**
In 1965, Gordon Moore, a co-founder of Intel and now the company's chairman emeritus, was preparing a speech for a gathering of the computer industry. He began to plot a graph showing the growth in chip performance (see Moore's Law graph box, left), and in doing so noticed a striking trend. Each new chip appeared within 18-24 months of the previous one and although each contained roughly twice the processing power of its predecessor, it sold at the same price. Hence, Moore observed, computing power doubles every 18-24 months, but costs the same.

Moore's observation predicted a continuing growth in computing power that many experts found very hard to swallow at the time. Yet Moore's Law proved to be remarkably accurate, pinpointing a trend that has continued for more than 35 years.

MOORE'S LAW GRAPH

This graph from chip manufacturer Intel clearly illustrates how Moore's Law has held over the years. The scale on the left shows the number of transistors per chip, while the scale running from left to right shows time measured in five years. By 1985, the Intel 80386 chip had more than 100,000 transistors while the 80486 exceeded one million before 1990. Today's Pentium 4 has more than 42 million transistors on a single chip.

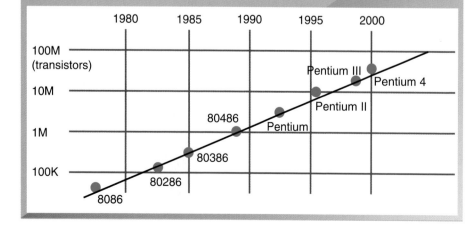

During this time, the Law has become a core computer industry belief, on which chip and computer makers, as well as bulk-buyers of computer equipment, base their plans and forecasts. Soon, however, Moore's Law might need to be revised as it comes into conflict with the more powerful laws of nature.

● Size matters

The trend over the past 35 years has been for more and more transistors to be crammed into less and less chip space. This allows designers to add new features, while overall speed also increases because there is less distance for data to travel between transistors. But in a speech in September 1997, Moore voiced his concern that designers might come up against limitations set by the size of atomic particles. According to some studies, this point could be reached by 2017.

Chips are made by an optical lithography process, effectively a very sophisticated form of printing that builds up microscopically thin layers of components (see Stage 6, pages 100-101). Most current chip manufacture uses so-called '0.18 micron' technology – a measure of component size. In the coming months, almost all processor manufacturers will move to a 0.13 micron production process, using components that are less than half the size. But it has been suggested that the process might reach its limits

within ten years or so, while the insulators currently used, only four or five atoms thick, simply cannot get much smaller.

There's a power problem, too. Moore compared a 200MHz chip made with a 0.35 micron process to a notional 1,000MHz chip made with the 0.18 process. He estimated that the effect would be to double the physical size of the chip and to increase power consumption to 40 watts – at which point the chip would be producing dangerous heat.

Anyone who has taken the lid off a Pentium III PC that has been running will know that processors are already quite big and fairly hot. And in the case of supercomputers, finding new ways to dissipate the heat from ever-faster chips is a challenge for the industry. Using inert gases (such as freon) as a cooling agent might be fine for expensive computers in government labs, but it remains to be seen whether it will be viable for the home or office user.

● An end to progress?

Intel and other microprocessor makers, such as AMD, face another massive difficulty

– the huge investment needed to develop chips and build the manufacturing plants. As chips get more complex and production processes shrink to a smaller micron count, the cost of building a plant increases exponentially.

Intel's success has allowed it to build up enormous cash resources, but other manufacturers are far less wealthy. Even when a chip has been developed, it still costs between $2 billion and $4 billion to build a manufacturing plant. That's money that even Intel, the most dominant company in the industry, has to think very hard about spending.

So, for the next decade, it seems that Moore's Law is likely to hold true. As chips become more powerful, they will also get cheaper in relative terms. That's good news for the consumer, although it does bring into play another 'law', which is that the PC you buy today is always likely to be 50 per cent cheaper if you wait a few months.

Microprocessors (above, left to right) have rapidly gone through many stages of development, from the first Intel microprocessor to the modern Pentium 4, with 18,000 times as many components packed onto the chip. But modern manufacturing technology (right) may be fast approaching an absolute limit.

Home Learning & Leisure

Airline ticketing systems

When you buy an airline ticket, you're not just buying a ticket to fly, you're buying a piece of information in a massive worldwide data network.

It has been estimated that the travel business worldwide has an annual expenditure on information technology of around $20 billion. It's a business that has always striven to be at the forefront of technological and commercial developments, as individual companies have tried to get an edge on their competitors by offering customers faster and more efficient service. And nowhere is this more true than in the air-travel sector.

Even though the Internet is changing the travel industry in some radical ways (see opposite), most people still buy their tickets from travel agents. And pretty much every travel agent in the developed world is linked to one of the big global reservation and ticketing systems. These systems, such as Galileo, SABRE and Amadeus, are among the largest and most heavily used data networks in the world. Typically, they are partly owned by consortia made up of the airlines themselves, but managed as independent companies.

There's much more to flying than meets the eye. For instance, behind the apparently simple process of being issued with a ticket and handing over your money, lies the very latest in superfast, reliable, high-tech computer systems.

● Information online

The core business of these ticketing companies is to maintain an accurate database of flight details and ticket availability, and to make that information available to participating travel agents and airlines, 24 hours a day, 365 days a year. With access to this information, sales staff can sell you a ticket and confirm your seat on the spot. This business requires some of the most sophisticated networking hardware and fail-safe computer systems around.

From the traveller's point of view, however, all that is seen is likely to be a common PC on a travel agent's desk. These PC systems are normally supplied by the ticketing company, often free of charge if the agency does a sufficient volume of business. The PCs are fairly standard desktop machines – except that they might be linked by leased telephone lines to the ticketing company's central database. The software they run (apart from the standard set of word processor and other everyday applications) is the proprietary 'front-end' to the exclusive data held by Galileo, SABRE or Amadeus.

● Windows interface

The user interface for the travel agent has become increasingly graphical, with 'point and click' functions replacing older text-based systems. Although each company uses a different version, Windows forms the basis of them all. Using the software, the travel agent can call up information on flight times, seat availability and just about anything else in the world of air traffic. Much of the huge investment in technology is spent on ensuring that this happens quickly and accurately.

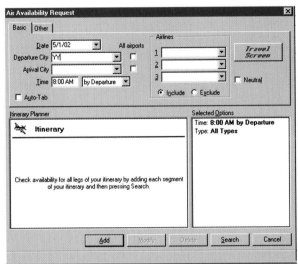

Viewpoint is Galileo International's latest software for travel agents, with an updated graphical interface. It helps to make booking a journey easy.

Each company has its own huge centralized data centre. Galileo International, for example, has its main installation near Denver, Colorado. It links 43,000 travel agents worldwide, using 160,000 terminals and supplying tickets from over 500 airlines. It also deals with many hotels and car rental companies. The amount of data flowing back and forth is astonishing: the Galileo data centre processes 255 million requests for information every day and over 92 billion transactions are being made each year.

● Hardware and networks
You need a solid hardware and network infrastructure to run such a system, and some reliable backup systems in case anything goes wrong.

Such data centres typically run their information systems on large mainframe computers with massive amounts of storage space and extremely fast parallel processors. Galileo and its parallel Apollo system run on 21 such mainframes, housed in a massive building with a floor space equivalent to 84 tennis courts, equipped with all sorts of sprinkler and alarm systems, and backed up by large emergency power supplies. Connections to locations throughout the world are maintained by a hugely complex combination of communications and networking technologies. These range in scale from the simple modem in the office of a small travel agent, to bunches of private high-speed lines carrying the heaviest traffic. The purpose of this technology is to allow you to walk into a travel agent and, in a matter of minutes, book a seat on an aircraft to your desired destination.

● Satisfying public demand
Travel and airline businesses have only invested in this kind of technology because of the laws of supply and demand. Some 30 years ago, air travel was the province of the rich, while now many can afford it. With much larger numbers of people

travelling by air, it has become increasingly important that airlines and agents have more or less instant access to reliable information on flights and seat availability.

Now travel agents and the airlines are faced with another revolution involving the public – the Internet. Much of the information that was until recently hidden from public view is now widely available on Web sites, many of which are the airlines' own sites. It's a quick and safe business to buy airline tickets on the Internet, and in the coming years more and more people will do just that. That's fine for the airlines, but it leaves the travel agents without their commission payments. So they too are joining the e-commerce revolution, using Web portals to get quick access to all sorts of extra opportunities, such as hotels and holidays, that they can sell on to their airline ticket customers.

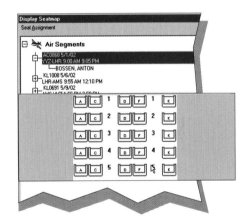

Viewpoint software allows sales staff not only to check flight times and seat availability but also to book a specific seat on an aircraft for you.

Viewpoint can show you maps of locations enabling you to find the most convenient hotel in the area you are visiting – and then book the hotel as well.

CUTTING OUT THE TICKET

Airlines are now moving towards ticketless travel. There are good reasons for this: lower costs, increased efficiency and greater customer satisfaction. Electronic ticketing is now used by most major airlines and all the major ticketing systems mentioned in this article. There's no single accepted standard, but the principles are very much the same, no matter who is issuing the ticket. In an electronic ticketing system what you do, in effect, is cut out the middleman – the paper ticket – by going straight from payment to boarding pass. You buy a 'ticket' (either at a travel agent, or on the Internet, or from a self-service kiosk) and are given a unique code, which you then use to get your boarding pass at the airport, either from a member of staff or from an automatic kiosk. The airlines and travel agents save time and money in administrative, paper and delivery costs, while the passenger saves time and stress by not having to queue up at a counter.

Wireless networks

Staying in touch and keeping track of business while on the move are both easy to do with wireless networking.

With the proliferation of mobile computers and phones, it was only a matter of time before the technology converged to create wireless networks.

The basic idea underlying a wireless network is straightforward. Rather than using a physical wire to carry data between points on a network (as with a traditional Ethernet-based office network), wireless networks use electromagnetic airwaves such as radio, infrared or microwave. This idea has actually been around for quite a long time, but it hasn't been possible to implement it successfully until recently.

Radio links from a truck through a service provider, such as RAM Mobile Data, mean that valuable cargoes can be tracked across a country to ensure their safety and to measure their progress and location.

● How does it work?

Here's how the system works in a typical modern wireless setup. A transceiver, known as an access point, is attached to an existing wired network (although a wired network is by no means necessary) and transfers

information between it and the wireless network. This network might be a group of users who have the necessary hardware installed within their machine: a wireless Local Area Network (LAN) adapter. This would come on a PCMCIA Card for a notebook computer; a PCI Card for a desktop computer; or would be built-in into a palmtop or similar device.

Generally, the physical range of such networks is anywhere up to several hundred feet. Crucially, the network operating system won't notice the difference: it will treat a wireless network and its attached users in the same way as it would a physical network.

● No need for cable

There are many obvious advantages to wireless networking. Mobile users, for example, can turn up at the office and log on to the network from any desk – what's known as 'hot desking',

without the physical network points that were traditionally required. This means that they can stay mobile, even in the office. Wireless networks do away with much of the nightmare of installing a physical network as there is no need to lift floorboards and make holes in walls in order to lay cables.

Going one stage further, they can also be immensely useful for connecting different LANs together, in adjacent buildings, for example. They are also much easier to customize gradually. It's easy to expand the network further (known as 'on-demand' networking) and it is also very mobile, which provides a couple of major advantages in itself. First, you can set up, configure and test the network off-site before you install it; second, if the office moves, the network can be picked up and moved with it, an operation which is difficult at the best of times with a physical installation.

There are a few drawbacks but they're getting fewer all the time. Speed was traditionally an issue, but now wireless networks can achieve speeds high enough to rival those of physical networks. With the approval of the IEEE 802.11 wireless networking standard, 11Mbit per second (Mbps) cards are already on the market, at a cost of around £100. At this price, a wireless LAN could well be cheaper than a physical network, once you've taken installation costs into account.

An office has to be laid out sensibly, particularly for an infrared network.

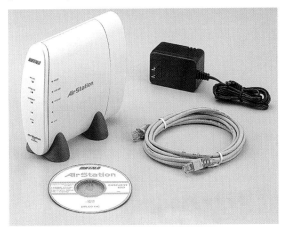

The Buffalo AirStation is a complete wireless networking kit for a home or small office. It is robust, compact and easy to set up.

WIRELESS HOME NETWORKING

If you have more than one PC in your home, it makes sense to network the machines so that they can share printers and Internet access, for example. Wireless networking combines mobility with an absence of messy cabling work. Intel's AnyPoint Wireless Home Network can connect up to 10 PCs located no more than 50 metres apart. You need a PC Card for each machine and the AnyPoint software at around £120 per machine. It's not the fastest system, however, with a maximum data transfer rate of 1.6Mbps.

If you need something faster, then the Buffalo AirStation could be a good option. This works at 11Mbps. You need a stand-alone network access point (around £250) and a network card per PC (around £180). The system is also expandable – you can connect up to 255 PCs in a network.

The transceiver would typically be placed high up, without any obvious obstructions. However, such considerations are far less important for the more common radio networks, as the waves pass straight through many walls and objects anyway.

● Crowded waves

Radio wireless networks have to be very clever, though, in order not to interfere with other services or each other. This is particularly important as radio LANs share the same frequency band, namely the Industrial, Scientific and Medical (ISM) band at 2.45GHz, which is available around the world. They avoid interference by using what's called 'spread spectrum'. This spreads the transmission over a range of frequencies, spending such a short time on each that it does not cause any disruption to other transmissions. This technology was originally developed by the military to avoid jamming and eavesdropping, and is also useful for corporate security. Only the transceiver and the receiving computer, for example, would 'know' the algorithm by which the frequencies could be switched for sending the data, making it very difficult to intercept.

● Expanding bandwidth

Wireless networks will undoubtedly grow very fast over the next few years. Ericsson, IBM, Intel, Nokia and Toshiba have joined together in a consortium to develop Bluetooth, the code name for a radio technology specification to link mobile PCs, phones and other portables. This should permanently do away with the need for special cables for mobiles and will allow automatic connections between mobile devices.

Broadband Internet access using radio waves is in development, too. Billions of dollars are being invested in the US to construct a high-speed fixed wireless network on a cellular basis. A research project in

A small and very handy data-capture terminal fitted with a radio link. This is ideal for stock checks.

Cambridge, Massachusetts has linked up 20 locations by radio, with information transfers at an impressive rate of 25Mbps.

● Digital initiatives

Unfortunately, Europe will lag behind in broadband systems, as there is a lack of the necessary free analogue frequencies. However, this is due to change in the UK as a result of the new digital initiatives in TV. Digital TV, which uses bandwidth, is far more efficient than the traditional analog systems (see pages 120-121).

Already begun, the digital television revolution will be complete with the shutting down of the original analogue transmitters in some 10-15 years' time, so there will be plenty of space for all, and broadband wireless networking will come into its own.

A police constable is quickly able to check a car's details via a radio link to a police database.

Digital TV

There's been a huge amount of publicity surrounding the recent launch of digital TV in the UK. What's it all about, and will it make your TV more like a PC?

The promise of digital TV is that it can deliver more programs using less 'bandwidth' and with a higher picture quality than previous TV delivery systems. In addition, digital TV has also made it possible to deliver interactive services, such as home shopping, travel reservations and email, to homes that don't have personal computers.

Previously, TV transmissions in the UK were encoded in analog format using the PAL (Phase-Alternation-Line) system. PAL has been around since the black-and-white TV age, but it was struggling under the strain of the many additions that had been made to it since then, such as colour, teletext and NICAM stereo.

● Lack of radio spectrum space

PAL also, however, takes up a lot of space to transmit relatively little data. This is significant because the radio spectrum is becoming an increasingly overcrowded place, the astonishing growth in mobile phone use over the past decade being the main problem.

The broadcasters, of course, want to transmit ever more variety, in the form of increasing numbers of TV channels and interactive services. With PAL, there hasn't been enough room for them.

There is also the added problem that analog TV transmission is vulnerable to interference, and so might occasionally deliver even poorer picture quality.

The ever-widening world of television has taken a huge leap into the future by going digital. This will present many new opportunities for purchasers, broadcasters and, of course, the viewing public.

● How digital TV works

Digital TV uses the latest digital compression techniques to cram pictures into approximately one-tenth of the space used in the PAL system. (see How digital compression works box, opposite). Once the data has been compressed, it is then combined with sound, sub-titles and any other necessary information. The whole mix is then encrypted and sent on ultra high frequency (UHF) channels to the home, where it is received by your TV aerial or satellite dish. These digital signals have been encrypted not because they contain top-secret information, but because the TV companies can make you pay for receiving the services (although some digital services are free, see Free to view box, left). You can't decrypt the programmes without signing up for the service, which in the United Kingdom means either ITV Digital or Sky digital. In both cases you need a set-top box which decrypts the signal and then decompresses the pictures to send the output to your television set.

● New digital TVs

The TV set does not have to be a new one; older TVs can cope with digital signals perfectly well. There are, however, new 'digital' TVs appearing in the shops; these contain all the necessary electronics inside them, although they don't necessarily have smart-card readers (for ITV Digital) and, of course, you'll still need a satellite dish and set-top box to receive Sky digital.

Digital television sets are nearly all manufactured in the 'widescreen' format, which enables them to display pictures in the 'letterbox', 16:9 aspect ratio, which is ideally suited to films. So far, only some TV has been produced in this format; it's mainly useful for watching movies in the way they're shown in the cinema.

● What's on

For the first couple of years, digital TV channels offered pretty much the same content that you could find on any subscription channel. But gradually more use has been made of the possibilities of digital TV, and a much wider variety of programs is now available. Sport is the main area of interest here, with ITV Digital broadcasting interactive European football. In this, and similar systems, you not only see the action itself, but you can also access statistics, team information, updates on other games being played and you are even given the opportunity to take part in quizzes.

Where there's sport there is inevitably betting, and interactive gambling via digital TV is an area that both the broadcasters and the bookmakers hope will explode. The aim here is to achieve 'in game/race' gambling, where you can bet on the soccer action, say, all through the match, keeping up to date with the latest odds as they change. Although this is not yet possible, it will happen in the future.

● Interactive services

When digital launched, it was purely a TV broadcasting system. But interactivity was not far behind. Using your phone line and an additional

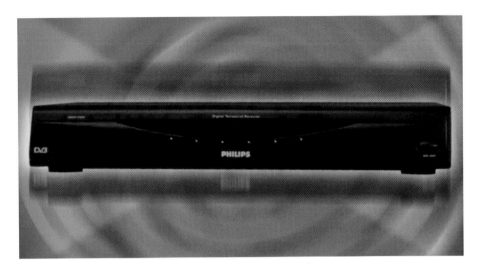

Digital TVs have widescreen cinema-type dimensions, superb picture clarity and great sound, all of which provide a better-than-ever viewing experience.

keyboard, you can turn your digital TV into a gateway to a variety of interactive services. However, the services offered here are not the equivalent of full Internet access. Instead, you get email and access to a limited selection of information and shopping services, supplied by partners and associates of the digital TV service provider. These are, by and large, the big high-street names:

WH Smith, Pizza Hut, Woolworths and so on.

There were great hopes that the large segment of the population without a PC and Internet access would enthusiastically embrace online shopping via the TV, but, so far, it hasn't really taken off. Only a small proportion of the 5 million or so digital subscribers use the additional online facilities. And many of those who do use them have been critical of their poor ease of use and limited range of services. The digital suppliers are addressing these criticisms and will doubtless revamp their services in a more attractive package.

● The future

By 2001, digital TV had gained significant market penetration and there were even rumours that Sky would abandon the old PAL system altogether by the end of 2001 – nine years before the system is officially abandoned. The UK government aims to encourage digital TV takeup by phasing out existing analog TV services from 2010. This doesn't mean, however, that we will embrace the idea of interactive TV. Whilst some people may wish to interact with a sports event or movie this is not likely to appeal to everyone.

A set-top box from ITV Digital. Devices such as these are essentially dedicated computers with MPEG-2 decoders that make the broadcast signal suitable for television.

The TiVo logo is found on many digital video recorders. These recorders store TV programmes on a PC-like hard disk so that you can watch them later.

HOW DIGITAL COMPRESSION WORKS

Digital TV compression is a process where only movement or detail in a digitized picture is used for transmission. A picture frame, when digitized, will be made up of 6.72 Megabits; at a rate of 25 frames per second, this equals 168 Megabits per second. After the compression, the same picture frame can be reduced to as little as 4–5 Megabits per second. As a result, more than one programme service can be transmitted on one UHF channel. The compression technique used, MPEG-2, is also used by DVD.

School computers

Classrooms in primary schools used to be technology-free zones. But now they're likely to have an IT system that's as sophisticated as those found in most offices.

It is the aim of the British Government to make the whole country PC-literate, harnessing IT and the Internet to increase skills and competitiveness in the global e-marketplace. The reason, of course, is that we are now at the beginning of a 'new knowledge economy', where IT skills will be essential to any job. Education, across the board, is key to this project.

In the world of education, it's not a simple matter of IT, but of ICT – information and communications technology. The government has made an undertaking to give all 5- to 16-year-olds training in this area, and it seems to be a commitment that is working out well in practice. School Web sites of all kinds abound, while there is no shortage of material for research and lesson planning.

● **Hardware**

What individual primary schools actually have in terms of hardware and infrastructure can vary substantially, depending on budgets and the decisions of the head teacher. Some teachers believe that computers are best used in dedicated 'ICT suites', with children timetabled to use them for a set number of hours per week. Another theory is that the computers are better used by being located in classrooms and becoming part of the everyday teaching apparatus whenever appropriate. In this way they can be 'embedded in the learning process', just as IT is in nearly all aspects of everyday life. Ideally, teachers would like the best of both

worlds, with a combination of suites and classroom computers, but budgets rarely stretch that far.

The base machine in primary schools is the PC, but the age and performance of these machines can vary widely. Many schools are using PCs that are several years old and have slow processor speeds, which is fine for simple software and basic tasks, but not so great when it comes to the Multimedia fireworks that really engage younger children.

When a school does have a significant budget, it is likely to buy PCs with a very similar specification to those used in the home or office: Pentium III Celeron processors of 633MHz or so for standard workstations; Pentium III or 4 processors with 800MHz and more for work such as sound editing, which requires extra processing power; and large monitors and hard disks. The large PC companies, such as Dell and IBM, all supply schools, but the

Computing in schools is moving on, but the early, slower computers still have a role to play in many schools.

leading UK educational computer supplier is RM (Research Machines), which provides a wide range of own-brand PCs, laptops and servers. Stand-alone PCs are not ideal for

The BBC Micro's famous turtle (right), which pupils can learn to program to move around the floor.

GridClub *is an interactive learning area for 7- to 11-year-olds. It provides learning materials, homework and Web advice, and displays examples of school work.*

Learning through play is a well-known concept but it is made even more enjoyable when lessons are conducted via a computer terminal and a mouse.

primary schools. Many have installed substantial networks, either as ICT suites or as school-wide teaching and administrative systems. Laptops, when schools can afford them, are growing in popularity, largely because of the flexibility they offer. And, increasingly, primary schools are examining the use of wireless networks to connect the whole building; they can be cheaper and less disruptive to install than fixed-wire systems and offer easier upgrading and expansion (see pages 118-119).

● Software

Just as the hardware in primary schools will be familiar, so will much of the software employed; children are taught to use the popular word-processing packages and Internet browsers. But they might well be ahead of many parents in their use of other business software. The presentation program PowerPoint, for example, is growing in popularity as a means for children as young as six or seven to structure their work and present it to a teacher or a whole class. Typically, they will have done much of the research on the Internet.

There is also plenty of specific learning software devoted to a given topic or Key Stage. Schools usually buy site licences so they can use multiple copies; the price per student falls the more licences are bought.

● Internet

Teachers in all educational sectors have welcomed the Internet as a liberating and exciting learning tool, but they also acknowledge that the sheer volume of material is daunting, and that some sort of sifting has to take place. Fortunately, there is a host of Web sites dedicated to the learning needs of different groups of children. Research Machines produce a highly regarded site called Learning Alive (www.learningalive.co.uk), which is packed with resources for specific projects, as well as giving plenty of tips on how to search the Web more effectively, and it also includes news sections for teachers.

As schools acquire PCs, they are able to make use of the huge range of Multimedia titles available, as well as standard Microsoft applications.

The government's own portal for education, the National Grid for Learning (www.ngfl.gov.uk), is a good starting point for all kinds of content. It will take children to the *GridClub* (www.gridclub.com) where 7- to 11-year-olds will find plenty of fun interactive learning content, as well as a library and the opportunity to post their own stories and poems. There's also a link to TeacherNet (www.teachernet.gov.uk) where staff can find out the latest news, links and initiatives in ICT learning. And for parents who are more perplexed than their children by all this 'new technology', the National Grid for Learning site also has a helpful area. As children outstrip their parents in IT skills, many schools are now finding it valuable to start after-school IT training so that adults can keep up with juniors.

THE BBC MICRO

The PC is a relatively recent arrival in the primary school. Through the 1980s and well into the 1990s, the BBC Micro was the dominant machine in primary schools that had any kind of IT equipment. It was cheap, sturdy, easy to use and rapidly spawned a wide range of excellent educational software. It was often supplied with a 'turtle' (see opposite), a small robot that could be programmed by children to move around in specific directions by using the simple LOGO language.

Computers in music

As so often seems the case, the technology used in the wider world of electronics – in this case the music industry – bears a close resemblance to the internal parts of your PC.

Computers are commonly used in the music business – and have been since the days of the Atari personal computer in the mid- to late 1980s. For example, the mostly widely used professional mixing application, CuBase, started life on the Atari. Apple Macs subsequently became popular, and now the home PC is often used, too. We'll return to this, but first some explanation is needed of how the sound system works.

For the purposes of music, a PC sound card is capable of two fundamental tasks: firstly, handling sounds, for example, for mixing, sequencing or digital recording; secondly, for generating sounds. Sound cards, in addition to playing audio and CD music, can generate their own sounds, and as such, work much like any professional synthesizer or sound 'module'.

Before music is turned into air-borne analog sound waves that we can hear, it very often takes the form of digital signals. Increasingly, computer technology is being used both to create and to manipulate these digital signals.

● Combining waves
Early PC sound cards were based on frequency modulation (FM) technology. This synthesizer sound was created by combining two simple sound waves (called carrier and modulator) to produce a complex third sound – that which comes out of the speakers. By controlling the two different waves, a wide range of sounds could be created. However, although FM can sound great for many types of electronic music, it isn't very good at producing acoustic sounds, such as guitar or piano. Only

by adding a wavetable chip to the sound card circuits could these sounds be made.

● Sampling sounds
Instead of using carriers and modulators, these wavetable cards use digital representations of the sound itself to create synthesized sound, which might well represent a real musical instrument. The quality of this sound depends on four factors.

Firstly, the quality of the original recording. Secondly, the frequency of the sample (this is typically 44.1kHz stereo, which is the same rate at which CDs are recorded – hence the boast of 'CD-quality' audio). Thirdly, the compression method used to store

the sound: given the fact that much of the data required to create these sounds is stored in the hardware, compression is important. Fourthly, the number of samples that make up each instrument. This last factor represents the way in which sound changes in various different ways when you attempt to play a real instrument 'enthusiastically', rather than just getting louder.

● Quality
An accurate representation of the subtleties of playing an instrument in different ways requires a great deal of sampling. For example, to accurately recreate the full range of sounds created by a piano would require

hundreds of megabytes of data. As you can see, the quality of a sound card (or indeed any synthesizer) for music purposes, depends as much on the quality of its samples as on the hardware itself. This is why any music studio will probably possess a mixture of different sound devices: a Multimedia PC, a couple of keyboard synthesizers and a rack of sound modules.

Apart from the obviously different functions of these devices, such as having a keyboard, the variety is necessary to get an interesting range of sounds beyond those available with a regular sound card – at a price, naturally.

● MIDI system

This is where MIDI (Musical Instrument Digital Interface) fits in. We've gone into MIDI in some depth before (see Stage 3, pages 110-111). MIDI is not actually a sound recording format, but rather one that tells an electronic instrument how to play. It contains various

A Yamaha sound card fitted to a PC uses DSP-digital signal processing-chips and enables a PC to function as a recording studio.

elements of information, including the note number and a velocity value – the details of how hard a key is struck. A MIDI file would contain exactly the same data on any system, and thanks to the General MIDI standard, it plays the right synthesized sound (trumpet, piano, etc) on any General MIDI system. However, the quality of that sound might vary enormously. And, of course, if it's played on a synthesizer that uses its trumpet, piano and any other instruments for other sounds, it might well sound startlingly different. (Contrast that with a .WAV file, for example, which is a straightforward recording format and which will sound exactly the same, with the exception of any differences that result from playing a sound on a cheap or an expensive stereo system.)

● Continuous controllers

MIDI on a computer is now invariably the very heart of a modern recording studio. A MIDI sequencer 'records' information from every input device. This information can then be layered into different channels, rather than being mixed, and can be adjusted with continuous controllers. This type of data allows you to change the nature of the sound, its frequency

and so on, to make interesting effects. MIDI and electronics don't cover everything, though. Musicians might well want to mix some 'real' sounds in with the electronic ones: they might want to play a real guitar, for example, or even sing. Until recently, this would require the use of conventional audio tapes – analog or DAT – because of the file size of CD-quality recordings: ten minutes takes up more than 100MB. It would also entail putting the MIDI and the vocals through an additional mixing desk. This has now changed.

● Recording to disk

Hard disk capacity has dropped so much in price that it is now possible to record straight to disk. Once the sound is recorded onto the hard disk, sound editing software can be used to improve it. Just as you can use a graphics program to retouch a photo, so you can use a sound editor to reduce noise, boost the signal in quiet passages, and even correct out-of-tune playing.

As long as the PC itself is fairly fast (700MHz or more is best), the recorded sounds can then be replayed from the hard disk in perfect synchronization with the MIDI music. This gives the best of both worlds, and is the method now used in almost all professional recording studios.

Once everything is laid down and mixed to your satisfaction, it can be recorded straight on to a DAT and taken to a CD pressing plant – or you can write a demonstration CD yourself.

Ocean yachting

It might seem an unlikely place to find the latest in high technology, but the modern ocean yacht is crammed with electronics and computer wizardry.

Until very recently, any improvements in designing, building and sailing a yacht were added piecemeal to centuries of accumulated wisdom. Drawings were done by hand, prototypes modelled and the yacht itself built by craftsmen using tried-and-tested techniques. Once the yacht was seaborne, its crew navigated using the traditional methods of dead-reckoning. But the advent of modern electronics and digital computers – and in particular the PC – has changed very nearly every aspect of traditional yachting.

● **New navigation**
The most revolutionary of these changes is in the navigation, steering and tracking of the vessels themselves. Thirty years ago, mariners used the techniques of dead-reckoning to find their way about the world's vast and featureless oceans. The tools of the trade were the compass, the sextant (to determine latitude and longitude from a reading of the stars), the paper chart and the chronometer. Using these, in conjunction with average speed and distance travelled, the navigator fixed a position for the vessel and plotted a new course.

Dead-reckoning was always an uncertain science, however. Any number of factors, including inclement weather, radio failure, being distant from well-used shipping lanes, incorrect calculations or equipment problems, could quite easily lead to navigational error. For

Underneath the classic billowing sails and deck planking, the very latest computerized equipment helps modern seafarers keep their ocean yachts on course with the minimum of effort. There is software and hardware that can pinpoint a boat's position to within a few metres and that can give vital, up-to-the minute weather forecasts.

instance, a chronometer which is inaccurate by just a small amount could mean that a navigator would miscalculate longitude by hundreds of nautical miles.

Nowadays, the sailor knows precisely, to within approximately 50 metres, where he is anywhere on the seas, thanks to the Global Positioning by Satellite (GPS) systems. The on-board GPS receiver is updated every second or so from the system's network of 24 satellites, so knowing your exact location need never be a problem for sailors any more.

The GPS system can do even more for the sailor, however. By keying in the co-ordinates of a destination, it can even plot your course for you. The benefits for the leisure and the professional sailor, in terms of both safety and time savings, cannot be underestimated.

On most ocean-going yachts, and on many smaller ones, too, the GPS will be connected to an on-board PC. In theory, at least, the computer used could be an ordinary PC just the same as your desktop machine or

INMARSAT

The global satellite system that keeps sailors in touch on their mobile satellite phones is managed by the Inmarsat consortium, to which many of the world's leading telecommunication companies belong. Inmarsat was founded in 1979 to develop satellite communications and distress and safety applications for the shipping industry. It has since expanded to provide mobile communications for remote locations where terrestrial communications are not reliable. Its main focus, though, remains on maritime communications.

portable; in maritime practice, it's more likely to be a 'marinized' machine (perhaps even a fully waterproof portable) designed to withstand the buffeting of the yacht and being lashed by the elements.

Once the PC is linked to the GPS data and to various other instruments on the yacht that measure variables, such as wind direction, tides and boat speed, the navigator can almost sit back and wait to be told what the optimum course to take is.

To do this, of course, you need a chart – the sailor's equivalent of a map. Before the electronic age, you would have needed to buy bulky and costly paper charts of all the regions in which you were intending to sail. Nowadays, many of these charts have been digitized and are available to the sailor on CD-ROM. The chart can then be loaded into the PC and used together with GPS to plot routes. Some of the PC software that manages all this will even give you a constant display of your ship's position on the PC monitor.

The Furuno GPS Navigator is a compact and waterproof GPS device, with LCD. It has 12 GPS channels and can store up to 950 waypoints in its memory.

● Weathering the storm
Knowing where you are and where you are going are vital when at sea.

The NX300 can display early warnings about hazardous weather and navigation reports from around the world. You can also connect it to a PC to get a print-out.

But it's just as important to have accurate meteorological information; after all, there's not much point in plotting a course, if it's only going to take you into the middle of a hurricane. This is where suppliers such as PC Maritime are useful. Their software takes data from meteorological satellites and allows the sailor to view the weather charts and satellite pictures on screen, save them and then plot the development of weather systems on and near the desired route; if the planned route becomes treacherous the navigator can plot an alternative course.

● Keeping in touch
The development of satellite phones means that seafarers are able to keep in touch wherever they are – and, of course, this gives them another distress signal option in addition to the traditional 'mayday'. These telephones use the Inmarsat satellite system (see Inmarsat box, opposite). Originally, satellite phones were bulky items, but in recent years they have become much more compact and, on some models, both the main unit and antenna weigh less than 5kg each. Just like terrestrial mobile phones, these sea-going models are increasingly used to connect to PCs and fax machines. The mobile office

on the high seas is already a reality, but fully featured satellite phones are not cheap; you can expect to pay in excess of £3,000, with usage costing around £2 per minute.

● Safe sailing
As the price of digital equipment generally continues to fall, however, the leisure sailor can expect to see much of the equipment that was previously the exclusive province of the supertanker appearing in his small yacht. This should considerably improve the safety of sailing.

SITES TO @ VISIT

PC Maritime
www.pcmaritime.co.uk
The UK's main supplier of maritime software, including charts and weather analysis systems.

Furuno
www.furuno.com/
Manufacturers of all kinds of maritime electronics, including navigation and communications equipment.

Nera
www.nera.no
Specialists in a number of satellite communications devices, including compact satellite phones.

Doctor at a distance

Sophisticated medical diagnosis and even treatment from a distance are now both possible, thanks to the marvel of telecommunications technology.

Although they might not know it, the medical profession have long been using what is called 'telemedicine'. At its very lowest level of technological complexity, this field includes simple medical diagnosis and treatment of complaints over the phone. For example, if your child has a temperature and a rash, you call the doctor, describe what the rash looks like, and the doctor tells you to give the child some junior paracetamol and call again if it doesn't clear within a couple of days.

Now, with the range of computer and telecommunications systems made available within the last few decades, telemedicine – medicine carried out at a distance with the use of telecommunications technology – is a growth industry. It covers a range of techniques, from the simple everyday case described above to surgery carried out by robots under the command of a skilled doctor located thousands of miles away.

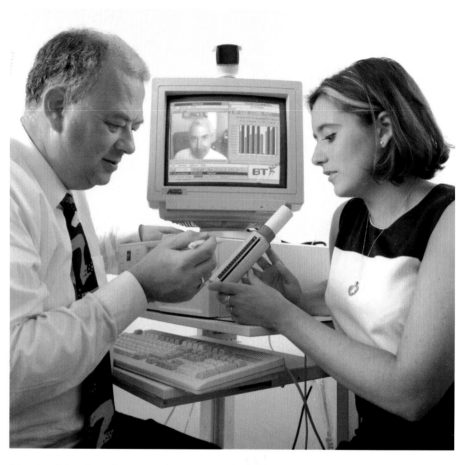

Telemedicine helps a doctor diagnose and treat a patient many miles away. To provide this type of medical video conference, the doctor and his colleague both need a PC, a Webcam and a high-bandwidth telephone connection.

● NASA beginnings
It's only in the past four or five years that the buzzword 'telemedicine' has become frequently heard, but it's something that's been around in quite a sophisticated form for a lot longer. Much of the early serious experimental work was, as with so much in the fields of computers and telecommunications, carried out by NASA as part of the US Space Program. In the 1960s NASA was, understandably, keen to keep an eye on the well-being of its astronauts and therefore devised telemetry methods

and systems for monitoring both the astronauts and their spacecraft. These early steps led to a number of experimental US programs in which NASA was involved.

● Rural medicine
One of the earliest experiments, on the Papago Indian Reservation in Arizona, highlights a major area of application for telemedicine: the remote, rural community. In such places, highly trained medical personnel are scarce, as is modern and expensive diagnostic hardware (scanners and so on). In the Papago project, two paramedics toured the area in a van fitted out with medical equipment, including an X-ray machine and an electrocardiograph. The van transmitted the test results

to a hospital, where they were analysed and the appropriate action was then recommended.

● Remote analysis
Today, this sort of setup is still representative of much telemedicine in remote areas, from Norway's frozen north to Australia's Gulf of Carpentaria. Indeed, a few of the latest telemedicine projects in some of the most advanced countries are concentrating on the lowest-tech options possible. In the UK, for example, the NHS Direct pilot scheme uses just a telephone; callers speak to a nurse, who then directs them to the appropriate form of care. This scheme has resulted in considerable savings in terms of time and money. The available technology has developed

EDUCATION

One of the biggest growth areas for telemedicine is in education, not just as a means of teaching large groups of students, but as a way of encouraging the ongoing education of healthcare professionals and specialists. Specialist instruments – such as the telemedicine stethoscope – help teachers reach a wider group of students. But it is streaming video on the Internet that is the key to the most powerful educational applications of telemedicine. A single lecture or surgical demonstration can be viewed by many people on their own PCs. Experiencing such a lecture remotely can be more fruitful than attendance, as the images and explanation can be saved, replayed and studied in detail.

rapidly over the past 20 years and now telemedicine can and does cover some very sophisticated applications.

● Teleradiology

Teleradiology, the remote analysis of X-rays and scans, uses techniques known in the telemedicine world as 'store and forward', in which the images are first captured (and stored), by a digital camera or other device, and are then forwarded to another location to enable expert analysis and diagnosis to be carried out.

With the advent of the Internet and other communications networks, this other location need not be physically close; you could send scans taken in Sydney to the world's top specialist in, say, San Francisco, and have an expert opinion back within hours.

● Web cam consultations

In theory, a doctor could show his consultation with a patient to another doctor located anywhere in the world, as long as both had a desktop computer, a simple Web cam and a reasonably fast Internet connection. In practice, a host of specialized equipment is available, produced by dozens of companies, mainly in the US. It's quite difficult, for example, to share the results of a simple stethoscope examination (auscultation). But, if you have a special telemedicine stethoscope fitted with a transducer and amplifier, you can share examination results with a number of local listeners or transmit them to specialists at remote locations.

● Telemedicine in the home

For the next few years, most of us will see the benefits of telemedicine mainly as increased efficiency in using scarce resources, largely through the use of the telephone or even email as the first step in a diagnosis. In remote areas, healthcare consumers will find they save time and get quicker specialist help with the use of some of the techniques described above. In the future, however, it seems likely that telemedicine will reach right into the home in the form of some kind of medical module that will carry out a variety of health checks – on the heart, blood pressure and so on – and then transmit the results elsewhere for analysis.

A consultant analyses a baby's ultrasound image, which is being transmitted live over an ISDN network. The camera on top of the monitor is used to relay the doctor's voice and the image to the scanner and consultant at the remote site.

PROJECT MISSION

NASA were involved at the start of telemedicine and are still heavily involved in its development. One of their latest projects is an attempt to use satellite networks for the transmission of medical data. This is because many truly remote areas are not sufficiently 'wired' to receive data-intensive information, such as 3D images or streaming video. Project Mission uses NASA satellites for the test, together with supercomputers at the Ohio Supercomputing Center. Researchers hope to move over to commercial networks when these have the required speed of transmission.

Garden design software

A fragrant rose and a home computer might not seem to go well together, but there's a wealth of impressive software available to help you design and enhance your garden.

Whether you've just bought a new home and want to design a landscaped garden from scratch, or are simply looking for a hardy perennial to provide a splash of colour, there is software available to suit your needs.

Novices and experts alike can benefit from the visualizing options that garden design software offers. Gardeners of any level will find the encyclopedias and plant finders included in these packages of enormous help, with their vast illustrated plant databases and their ability to find the type of plant you're looking for in seconds. Of course, such software can also be immense fun to browse through and play with.

● **3D Landscape Professional**
FastTrak's *3D Landscape Professional* is produced 'in association with Monty Don', a well known press and TV gardener. This is something of a giant compendium software package: it contains 3D garden design software; a Garden Encyclopedia with plenty of data and pictures of plants;

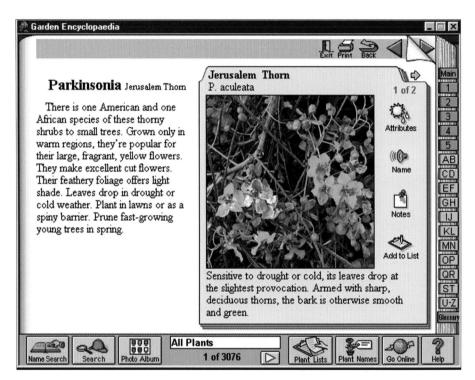

3D Landscape Professional's *Encyclopaedia gives you the low-down, with photos, on thousands of plants.*

a 3D Deck which allows you to design for outdoor decking; and Photo LandDesigner which enables you to develop a design on the basis of an imported photo. The whole package takes up a substantial

amount of hard disk space but you can pick and choose which components you want to install.

The garden design software itself is extremely easy to use, largely because you can get started very quickly with the help of the design wizard. You can set up a plot of your land, add your house and then the plants. As you refine your garden design, you can switch between 2D and 3D views. And, if you're interested in longer term development, you can set the software to 'grow' the garden over any period you choose.

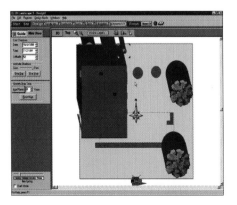

3D Landscape Professional's *wizard helps you to select a plot shape and then add building and plant elements (above left) such as trees and flower beds. When you're ready, just select the 3D view to get an idea of the magnificent home and garden you've created (above right).*

● **Water features**
Garden makeover shows on the TV have made a number of gardeners into household names, and even, as in the case of Charlie Dimmock, into a minor celebrities. Through the BBC's

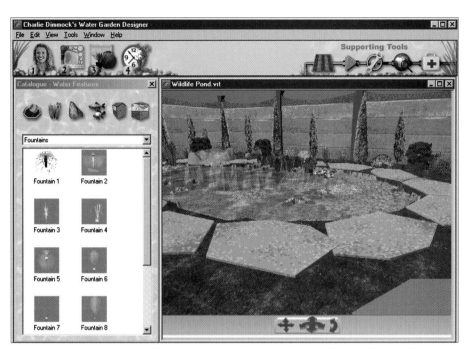

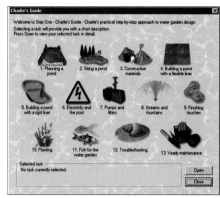

Charlie Dimmock's Water Garden Designer covers all aspects of how to create your perfect water garden.

popular *Ground Force* programme, her speciality – water features – has become a must-have element in the modern garden.

If you want to add a water feature to your garden, the first port of call must surely be *Charlie Dimmock's Water Garden Designer* CD-ROM by Europress. It is packed with all the know-how that there simply isn't the time for in a 30-minute television programme, and this software guides you through all of the necessary stages, from planning and design to construction and maintenance.

In the design phase, you can choose the type of water feature that you want. The program gives you good illustrations of your choices, such as babbling cascades, fountains or static pools. In terms of size, you can design small patio fountains, larger formal ponds or less formal wildlife ponds, and also bogside gardens. The program also highlights issues such as buying and caring for the fish in your pond.

The CD-ROM also goes into great detail about the planting options for your water feature, covering 200 pond plants and 50 rockery plants. Importantly, the 3D-view lets you preview your design in both flowering and non-flowering periods, so that you get as much enjoyment from your efforts as possible.

● Plant Finder

Garden design software is aimed largely at those planning a new garden or making changes to an existing one. But there is also a category of software suitable for both grand-scale design and for the mature garden. Dorling Kindersley's *The Plant Finder Reference Library*,

available from GSP, is a combination of plant database and gardening guide, with many extras thrown in. *The Plant Finder Reference Library* outranks everything in terms of the sheer size of its database. It contains a list of over 70,000 plants, and also provides details of where you can buy them. The database is taken from the Royal Horticultural Society's book of the same name, so its comprehensiveness and authority are to be expected.

And, if it doesn't quite have the Multimedia glamour of some other CDs, it more than compensates for that in its exhaustive volume of information and usefulness. You can also visit the Royal Horticultural Society's Web site at www.rhs.org.uk.

The Internet can provide a huge range of information on gardening, including gardening suppliers, trade associations, directories or nurseries.

The Plant Finder database allows the user to select any one of its 70,000 database entries (above left). Having made a selection, it then provides the names and addresses of nurseries that can meet your requirements (above right).

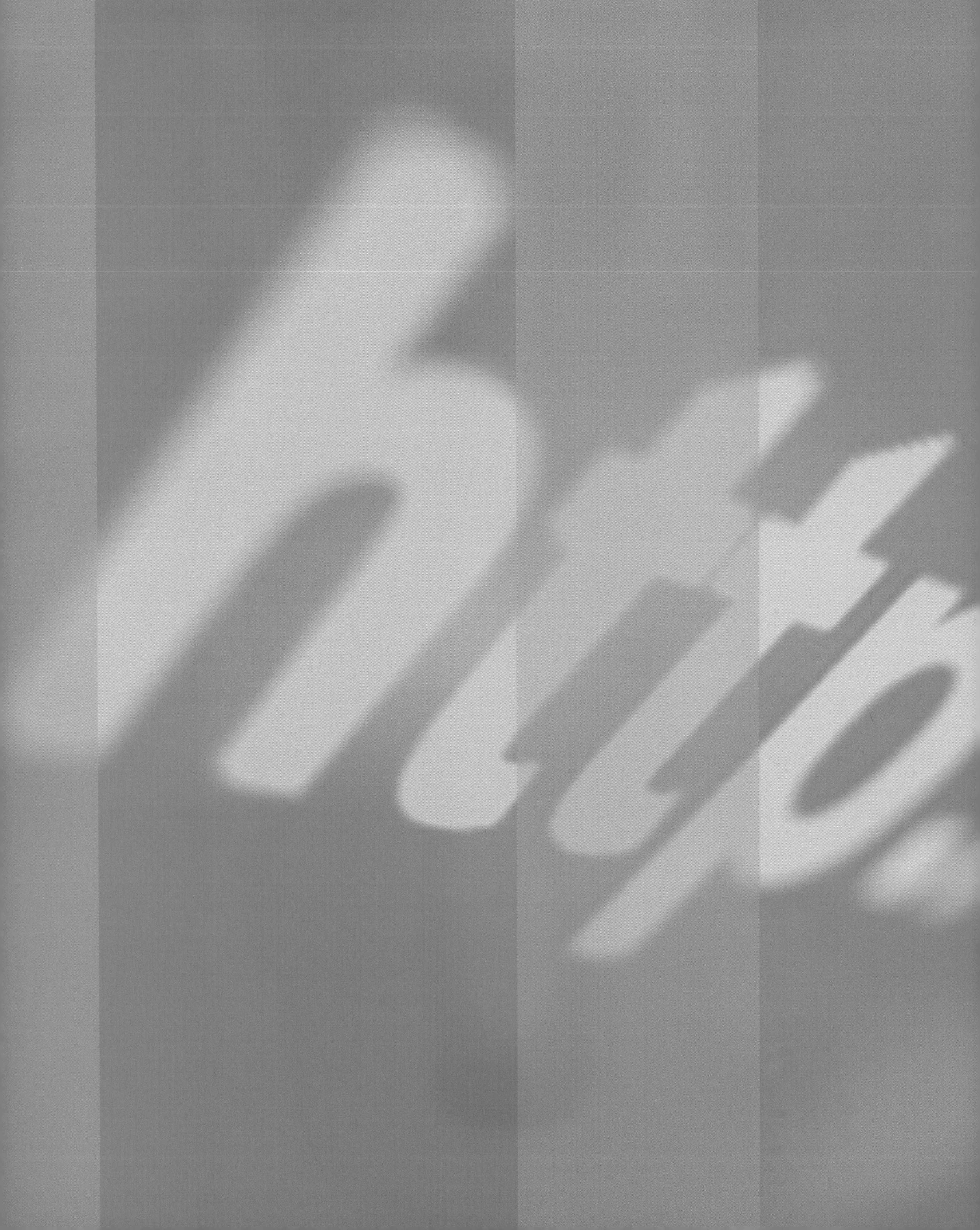

The Internet

Audio-visual plug-ins

The World Wide Web is full of
Multimedia of all kinds.
To take advantage of it, you
need to download and install
a few essential audio-visual
plug-ins and programs.

I n its early days, the Web was a
fairly static, one-dimensional
experience. Sites were very much
like online magazines. When you
went to a Web address a single page
loaded into your browser. Clicking on
a link loaded another, different, single
page, just as if you were flicking
through pages in a magazine. There
were pictures, but no animation,
sound and interactivity.

Today, though, Multimedia
interactivity is part of almost every
professional site and a large number
of amateur ones. Sound and moving
objects are the rule rather than the
exception. As the top browsers –
Internet Explorer and Netscape
Navigator – have developed
they have become more adept at
loading this type of material. But to
get the most out of the Web, you
may need to install a range of
audio-visual plug-ins.

● Instant sound

Audio plug-ins are vital if you want
to hear the full range of music and
atmospheric sounds that many sites
now use. These effects have to be
delivered instantly when you interact
with the features of a site, for
example, when you move your mouse
over a portrait photo and it says 'Hi,
I'm Dave'; nobody wants to wait for
a simple jingle or sound effect to
download. But sound, and especially
music, is not easy to deliver instantly.
File size is a crucial issue. While MP3
files provide very high quality, they

are also quite large and require a
considerable wait while they
download. This is why other file
formats – MIDI (see page 125 and
Stage 3, pages 110-113) and a variety
of proprietary formats, depending on
the plug-in – are preferred for instant
sound. Site designers may use
software such as Beatnik or
Crescendo to add sounds – but the
user then needs the relevant plug-in
to take advantage of the sounds that
are available.

● Animation

If you want your Web site to be able
to display eye-catching animations
and interactive games, and if you
want to view a range of sites that do
this, then there is really only one

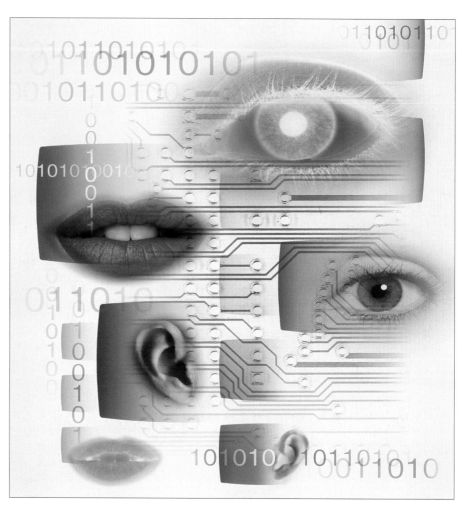

Adding sound and animation to a Web page makes it
instantly more noticeable.

choice of plug-in these days –
Macromedia's Shockwave and Flash
players. Both of these allow Web
designers to add small but effective
interactive objects to their Web
pages. Macromedia is the market
leader in the field of multimedia
plug-ins, with over 240 million
downloads of its players. So many
sites now use Shockwave and Flash
that you'd be missing out on a lot of
interesting action if you don't have
them. Flash is the simpler of the
two systems, while Shockwave
offers more options to the web
designer, and so gives the user a
richer experience.

● Streaming media

'Streaming' describes the process whereby audio or video material is downloaded and played in real time, with little or no pause as the data is loaded onto your PC. That's the theory, at least; with a 56K modem the practice lags far behind. However, as broadband Internet connection becomes more widely available (see pages 110-111) true streaming will become a possibility, letting you watch and listen to 'Webcast' events worldwide.

To make the most of this sort of data – video files and MP3 music files – you need a more sophisticated plug-in. A breed of software known as the 'media player' is required. Media players allow you to play streaming media live from the Web, and act as off-line players for sound and video files stored on your hard disk, letting you catalogue, organize and play your collection of MP3 music. Also, they come with pre-selected Web sites where you can find media of all types to suit all tastes.

In the Windows world there are two competitors vying for dominance: Microsoft, with Windows Media Player, and RealPlayer. There's also the QuickTime system from Apple, which is available for Windows.

BUFFERING

Streaming audio and video sites use a technique known as 'buffering' to give you the illusion of a seamless media experience. Data sent from the site is stored in an area of memory known as a buffer, and is retrieved from there when needed by your browser or plug-in. This way, the data can be displayed long before the whole file has been transmitted. With a 56K connection you are likely to get lots of jerky motion or stuttering sounds as there will be gaps in the delivery of different segments of the file. However, at higher speeds and with faster processors the streaming should become seamless.

Sites for plug-ins

Here we take a look at the sites for those special plug-ins that allow you to experience rich Multimedia content on the Internet.

Beatnik Player 2.1

www.beatnik.com/

'Sonified graphics' are what Beatnik Player offers developers and Web users. It uses principally its own file format, .RMF, which is much smaller than most streaming music formats and so downloads with no discernible time lag. The result is that sites developed with Beatnik give a rich sonic experience; moving your cursor over a graphic might produce something as simple as a beep, or as complex as a burst of rock music. Web designers can also make the music respond to your keyboard input or the choice of pages you browse on a Web site. It's worth downloading Beatnik Player in case you come across sites that use it – the Sonified Showcase area at the above address displays some of these sites.

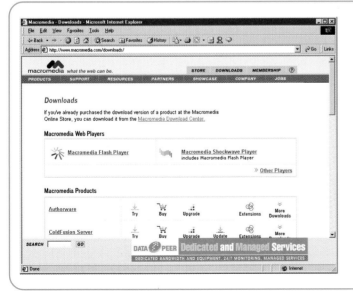

Flash and Shockwave

www.macromedia.com/

If you don't have these plug-ins, then get them right away. Without them, you just won't be able to take advantage of the creativity and interactivity on the Web. Any interesting interactive site is likely to be using one or both of these. Although they are two separate plug-ins, Flash and Shockwave work well together. The former produces relatively simple animations, while the latter brings you myriad interactive Multimedia presentations, games and learning activities. You can download them separately, but it is better to download Shockwave, which also includes the Flash plug-in. You will find sites using Shockwave are frequently described as being 'shocked' and often present users with a 'shocked' or 'non-shocked' option on an introductory page.

Liquid Audio

www.liquidaudio.com/

Liquid Player 6 is a very popular streaming and MP3 player. It covers the main file formats and also has its own proprietary Liquid Tracks format, so you'll need the plug-in for sites that use this format.

If you download MP3 files, Liquid Player 6 gives you powerful organizing features, as well as allowing you to 'burn' your own CDs. You can also use it to turn your own CD tracks into MP3 files. You can then download them on to a portable MP3 player, for example. If you're already a devoted fan of the WinAmp MP3 player or Real Player, you can download a smaller plug-in instead of the full program. This upgrades WinAmp or Real Player so that they can play music in Liquid Tracks format. Liquid Audio also runs www. liquid.com, a Web site that lets you preview clips of commercial music releases so you can decide whether or not to buy them.

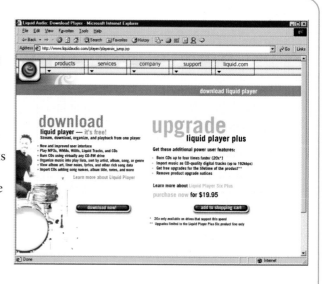

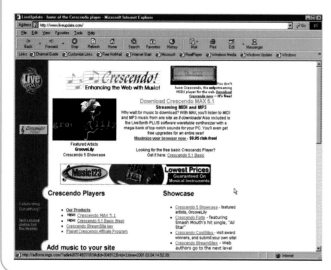

Crescendo

www.liveupdate.com/

Crescendo 5.1 Basic claims to be 'the only streaming MIDI player for the Web'. As such, it is worth obtaining, since it covers a lot of audio options. The Basic player is free, but for $9.95 (around £6) you can download Crescendo MAX 5.1, which will stream both MIDI and MP3 files. This is quite a useful combination, as it incorporates very nearly all the main options.

There are links to sites where Crescendo is demonstrated, so once you've installed the software, you can have a look at how effectively it can be used to generate musical accompaniment for Web pages. If you have taken advantage of Crescendo in making your own Web pages, you can submit your site for possible inclusion in the Crescendo 'Showcase'.

NookNak/NoiseNak

www.comsoft.co.nz

Not everyone wants music, or at least not all the time. When you have a CD blaring away and the phone rings you'd rather not have to fiddle around with Windows' volume control settings first. The NoiseNak and NookNak plug-ins from New Zealand give you a wide range of easy controls over the sound on your PC.

NoiseNak offers such features as automatically setting volume limits for times of the day or week and reducing the volume after a set period in which the PC is not used. NookNak allows you to alter various settings of your PC simply by moving your mouse over a corner of the screen. You can instantly mute the PC, for example, by moving the mouse to the bottom right; it's a lot quicker than using the volume control settings.

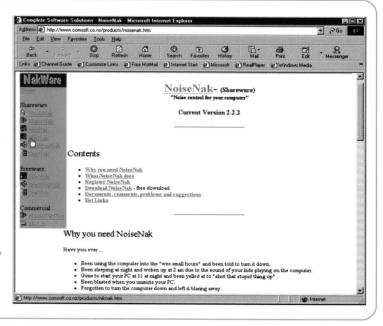

Media players

If you really want to have access to all the streaming media on the Web, make sure you have all three of the programs covered here.

RealPlayer

www.real.com/

The longest-standing name in this field is RealPlayer, which you can download from www.real.com. At one time this had a monopoly, and quickly established a dominant position in the market. The player is a single program that uses RealAudio 8 and RealVideo 8 streaming formats. Almost every streaming site on the Web is compatible with these formats, so if you are going to limit yourself to one media player, this is the one you should choose. RealPlayer offers all sorts of extras, including many 'channels' for streaming content, a list of Internet radio stations, and the ability to organize and play your MP3 collection.

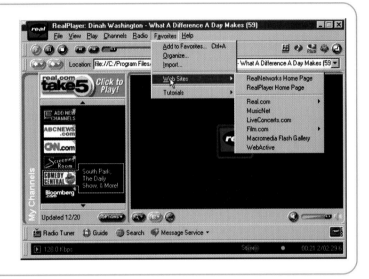

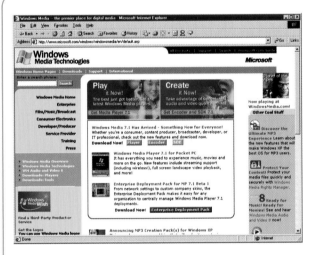

Windows Media Player

www.microsoft.com/windows/windowsmedia

RealPlayer's competitor is Microsoft's Windows Media Player. This may be installed on your computer, especially if you have bought your PC in the last year or two. Go to Programs, Accessories and then Entertainment to see if it's there. If not, you can download it from www.microsoft.com/windows/windowsmedia, which is also where you will find updates. Its capabilities almost match that of RealPlayer and it adopts a very similar approach. It plays MP3 files as well as files that are stored in Windows Media Format, which Microsoft claims is much better than MP3. But, as much more high-quality music is available in MP3 than in any other format, this might not be such a big attraction. As with any streaming technology, you'll have more fun, and faster downloads, with a high-speed connection.

QuickTime

www.apple.com/quicktime

You should have both of the above media players, but you might also want to get hold of QuickTime, Apple's technology for delivering Multimedia sound and video. This is built into the Macintosh operating system, but you can download a driver from www.apple.com/quicktime to run QuickTime files on a PC. In fact, there's a good chance you may already have a version on your system, since many Multimedia CDs use QuickTime and install it on your system with the program itself. Examine the Programs menu to check. QuickTime is widely used in the Mac world, in which many Multimedia designers work, so there's a lot of good material. But you won't be able to run QuickTime files in other media players since it uses its own file format.

Encryption explained

If the privacy of the information you send across the Internet is important to you, encryption is the answer. One thing you might want to do, for instance, is encode your email messages so that they can be read only by people to whom you have given your own special code.

Please charge £150 to my credit card, number 5555 1236 5678 9876.

LNGKIJBrniTmAFr YMgGgzk7EDzCHVj Wfx7qgmcL1vw8Zvj72 R/HtwpxiHEw

Encryption – the encoding of computer information so that it can be read only by people who have a special code – may sound as if it belongs to the realm of spy fiction, but it's an increasingly important part of Internet computing.

You might already be using encryption without realizing it. When you use a secure server for ordering goods from a Web site, for example, your credit card information is sent in an encoded form so anyone who intercepts it can't read it and use it fraudulently. Once it is received at the Web server, it's decoded so the company selling you the goods can debit your account as in a normal transaction.

● **Inside encryption**

Encryption is one of the most complex areas in computing. There's a good reason for this: there wouldn't be much point in encoding information if it was easy to decode. The companies that devise encryption routines use advanced mathematics to make sure that the encoded information is almost impossible to crack. The very best codes produced by encryption techniques are, quite literally, uncrackable.

It's for this reason that encryption is a controversial issue, involving free speech and even anti-terrorist concerns. It is also therefore an area where international government legislation and shadowy intelligence agencies are closely involved.

In fact, the issue of encryption affects just about every area of the Internet, from the companies using the Web to make money, to the lunatic fringe. People are usually either pro- or anti-encryption.

● **Arguments against encryption**

The anti-encryption argument says that if you want to code your email, then you must have something to hide: you're a terrorist, a drugs dealer, or some other kind of dangerous criminal. Clearly, government agencies are concerned about being unable to read any intercepted communications sent between suspected criminals or disreputable organizations.

The pro-encryption argument insists that there is such a thing as privacy, that the anti-encryption argument is paranoid and that your personal email messages should be just as sacrosanct as your personal letters or your diary. This lobby is certain that everyone should have the right to encode personal information.

DID YOU KNOW?

If you aren't already using encryption, every email you send can be read by anyone with the desire to do so and the necessary technical knowledge. Such a person could be a mischievous hacker doing it for idle fun, much like the people who scan mobile phone conversations; it could be someone who has targeted your email specifically for commercial espionage; or it could be a government agency trawling for potentially suspect communications.

The Clipper chip

Probably the most significant development to bring this encryption argument to a head, was the uproar surrounding the US government's Clipper chip initiative.

The Clipper chip is a sophisticated device the US government wanted to have installed within any equipment that might use encryption: computers, modems, digital TVs and so on. The Clipper chip uses a complex mathematical encryption procedure that's designed to be impossible to crack. However, there would be an important exception: the US government and its agencies would keep a record of everyone's encryption key in order to be able to decode anyone's encrypted information.

Although it seemed to take the US government by surprise, this proposal naturally led to a public outcry.

Other benefits

Encryption can have other benefits in addition to the privacy aspect. For example, it confirms the identity of the sender. This is important, as it's very easy for unscrupulous users with a little technical knowledge in this area to fake an email, making it appear to have been sent from someone else. If you receive an encrypted email and then decode it using the sender's key, you can be assured that it was sent by them.

Encryption also ensures that the message is received precisely as it was originally sent. As part of the encoding process, extra data is added to the information that can be checked on decoding to make sure that nothing has changed. This ensures that the message hasn't been tampered with and that it hasn't been corrupted during transmission.

WHAT IT MEANS

KEY

When information is encrypted, a special code is used to turn the normal legible text into what looks like gibberish. This code is called the key. Many encryption schemes use two keys – a private and a public key – so that only the sender and intended recipient can read the message.

EASY-TO-USE SOFTWARE AND COMPLEX TECHNOLOGY

Despite the complexity of the encryption process itself, the most popular software, PGP (Pretty Good Privacy), is easy to use. It's based on public key cryptography. This works through two keys, a private key which you keep entirely to yourself and a public key which you let everyone know.

When you want to send an encrypted message to someone, you use the recipient's public key. This scrambles the information so that it can be read only by someone who knows the corresponding private key, ie the recipient. You can also use your own private key to 'sign' an email. The recipient can verify this digital signature through your public key and ensure that it was sent by you and that the contents haven't been tampered with.

The PGP software

The PGP program does an excellent job of leading you through this complex process. The creation of the keys is vitally important and is carried out by a slick Wizard-style process. After that, most functions can be controlled from within your email software, to which the necessary plug-ins are added during the installation. PGP includes plug-ins for both Eudora and Microsoft Outlook. If you have a different email program, you can encrypt and decrypt messages using the Windows Clipboard. The

software also includes extensive online help and if that's not enough, you can download the 150-page manual in Adobe Acrobat format from the PGP Web site (www.pgpi.org). We recommend that you download this and read through it before you start using encrypted messages.

Using your keys

Once you have generated your key pair, you must pass on your public key to whoever might need it. This key is no more than a block of gibberish text, so you can distribute it via normal unencrypted email (it's useless to anyone intercepting it). You can also post it on a Web site for others to download – there are dedicated key servers for this purpose and PGP software will handle the upload.

It's important that if you are sent a key via email, or if you retrieve one from a public key server, you should check that it really has come from the person that it purports to. The safest way to do that is to call the person and have

them read their unique 'fingerprint' over the phone, or have them write it down and post or fax it to you. You can see the fingerprint code by clicking on the key in the PGPkeys window and selecting Key Properties from the Keys menu.

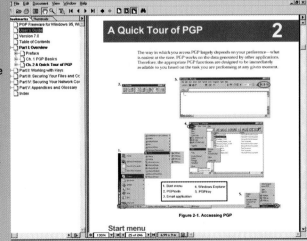

A typical fingerprint (above) does appear to be extremely complicated, but everything is clearly explained in the comprehensive downloadable manual (below).

Go-faster Internet

The Internet was once an exciting development for a few scientists. But now there are hundreds of millions of users, and Internet traffic is increasing phenomenally. How will the Net cope? And how will your connection improve?

For most users, the Internet appeared like a virtual Big Bang. First there was nothing, then, suddenly, there was a huge and ever-expanding universe. The Internet appeared everywhere: magazines, radio, TV and on business cards and letterheads.

The huge burst of interest and use has caused a correspondingly huge explosion in the amount of data that the Internet is being asked to transfer from site to site – and it can barely cope. As anyone who has tried to download files during US daylight hours knows, sometimes the Internet simply gets bogged down. Even a fast modem that can download 3,000 characters per second can leave you twiddling your thumbs as data is sent at a mere 300 characters per second. At times, it's more of an information gridlock than a highway.

● Internet beginnings

The Internet began life in the late 1960s with the development of packet-switching networks. Information on these networks didn't go straight from computer A to computer B; it often took a circuitous route, such as from A to P to L to D to Q to B. Furthermore, not all packets travelled the same way. A little like a technical pass-the-parcel game, every computer along the line simply concerned itself with passing the packet on to the next, until it eventually got to the computer it was

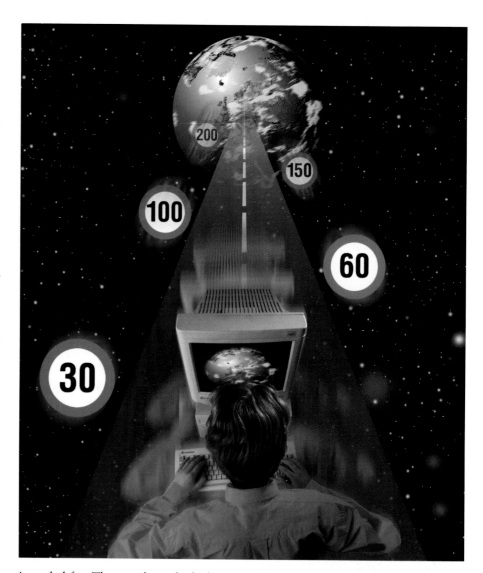

intended for. The speed at which the packets could be transmitted along the links that connected Internet computers was extremely sluggish compared with the modems of today.

The Internet first emerged in something like today's form when in 1985 the US National Science Foundation (NSF) linked together their five national supercomputer centres across the country via a 56Kbps national network. This was the original backbone of the Internet. As more and more people realized that the network was a great way of not just accessing the supercomputers for research but also for transmitting email, files and newsgroup messages,

With increasing Web traffic, it's not surprising that jams occur. Developers are preparing for the future to ensure your browsing stays quick and trouble-free.

BANDWIDTH LEAPS

Bandwidth refers to the amount of data that can be transmitted in a given amount of time. Usually, this is expressed in bits per second. A typical modem connecting a home computer to a telephone line, for example, could handle 33,600 bits per second (bps). However, even a top-notch modem running at 56Mbps is slow, compared to the flood of asynchronous transfer mode networks which run into gigabits (one billion bits) per second. Fibre optic networks improve the performance even more, offering the equivalent of 1,700 gigabits per second.

traffic soon exceeded the network's ability to cope. Consequently, the backbone was upgraded in 1988, this time connecting 13 sites with a newer, faster 1.544Mbps line and the old one was closed. But the increase in traffic continued and during 1989-91 the backbone was upgraded and extended again. Other networks were developed independently, each one hitching onto this main backbone and by 1991 there were nearly 4,000 of these 'hitch-hikers'.

In 1995, realizing that the network was under strain, the NSF transferred responsibility for the development and implementation of the Internet from the government to more commercial parties. It was decided that, rather than a long, strung-out backbone, along which other networks could connect, instead there would be four connection points through which the global Internet traffic would operate. These Network Access Points (NAPs) are located in San Francisco,

Washington DC, Chicago and Pennsauken, New Jersey and they took over the Internet operation from the NSF on 30 April 1995. Today they run at a staggering 622Mbps.

Under the current system, sending an email to someone in another office down the road can be a lengthy process. It's likely that the email will leave your computer, travel across the Atlantic to your Internet service provider (ISP) in, say, Chicago, and back through the recipient's ISP before arriving on the other person's computer. It would be much more sensible to have the email carried by a localized network and to use the NAPs only when the circumstances demand it, which is now happening.

Although an exciting development, high-capacity fibre optics is still in development.

High bandwidth Metropolitan Area Ethernet (MAE) systems already exist in big cities around the world. MAEs help enormously to siphon traffic off the Net. The London Metropolitan Area Network connects numerous academic institutions, with more joining all the time. It was supplied and installed by a consortium of cable TV firms. Cable modems that can utilize the broader bandwidth offered by cable – rather than telephone lines

– have been at breakthrough point for some time now. A cable modem can give you a connection to your ISP that is about as fast as an office network.

● Network upgrade
The latest attempt to upgrade the Internet's capacity and reliability is IPv6 (Internet Protocol version 6). All the world's major companies that are interested in the Internet are involved: Cisco, Intel, Nokia, Microsoft and many others. The idea is to upgrade the network to cope with a predicted massive increase in users, in the amount of data transferred, and the need for faster, more fault-tolerant and reliable systems.

Faster processors from companies such as Intel will enable the Internet's file servers to handle more data more quickly, while new routers from companies such as Cisco will allow the data to get to its destination much faster. Only by making sure that no single link in the Internet chain is holding back the performance of the PC-to-Web-site connection will we finally see real performance gains.

ORGANIZED CHAOS

Because the Internet is a worldwide phenomenon encompassing both community-minded technology experts and IT companies keen to make money by developing newer, faster technology, its development can seem chaotic.

It's not uncommon for many months of development of one method of improving performance to be sidelined as a more recent breakthrough makes a larger leap forward. Although potentially frustrating for the technology experts who have wasted their time, the good news for the rest of us is that this worldwide competition makes the Internet develop faster than any other applied technology.

Wireless Internet

IN THE UK, a company called Tele2 is introducing a new wireless connection: data is broadcast over the airwaves rather than carried down wires. This service is quick: from 512Kbps to 2Mbps. The plan is to offer it to 60 per cent of the UK by 2003. Wireless Internet technology looks set to develop very quickly.

Keep up to date with wireless Internet developments by visiting Tele2's Web site (www.tele2.co.uk).

Fishing on the Net

If you're an avid angler, the Internet is a great place to learn about tackle technology developments – and everything else to do with fishing.

To the uninitiated, fishing might seem one of the simpler, less structured, sports. Some might suppose that the only tools required are a reasonably long stick, a length of line, a hook and some bait. Of course, anyone who goes fishing regularly knows that the truth is very different. Technology has not overlooked the tranquil sport of fishing, and the odds are now firmly stacked against all fish, as anglers employ everything from state-of-the-art composite rods, to underwater sonar units and specially created bait.

● Regional variations

Just as for any other popular pastime, there are numerous Web sites dedicated to the sport of fishing and related topics. However, as fishing is popular world wide, it is necessary to dig around a little more carefully than

usual to ensure that you find information that relates to a given locality. Because the Internet is largely a US-dominated medium you will need to search carefully for Web sites covering popular spots in Cornwall or Scotland, as opposed to those for fishing in California or Florida.

As ever, try to narrow your search by using terms that will restrict the hits to specific places – for example, 'fly-fishing AND Scotland'. Of course, it's easy enough to spot an American fishing site simply by its content – bass and muskie are not the sort of catch to be found in rivers all over the world.

Over the next few pages we'll be looking at some of the more prominent fishing sites and the sort of information they offer. Many of the sites listed are entirely amateur, and are none the worse for that; they're produced by fishing enthusiasts in an attempt to help out their fellow anglers, or simply to show off their

biggest catch. But there are plenty of other sites produced by companies that organize professional fishing trips or holidays. These are worth checking out, as they can be a great way to discover resorts that you might not find otherwise.

UNUSUAL CATCHES

As rich as any one locality is in species, there is, of course, a much greater variety of fish – and fishing techniques – to be found elsewhere in the world. The Web offers sites featuring such pursuits as ice fishing, spear fishing and deep-sea fishing, as well as pages all about species that may be unfamiliar, such as bass, muskie and walleye. These sites are easy to find and offer an interesting insight into fishing in other parts of the world. They may also give you holiday ideas – and several of these sites will actively help you to organize a fishing holiday.

PC TIPS

There are a number of newsgroups set up to discuss various types of fishing. A newsgroup is essentially a dedicated noticeboard where you'll be able to hear the latest news, tips and forecasts, and have a chat with fellow angling enthusiasts. To visit one of these groups, you will need a special newsgroup reader, such as Netscape Messenger, which comes with the Netscape Communicator package (see Stage 4, pages 142-145). You can then subscribe to these three (UK-based) groups: uk.rec.fishing.coarse, uk.rec.fishing.game and uk.rec.fishing.sea.

Fishing sites

There are, of course, many more fishing Web sites than we can cover here. Consider these as the bait to hook you on more Web site angling.

Fishing.co.uk
www.fishing.co.uk

This is a very professional and informative site, with something for every fishing fan, whether your interest is coarse, game, sea or whatever. There are plenty of sections that add to your knowledge and pleasure, and give practical help. There are regular articles from fishing expert Geoff Maynard as well as a 'trophy room' where you can display your own magnificent catch. Other regular articles appear on a weekly or monthly basis and cover all aspects of fishing. There's a good online interactive locator for all your fishing needs, from bait and tackle to fisheries and boat hire. Similarly, there's an e-shopping area that enables you to buy whatever you need via the site. There is also a Clubroom where you can take part in forums with other fishermen.

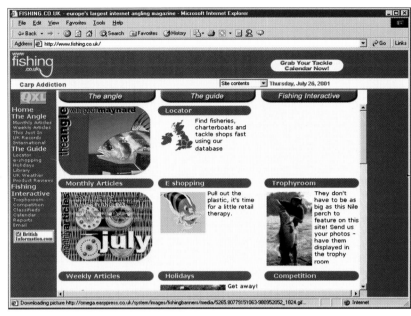

U.K. Sea Fishing FAQ
www.gorp.com/gorp/activity/saltfaq.htm

This site contains one of the few sources of information for sea fishing in the UK. It is organized as FAQs (Frequently Asked Questions), and so there is little attempt to provide the range of features offered by other online fishing magazines. However, this is not to say that the FAQs are anything other than complete – far from it. They provide answers to all the common queries about fishing and information which in many cases is unavailable elsewhere. The FAQ is organized into sections, the main ones being: UK Sea Angling And The Law; UK Sea Fish, Baits, Techniques, Tackle, Organisations & Clubs; and UK Sea Angling Publications & Software.

Fishing Licence Online
www.fishinglicence.co.uk

Apart from your bait, tackle and waterproof jacket, there's one other very important thing you will need for certain types of fishing in Britain – a licence. This is not a permit to fish a particular lake or river, but a government licence to fish. This site allows you to register over the Internet, and the licence will be posted to you, so that you don't have to visit the post office. Simply select the licence you want (coarse, game, and so on), the date you want it to start, and when you want it to finish. Clicking on the fish icons takes you to each stage. Once you've completed the relevant sections, you can sit back and wait for the licence to arrive in a few days' time. Note, however, that there's a basic £1.50 handling fee, which covers first-class postage, and an additional 63p if you want the licence sent by recorded delivery.

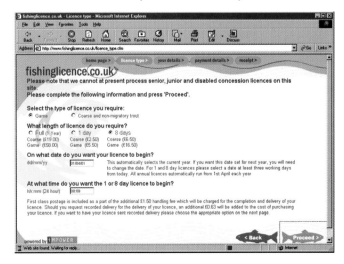

Special-interest sites

If you have a special interest in certain species, need your prize specimen preserved, or want to promote angling, here are some sites for you.

Fish & Fly

www.fishandfly.co.uk

Another online-only fishing magazine, Fish & Fly is very much for the hardcore angler, specifically those who enjoy fly-fishing in the UK. This is a site created by enthusiasts for enthusiasts, and it is all the better for it. The articles are extremely in-depth and detailed, but at the same time, often very entertaining. This might not be a site for fly-fishing novices, but it does have a sense of humour, and avoids being snobbish or geeky. The site is organized into various sections, such as features, fly tying and resources.

Carp Net

www.carp.net

As is obvious from its name, this site is dedicated to carp – although to a lesser extent it also embraces other freshwater fish. All the various needs of the carp fisherman are covered here, from product reviews to fishing locations. There are regular sections on bait and tackle, carp fishing articles from around the world and an excellent tactics section with diagrams. Due to its fairly basic design, the site doesn't look very attractive, but it's worth persevering because the information it contains is, quite simply, first class.

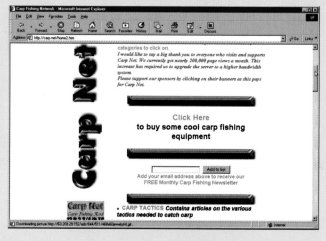

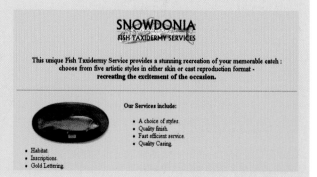

National Federation of Anglers

www.the-nfa.org.uk

This site is intended to further the NFA's goal of protecting and organizing the UK's angling industry. It is concerned with environmental problems that affect angling, specifically water pollution, abstraction and land drainage. The NFA is also a leader in the European Anglers' Alliance, formed to monitor European legislative proposals that are likely to affect angling, and to press the European Parliament to pass laws to protect the aquatic environment and anglers' rights.

Fish taxidermy services

freespace.virgin.net/sts.northwales/intro.htm

For the less 'politically correct' anglers who prefer to keep what they catch, there are other ways to show off a fish, rather than frying it up and making it the centrepiece of a dinner party. This company deals with all animals, but specifically advertises its expertise in stuffing fish.

SNOWDONIA
FISH TAXIDERMY SERVICES

This unique Fish Taxidermy Service provides a stunning recreation of your memorable catch : choose from five artistic styles in either skin or cast reproduction format - recreating the excitement of the occasion.

Our Services include:
- A choice of styles.
- Quality finish.
- Fast efficient service.
- Quality Casing.

- Habitat.
- Inscriptions.
- Gold Lettering.

Where To Fish

www.where-to-fish.com/

This is the Internet version of the very popular Where To Fish directory. The site boasts over 3,000 pages of information, covering thousands of fishing locations in the UK and abroad. The information is split into six main areas: England, Scotland, Wales, Ireland, Northern Ireland and 'Abroad'. The facts that you find for each individual location may, at first, seem a little basic, but all the necessary contact details are provided along with a concise listing of the fish available, fishing conditions and directions to the site.

Regional-interest Web sites

Here are some sites that cover specific areas of the British Isles.

Fly Fishing in Scotland

www.beith.demon.co.uk

Almost everything you need to know about classic fly-fishing is included on this comprehensive site. At its core is solid and practical information about Scotland's rivers and lochs, such as when and where to fish them. And this site proves that fishing in Scotland is by no means limited to salmon and trout; whilst those fish do, of course, feature strongly, there is also plenty of information regarding other species, such as ferox and char. A good selection of pictures of flies suitable for Scotland provide an additional bonus – and they'll even send you tying instructions if you make a request by email.

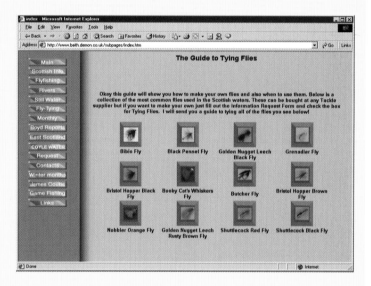

Fishing in Northern Ireland

www.interknowledge.com/northern-ireland/ukifish1.htm

This is another Web site specializing in a particular area of the UK. It is easy to overlook Northern Ireland when you organize a fishing trip, but this site will whet your appetite for some of Europe's most fish-productive waters.

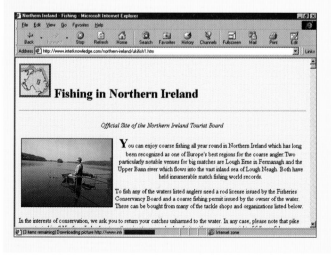

Fishing in Wales

www.fishing-in-wales.com/

This is an extremely extensive site on fishing in Wales. All the best fishing areas are detailed, as are nearby shops and accommodation. There is also much general information about fishing techniques and fish species.

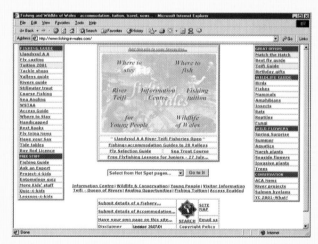

Cooking on the Internet

No matter what type of meal you are interested in preparing, or what exotic vegetable you want to include in a recipe, the Internet will almost certainly provide you with what you need.

If you want to find great recipes or new places to eat, discover more about the nutritional benefits of certain foods or find out about the different cuisines around the world, the Internet is undoubtedly the best place to look.

Food has become one of the great lifestyle pursuits of our time. We eat out more often and we're more interested than ever in cooking at home. A trip to even a modest supermarket reveals a vast array of exotic ingredients from around the world. And when we're not eating or preparing food, we might well be watching a food programme on the TV. You won't be surprised to find that this interest is matched on the Net, where food sites abound – from vast recipe databases to chatty e-zines with plenty of pictures and strong opinions.

● A world of food

Every culinary interest you can think of is catered for on the Web. As it's a truly global medium, the Internet is a great place to find details on your favourite ethnic cuisine and also to discover other cookery styles that you might never have otherwise encountered. It's also a good place to find recommended and specialist restaurants in your own area.

There are many sites created by enthusiasts for a particular cuisine that invite surfers to send in their views and provide a forum for exchanging ideas and recipes. And, as with any shared-interest sites, they can be a good way of making new friends. Try a search for 'curry', for instance, and, even when restricted to UK sites, you'll find a wealth of information on good restaurants, in many cases expressed with appropriate piquancy.

● Healthy eating

We are all more health-conscious these days and much better informed about the health effects of the food we eat and how it is produced and prepared. The last decade has also seen many people changing to a vegetarian diet. Both healthy eating and vegetarianism are covered in many Internet food sites, and even the most difficult-to-please gourmets will find a wide range of recipes and ideas to stimulate their appetite.

Online shopping has boomed in recent years. Whereas in the early Internet days, you could find only outrageously expensive luxuries for purchase online, now you can locate just about anything.

Within the UK it is possible to place online orders for organic fruit and vegetables, and in many areas you can now log on to the site of a major supermarket, order your groceries and have them delivered to your home (see Stage 4, page 153).

However you order your food, preparation remains important and to help you there is a veritable cornucopia of recipes on the Web – in fact, enough to keep you in three different square meals a day for the rest of your life. A massive database, RecipeSource (see opposite), offers more than 70,000 different recipes.

Sites to visit

There is such a wealth of information on the Web for both the budding cook and experienced chef that it's difficult to know where to begin. Here, we give you a taste of some popular and unusual sites.

SOAR – RecipeSource
www.recipesource.com/

This online archive of recipes is an astonishing free resource for the cook. There are over 70,000 recipes in the database and all are easily searchable, so that you can quickly find something quite specific, such as recipes using tofu, for example. If you don't feel like searching, browsing is an entertaining alternative, as the recipes are listed both by ingredient and ethnic origin. There are no frills on this site, but what you do receive is an incredible depth of information.

ChocolatEpicure
www.chocolatepicure.com/

Chocaholics who have no wish to kick the habit should call in here, as should anyone keen to find out more about chocolate and where to buy the best. This site offers details of Europe's top *chocolatiers* and gives you the chance to buy their products over the Internet. In addition, you'll find out what distinguishes great chocolate from the everyday variety, discover interesting recipes using it and read interviews with the key players in the chocolate world.

THE RECIPE RING

When browsing sites devoted to cooking, you might come across icons similar to those below. This is because many culinary enthusiasts have created Web sites with the sole intention of spreading their favourite recipes around the world, with no thought of commercial gain. If you create a Web site of your own, perhaps featuring favourite family recipes, you can add it to the Recipe Ring by just following the simple instructions. You can rest assured that any site you visit via the Web ring won't be trying to sell you something, but will be the loving creation of an enthusiast and contain lots of interesting information.

Fresh Food
www.freshfood.co.uk

This site gives you the chance to combine health and tasty eating – in the form of organic vegetables – with the ease of Internet shopping. The idea is simple and is based on what is called a box scheme. You make your order and every week or fortnight, a box of organic produce is delivered direct to your door. There's organic wine as well.

Chopstix

www.chopstix.co.uk

This is an excellent e-zine site devoted to Chinese cookery in all its manifestations. There are several distinct areas: Lifestyle & Culture is a chatty section where you can read interviews with celebrity chefs such as Ken Hom; in Ingredients you'll find information about the ingredients used in Chinese cooking; and in Recipes there are recipes, tips and techniques for successful Chinese cookery.

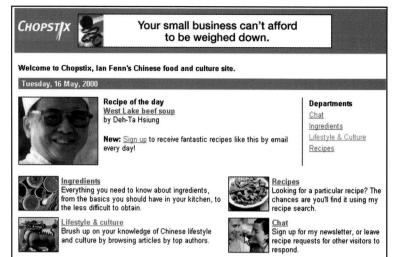

Foodwatch

www.foodwatch.com.au

Healthy eating is the watchword of this site from Australian food broadcaster and writer Catherine Saxelby. There's a good variety of sections on the site, covering material such as the small print on labels and how to lose weight and including a page where you enter your personal details and your weight rating is assessed. The site's recipes are very clearly and attractively presented, and there is also a fun food quiz to test how much you know about food.

Vegetarian Society

www.vegsoc.org/

This is the official site of the Vegetarian Society of the United Kingdom. As such, it has all sorts of information about how you can join and about vegetarianism in general. There's also plenty of useful material here about food and drink. The site offers information on the Cordon Vert vegetarian cookery school and has loads of recipes that incorporate a wide range of ingredients. There's also an online store where you can buy books and gifts although it does not sell food.

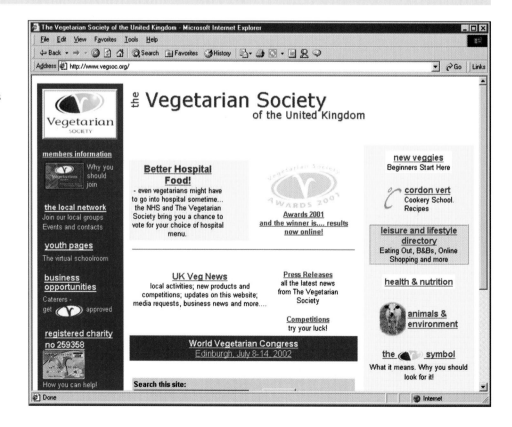

BBC Food

www.bbc.co.uk/food

Given the omnipresence of cooks on the TV, you would expect the BBC to offer a rich mix of cookery topics on their Web site and they do not disappoint. In fact, if you are only ever going to look at one food and cookery site on the Internet, this should probably be the one. The site's home page is more of a portal – a collection of related sites. You can use the pull-down menu to navigate to separate areas for TV programmes, such as *Food and Drink*, *Fresh Food* and *Gary Rhodes' Classics*, where you'll find all your favourite personalities. You can also click on links to Ask the Chef for answers to all your cookery questions, such as, 'Can you tell me the difference between Cottage Pie and Shepherd's Pie?', Global Cooking, Healthy Eating and, of course, good old-fashioned recipes. There's lots of light-hearted content as well: you can send in your recipe to Jamie Oliver for a competition, or even chat with him online.

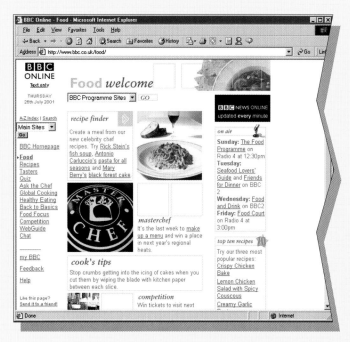

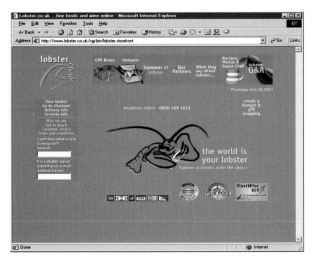

Lobster

www.lobster.co.uk

If you crave the finer things in life – such as Beluga caviar or smoked salmon – this is the site you should visit. You'll find nothing but the best on the attractively designed Lobster site, with price tags to match. You can buy individual items or select a gourmet hamper, and they offer same-day delivery in London, or next day delivery nationwide.

The Grange

www.cookery-grange.co.uk

To further stimulate your enthusiasm, and develop your cooking skills, you could take a cookery course. At this site you can peruse details of the courses offered at The Grange, a 17th-century coach house in the Somerset countryside – just one of many cookery schools around the world. For lists of schools just about everywhere in the world, try www.cookingschools. com for more options.

Amazing plants

If you want to find out about the more bizarre or exotic-looking species of the plant world, then the World Wide Web is the place to go.

Until gardening programmes on the TV became popular, plants and botany were not viewed as particularly interesting subjects. Now, television schedules and newsagents are packed with all kinds of gardening and nature promotions.

The subject of botany covers the physiology, structure, genetics, ecology, distribution, classification and economic importance of plants – and the Internet has abundant information concerning all of these different areas.

While you will find plenty of conventional gardening sites that help you to trim your geraniums and prune your roses, there are many others that deal with the more unusual side of plants and plant habitats. These Web pages tend to be either serious botanical sites, created by researchers and students, or ones that have been produced by amateur enthusiasts. Gardening newsgroups

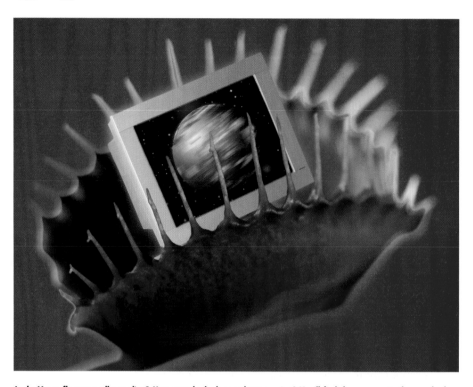

Is the Venus fly-trap really an alien? How exactly do desert plants survive? You'll find the answers to these and other unusual botanical questions – including many you never even thought to ask – on the Internet.

also abound. Whoever the author, and whatever the nature of the site, you'll find that most of these sites are well put together and totally absorbing.

● Carnivorous plants
The strangest plant that most people can think of is the Venus fly-trap. Although they are fascinating – and

there are dozens of Web sites dedicated to these weird plants – there are plenty of other bizarre and wonderful types of plant. Consider the *Rafflesia Arnoldii*, with a beautiful flower that grows up to a metre in diameter and stinks of rotting flesh – which makes it a pleasure to view but a horror to smell, unless you are a particular type of fly.

Plant life does not have to be quite so extreme in appearance, scent or behaviour to be interesting, however. Many people are just as fascinated by, for example, the 20,000-plus species of orchid in the world. With so many plants to choose from, each with their own specific horticultural needs, you require an information resource as large and versatile as the Web to keep well informed.

● Plants in the environment
Many of the plant Web sites are concerned with education, not only for school children, but also for a

ALIEN PLANTS

The idea that bacteria from passing comets and meteors might have originally 'seeded' life on earth is currently a popular theory. Some people have taken this concept a step further and suggested that there is a species of plant – specifically the Venus fly-trap – that could be of extraterrestrial origin. They argue that the fly-trap exists as only one species and grows in only one spot on Earth: a 100-mile radius around Wilmington, North Carolina. In the centre of this circle is what appears to be a series of craters from an ancient meteor shower. Drawing a parallel between the two facts has led to the belief that the fly-trap is alien in origin.

wider audience. These sites aim to promote a greater understanding of our natural environment and to draw people's attention to some of the richest plant environments in the world that are in danger of being destroyed.

The mangrove swamps of Indonesia and Australia, for example, have been gradually disappearing over the years because people considered them to be nothing more than breeding grounds for mosquitoes and crocodiles. It is only in recent years that we have become aware of the abundance of plant life they contain – and many plants that grow in these areas have never been properly researched.

Here we'll be looking at Internet sites covering many different aspects of botanical study and unusual plants. So, if you're interested in finding out more about all the different exotic species of plants, head towards one of the following sites.

LITTLE SHOP OF HORRORS

Although the Venus fly-trap is the most violent of carnivorous plants, it is not the biggest. In terms of sheer bulk, the largest meat-eating plants are those of the genus *Nepenthes* (see Borneo Exotics, below). The largest of these vine-like plants can grow up to 10 metres long. Their traps are reactive rather than proactive – animals just fall into them and die. Even so, they appear to be effective, since creatures as large as frogs and rats have been found inside them, although the victims were probably sick or wounded when they fell into the plants' traps.

Botanical sites
Whether you want to find out about rare plant species or unusual plant habitats, you'll find it all on the Internet's botanical sites.

Botany.com the Encyclopedia of Plants
www.botany.com/

It is quite rare to come across a site, such as this one, that deals with the wider world of plants in an accessible and entertaining way. An encyclopedia of plants, the main part of this site lists entries for plants in alphabetical order according to their common and botanical names.

Also included is a dictionary of botanical words and a set of links for various gardens, associations and societies. The site provides general descriptions of plants as well as information on the required methods of cultivation and propagation, and on the many different varieties and hybrids. The site lists just about every plant, from an ordinary rose bush to the most exotic species.

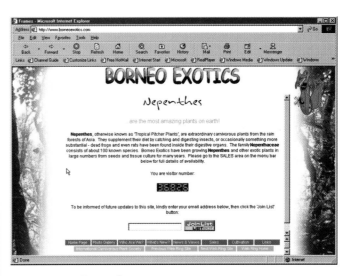

Borneo Exotics
www.borneoexotics.com/

The Venus fly-trap is unique, even when compared to other carnivorous plants (see Alien plants box, opposite), but while it is in a category all by itself, there exists in Borneo and other nearby countries a whole genus of insectivorous plants that capture and absorb insects. These plants are the *Nepenthes*, or Tropical Pitcher Plants.

Their common name comes from the oddly beautiful petals that form a pitcher-like shape in which insects are caught and killed, usually by drowning. There are currently about 90 known species of *Nepenthes*, although many of these are endangered by the destruction of their natural habitat. This excellent site includes all kinds of information about these amazing plants, with details on how to grow them as well as how to help protect them in their natural environment.

International Aroid Society, Inc.

www.aroid.org/

Aroids are plants related to the family *Araceae*, which includes Arums. This family comprises the largest flowering plants in the world. The *Amorphophallus titanum*, also known as the Devil's Tongue or Corpse Flower, has a flower that can grow up to 1.2m tall and 3.7m in diameter. Unlike most plants, which smell pleasant in order to attract bees for pollination, this plant actually smells of rotting flesh so that it can attract flies for the same purpose. As you can imagine, a huge plant smelling of rotting corpses is much more attractive when viewed from a distance!

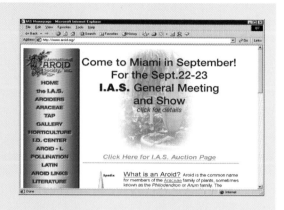

Aquatic Gardeners Association

www.aquatic-gardeners.org/

The Aquatic Gardeners Association (AGA) is an international organization of aquatic plant enthusiasts. Its Web site and its journal, called *The Aquatic Gardener*, are the only English language resources that are devoted primarily to aquatic plants. The main part of this Web site is dedicated to showing off the AGA's journal and enticing new members to join the association. The online bookstore also offers access to various books on aquatic gardening, which can be bought directly.

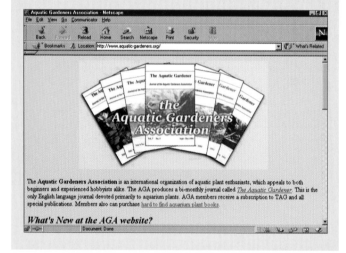

The Orchid House

retirees.uwaterloo.ca:80/~jerry/orchids/

The collection and cultivation of orchids was once the preserve of the rich, but an interest in orchids can now be enjoyed by anyone. A benefit of the previous exclusivity of orchid growing is that it is one of the best organized and most documented of plant hobbies. This means that information is easy to come by, but the sheer volume can make it difficult to research specific facts. The Orchid House has an excellent illustrated FAQs section that describes the basic features and needs of orchids. It also clarifies numerous false assumptions about the plants, for example, apparently none of the 20,000 species of orchids is a parasite.

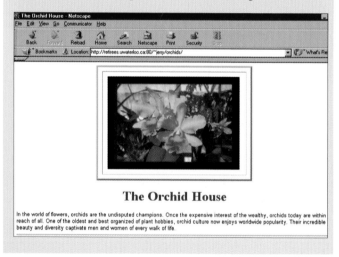

The Orchid House

The Silk Plant Company

www.silkplant.co.uk

Although artificial plants don't appeal to everyone, if you don't have green fingers, or if you simply haven't got the time, effort or space for a real plant, modern facsimiles do offer an interesting alternative. This is the Web site of a company dedicated to providing the most comprehensive selection of fine-quality artificial plants on the Internet. Trees and bushes seem to be the favourite type of artificial plant, but this Web site also offers a full range of other smaller plants.

Royal Botanic Gardens, Kew

www.rbgkew.org.uk

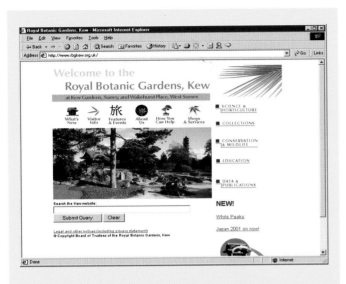

The Royal Botanic Gardens at Kew are probably the most famous and well-stocked gardens in the world – no mean feat in the inclement climes of England. Kew Gardens, and the associated gardens at Wakehurst Place, have been committed jointly to the scientific study and public display of all matters botanical since the 18th century. They owe their origin to Augusta, Dowager Princess of Wales, who in 1759 laid out 3.5 hectares of her estate as a botanic garden.

The Great Plant Escape

www.urbanext.uiuc.edu/gpe/

Botany is perhaps one of the most difficult scientific subjects to get children interested in. Luckily, this site, created by the University of Illinois, has gone to admirable lengths to make the subject as interesting and fun as possible. It is aimed at primary school students, who are guided through the various pages by Detective Le Plant and his partners, Bud and Sprout. The site is organized into six sections, with titles such as 'Soiled Again!' and 'Plantenstein is the Suspect!'. Despite the awful puns, the information on the site is serious and very well presented.

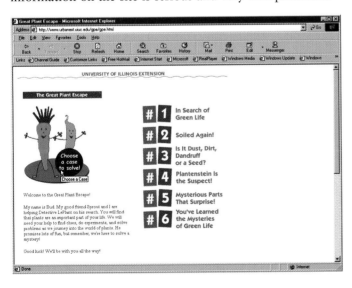

Wetlands and rainforests

www.env.qld.gov.au/environment/school/wetlands/

One of the most unusual and fascinating environments in the world is that of the mangrove swamps of Indonesia and Australia. This Web site comes from the Australian education board, and although aimed at primary and secondary school students, it is an excellent source of information for any visitor. The site deals with the concept of wetlands and rainforests. All the information on the site's pages is split up into bite-sized chunks to ensure that young minds stay interested. The site contains a useful list of FAQs and contact information for various Australian and worldwide authorities and organizations.

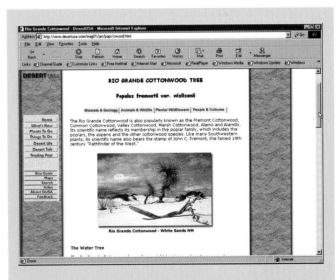

Desert Plant Survival

www.desertusa.com/du_plantsurv.html

This site, created as a teaching aid, is part of a larger Web site concerned with all aspects of American deserts. Every type of desert-dwelling plant is covered, from phraetophytes (plants that have adapted to arid conditions by growing very long roots) to ephemerals (some of which can complete an entire life cycle in a few months or even weeks). Many other fascinating facts await you at this excellent educational site.

Charities

With charities looking at every possible way to raise money and promote their work more effectively, many are now turning to the World Wide Web.

O nce Red Nose Day is over, many people assume that they have 'done their bit' as far as charitable donations go. Unfortunately, charities need a regular supply of donations or their work simply grinds to a halt. When the economy isn't doing so well, or when people think the Lottery is helping out as much as is necessary, the situation can become very bleak for charity fundraisers. As a result, most have quickly embraced the Internet as a way of getting their message across.

● Charity content
The content of the average charity's Web site is fairly standardized, and with good reason. Most people need only a quick reminder of the charity's work and those they could help before they decide to give a donation. No amount of sad stories or pictures will necessarily convince people of the

need to donate, and indeed too much 'persuasion' can easily put them off. So you'll find that many of the sites we look at over the next few pages are quite short and to the point. Added embellishments are unnecessary and a waste of the organization's hard-earned resources.

● Public education
Charity sites that offer more in the way of content are usually those where the problems they combat can be prevented more easily than they can be cured. Two obvious examples of this are the British Heart Foundation and The World Wide Fund for Nature.

Organizations such as these have realized that by educating the public about the causes of their problems, they can reduce the need for expenditure on research or damage limitation. As a result, these two charity Web sites in particular are

Charity sites work well as educative resources, helping to prevent disease or disability. Straightforward appeals for money are often less effective.

highly educational, usually to the direct benefit of the visitor.

● Helping charity sites
Of course, not every charity can afford to maintain a Web site. You'll notice that most of the sites we look at belong to the larger national or international organizations. Smaller regional charities are sometimes represented on the Internet through personal Web pages.

Also, sites such as CharityNet can help you to get in touch with those charities that do not yet exist in cyberspace. You might even be tempted to help these organizations make the move to the Web – something that would probably be more valuable than any modest donation.

● Fundraising

If your HTML skills aren't good enough for you to help a local charity with Web programming or design, most of the larger sites will suggest some sort of fundraising event as the best way to get actively involved.

Examples of previous events will be detailed on most of the sites, to give you an idea of what works and what doesn't. Of course, anything that generates money can be seen as a success, but each organization will be well aware of the best method for getting people to reach into their pockets. This might seem cynical, but with so many worthy organizations needing money, the fundraisers have to take a more professional view.

The next few pages provide details of some of the more interesting and impressive Web sites for national and international charities. Remember, though, there are a lot more organizations out there, and just because they don't appear in the following list, it doesn't mean that there isn't one doing something to raise funds in an area that is of interest to you.

INTERNET MONEY

The main obstacle to a charity's success online is the question of donations over the Internet. Despite the increasing popularity of online shopping, many people are still cautious about giving their credit card details over the Web, especially if they feel a charity site may not have the funds to spend on ensuring watertight security measures. For this reason, most sites promote their traditional phone numbers and postal addresses as the easiest, and safest, ways to donate money.

The sites

Here is a selection of the more impressive charity sites, which provide a clear message about what they do and how you can help them.

British Heart Foundation

www.bhf.org.uk

The British Heart Foundation is one of the largest and best-supported medical charities in the country. This well-designed site outlines the charity's work and how you can help it, but it also stresses the measures you should take to prevent heart disease. As the site ably points out, prevention is far better than cure.

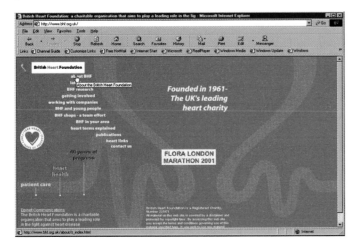

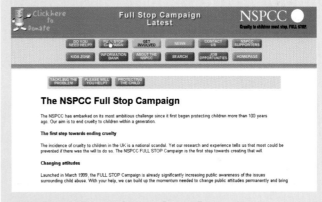

National Society for the Prevention of Cruelty to Children (NSPCC)

www.nspcc.org.uk

The NSPCC Web site is simple but it has all the information you need. Like most charities, the NSPCC focuses on explaining what it does and how you can help. There is also plenty of detail on the NSPCC's Full Stop Campaign, and a separate Kids Zone area to tell children what the NSPCC does.

International Committee of the Red Cross (ICRC)

www.icrc.org/

The Red Cross and Red Crescent are perhaps the most famous and active charities in the world. Although there are separate Web sites for various national Red Cross organizations, this is the main international site. As you might expect, the content of the site concentrates on the work done by the charity, rather than on fundraising efforts, which are often specific to a certain region or country. This site is an interesting and well-informed resource for various humanitarian concerns.

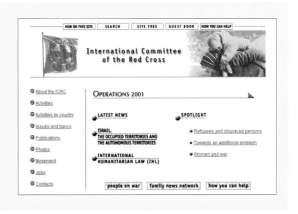

Comic Relief
www.comicrelief.com/

Comic Relief is one of the most well-known charities in the UK today and devotes itself to raising money and awareness of humanitarian problems in the UK and Africa, together with organizing self-help programmes. Its Web site is one of the most professional and attractive on the Net, and although that isn't really the point of charity Web sites, it probably helps to fire people's interest and enthusiasm.

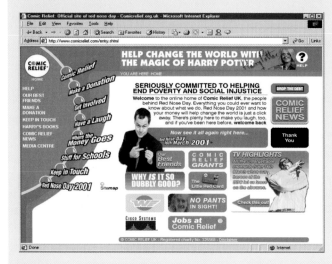

WWF Global Network
www.panda.org/

This is the main international site for the World Wide Fund for Nature (the site at www.wwf.org lists national branches). It's an excellent site that almost doubles as a full-scale natural history resource. The main reason for such expansive information is to educate people, particularly children, about the damage being done to the environment, and the animals and plants currently at greatest risk. This site pulls no punches in its reporting of news stories and is quite scathing of any government that it sees as failing in its responsibility to the environment.

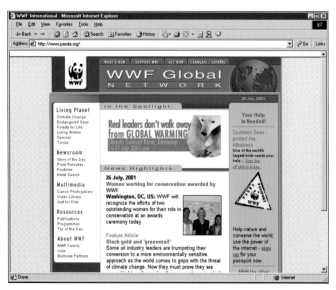

Oxfam International
www.oxfaminternational.org/

Although Oxfam started out as a British charity, since 1995 it has become international and is made up of 11 autonomous non-governmental groups. The charity's goal is to help fight global poverty. The site has been jazzed up and now reflects Oxfam's global importance, giving a thorough rundown on activities. There are numerous country-specific sites for Oxfam, of which www.oxfam.org.uk is the main British site, where you can make an online donation.

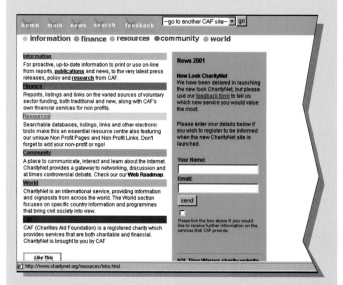

CharityNet
www.charitynet.org/

While much attention is given to the more famous and most widely supported charities, it can be easy to overlook the smaller, but no less deserving, organizations. The CharityNet site addresses this problem by providing a complete resource for information on charities around the world, with a bias towards those in the UK. For the casual surfer, the most useful section of this site is the well-stocked list of Web links. This helps you to get in contact with small and/or local charities that can't afford much publicity. If they don't have a Web site, their other contact details can be provided instead.

Royal National Lifeboat Institution (RNLI)
www.rnli.org.uk

Despite the fact that nearly everyone involved in the lifeboat service is unpaid, the Royal National Lifeboat Institution is always in need of funds – lifeboats and lifeboat stations cost a great deal of money to buy and maintain. This well-produced site explains the different ways in which you can make a contribution and outlines the services and work that the RNLI does. In addition, there's a special RNLI club for the under-16s and an extremely well-designed section entitled Safety on the Sea. This is actually a separate site aimed mostly at children, but it contains plenty of good advice for everyone.

Royal National Institute for the Blind (RNIB)
www.rnib.org.uk

The RNIB doesn't just help the completely blind, but also the 500,000 partially sighted people in the UK. The site is constructed with the visually impaired in mind and has various built-in options for larger font sizes and easily distinguishable colours. The site has lots of information on RNIB campaigns, especially the Good Web Design Campaign to encourage site designers to make their pages accessible to the blind and partially sighted.

Charity Commission for England and Wales
www.charitycommission.gov.uk

To find out about a particular charity, or to set up your own, you must contact the Charity Commission. They can provide details and verify the official status of a charity, so you can be sure you are giving your money to a reputable concern. Setting up your own charity requires verification of your status by the Courts and the Home Secretary, both via the Charity Commission.

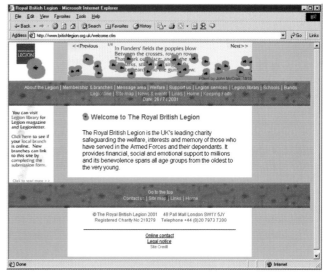

The Royal British Legion
www.britishlegion.org.uk

Many people assume that the Royal British Legion exists only to help veterans of the First and Second World Wars. In fact, it is dedicated to helping all ex-service men, women and their dependents. The charity helps up to 15 million people – nearly a quarter of the entire population of the United Kingdom. Most people will know the Legion from the work it does with the annual Remembrance Day Poppy Appeal, but this accounts for only 50 per cent of its necessary funds.

● **About the index**
Text in italics is used for cross-references within the index (as in *see also...*). Page numbers in bold type denote the main entries for a topic.

● **Acknowledgments**
Abbreviations: t = top; b = bottom;
r = right; l = left; c = centre;
bkg = background. All cartoons
are by Chris Bramley

8	Lyndon Parker/De Agostini
10	Lyndon Parker/De Agostini
12	Lyndon Parker/De Agostini
14	TRH
16	Lyndon Parker/De Agostini
18	Lyndon Parker/De Agostini
20	Robert Harding
21	Robert Harding
24	The Stockmarket
30	Tony Stone Images
34	Lyndon Parker/De Agostini
36	Lyndon Parker/De Agostini
38	Transocean/Warner/Kobal
40	Lyndon Parker/De Agostini
42	Lyndon Parker/De Agostini
44	Lyndon Parker/De Agostini
45	Lyndon Parker/De Agostini
48	The Stockmarket
52	Lyndon Parker/De Agostini
54	Lyndon Parker/De Agostini

58	Lyndon Parker/De Agostini
62	Courtesy Hewlett Packard
64	Lyndon Parker/De Agostini
66	Tony Stone Images
70	Tony Stone Images
72	Lyndon Parker/De Agostini
76	Tony Stone Images
78	The Stock Market
82	The Stock Market
84	Lyndon Parker/De Agostini
88	Images Colour Library
92	Tony Stone Images
98	Courtesy Cybermind UK Ltd
99bl	Lyndon Parker/De Agostini
100tr	Courtesy Cybermind UK Ltd
102	Lyndon Parker/De Agostini
103t,c	Lyndon Parker/De Agostini
103b	Courtesy Holdan UK Ltd
104	Lyndon Parker/De Agostini
105(all)	Lyndon Parker/De Agostini
106	Lyndon Parker/De Agostini
108	Corbis/Hulton Getty
109(all)	Courtesy Wadsworth
110	Lyndon Parker/De Agostini
112tr	Courtesy Intel
113b	David Parker/Seagate Microelectronics Ltd/SPL

113(all other)	Courtesy Intel
116	Tony Stone Images/Courtesy British Airways
118	RAM Mobile Data UK
119tr	Courtesy Buffalo AirStation
120	The Stock Market
121tr	Philips
121bl	Lyndon Parker/De Agostini
122tr	The Stock Market
122br	Marshall Cavendish
123	Marshall Cavendish
124	The Stock Market
125b	Courtesy Yamaha
126	Lyndon Parker/De Agostini
127(all)	Lyndon Parker/De Agostini
128	Lyndon Parker/De Agostini
129	Lyndon Parker/De Agostini
134	The Stock Market
138	Lyndon Parker/De Agostini
140	Lyndon Parker/De Agostini
141	Lyndon Parker/De Agostini
142	Robert Harding Picture Library
146	Lyndon Parker/De Agostini
150(all)	Tony Stone Images
154	Lyndon Parker/De Agostini